One Hundred Days
of Silence

One Hundred Days of Silence

America and the Rwanda Genocide

Jared Cohen

ROWMAN & LITTLEFIELD PUBLISHERS, INC.
Lanham • Boulder • New York • Toronto • Plymouth, UK

ROWMAN & LITTLEFIELD PUBLISHERS, INC.

Published in the United States of America
by Rowman & Littlefield Publishers, Inc.
A wholly owned subsidiary of The Rowman & Littlefield Publishing Group, Inc.
4501 Forbes Boulevard, Suite 200, Lanham, Maryland 20706
www.rowmanlittlefield.com

Estover Road
Plymouth PL6 7PY
United Kingdom

British Library Cataloguing in Publication Information Available

Library of Congress Cataloging-in-Publication Data

Cohen, Jared, 1981–
  One hundred days of silence : America and the Rwanda genocide / Jared Cohen.
    p. cm.
  Includes bibliographical references.
  ISBN-13: 978-0-7425-5236-4 (cloth : alk. paper)
  ISBN-10: 0-7425-5236-5 (cloth : alk. paper)
  ISBN-13: 978-0-7425-5237-1 (paper : alk. paper)
  ISBN-10: 0-7425-5237-3 (paper : alk. paper)
  1. Rwanda—History—Civil War, 1990–1993—Atrocities. 2. Genocide—Rwanda—
History—20th century. 3. United States—Foreign relations—Rwanda. 4. Rwanda—
Foreign relations—United States. 5. United States—Foreign relations—1993–2001.
I. Title.
  DT450.435.C64 2007
  967.57104'31—dc22   2006031325

Printed in the United States of America

∞™ The paper used in this publication meets the minimum requirements of American
National Standard for Information Sciences—Permanence of Paper for Printed Library
Materials, ANSI/NISO Z39.48-1992.

To Grandma Marilyn

"We are reminded of the capacity of people everywhere . . . to slip into pure evil. We cannot abolish that capacity but we must never accept it . . . Genocide can occur anywhere. It is not an African phenomenon. We must have global vigilance. And never again must we be shy in the face of the evidence."

— 42nd President Bill Clinton, March 24, 1998

Contents

List of Abbreviations

ADL	Rwandan Association for the Defense of the Rights of the Person and of Public Liberties
AF	State Department Bureau of African Affairs
APC	Armored Personnel Carrier
APLA	CIA Office of Asia, Pacific, Latin America and Africa
ARDHO	Rwandan Human Rights Association
ARG	Amphibious Readiness Group
ASD	Assistant Secretary of Defense
A/S	Assistant Secretary of State
BBTG	Broad Based Transitional Government
CDR	Coalition for the Defense of the Republic
CIA	Central Intelligence Agency
CLADHO	Liaison Committee of the Associations of the Defense of Human Rights in Rwanda
CND	National Council for Development
DAS	Deputy Assistant Secretary of State
DASD	Deputy Assistant Secretary of Defense
DATT	Defense Attaché
DCM	Deputy Chief of Mission
DepSecDef	Deputy Secretary of Defense
DIA	Defense Intelligence Agency
DoD	Department of Defense
DOS	Department of State
DRC	The Democratic Republic of the Congo
DRL	State Department Bureau of Democracy, Human Rights and Labor

DSAA	Defense Security Assistance Agency
Ex-FAR	Ex-Rwandan Armed Forces
FAR	Rwandan Armed Forces
FOIA	Freedom of Information Act
GOR	Government of Rwanda
HRW	Human Rights Watch
IAEA	International Atomic Energy Agency
ICRC	International Committee for the Red Cross
INR	State Department Bureau of Intelligence and Research
IO	State Department Bureau of International Organizations
ISA	Pentagon Bureau of International Security Affairs
IWG	Interagency Working Group
JCS	Joint Chiefs of Staff
LDC	Less Developed Countries
LICHREDOR	Christian League for the Defense of Human Rights
MEAF	Pentagon Office for Middle East/Africa Division
MRND	National Revolutionary Movement for Development and Democracy
NEO	Non-combatant Evacuation Order
NGO	Non-governmental organization
NSC	National Security Council
OSD	Office of the Secretary of Defense
PARMEHUTU	Party for the Movement of the Emancipation of the Hutu
PC	Principals Committee Meeting
PDAS	Principal Deputy Assistant Secretary of State
PDASD	Principal Deputy Assistant Secretary of Defense
PDUSDP	Principal Deputy Under Secretary of Defense for Policy
PDC	Christian Democrat Party
PDD-25	Presidential Decision Directive 25
PL	Liberal Party
PRD-13	Presidential Review Decision 13
PRM	State Department Bureau of Populations, Refugees, and Migration
PSD	Social Democrat Party
RPF	Rwandan Patriotic Front
RTF	Rwanda Task Force
RTLM	Radio Television Libre des Mille Collines
SecDef	Secretary of Defense

SO/LIC	Pentagon Bureau of Special Operations and Low-intensity Conflict
SVTS	Secure Video Teleconference System
SYG	United Nations Secretary General
UNAMIR	United Nations Assistance Mission for Rwanda
UNDPKO	United Nations Department of Peacekeeping Operations
UNHCR	United Nations High Commission for Refugees
UNHRC	United Nations Human Rights Commission
UNOSOM	United Nations Operation in Somalia
UNSC	United Nations Security Council
UNSCR	United Nations Security Council Resolution
UNTAF	Multinational Unified Task Force
USAID	U.S. Agency for International Development
USDP	Under Secretary of Defense for Policy
USG	U.S. Government
USIS	United States Information Services
USUN	U.S. Mission to the United Nations

Foreword

Jared Cohen provides a detailed account of the deliberations within the U.S. government's foreign policy bureaucracies during the 1994 Rwanda Genocide. His interviews with many key players answer the question why the United States gave such an anemic response to the horrific and systematic slaughter of over 800,000 civilians in a mere one hundred days. His focus on what went on inside the walls of government buildings in Washington while thousands died in Rwanda gives a different perspective from other books about the genocide. An excellent case study of the consequence of placing perceived national interest above moral imperative, *One Hundred Days of Silence* is a valuable, if disturbing contribution to the historical record of American diplomacy. These are lessons worth noting.

—Ambassador Prudence Bushnell,
Former Deputy Assistant Secretary of State

Preface

I spent the summer of 2001 living in the bush with the Maasai and conducting anthropological research on Maasai socialization of youth. After three months of interviewing, herding, and sleeping in a dung hut, I decided to be a tourist for a short period in order to see the rest of East Africa. In September 2001, I traveled from Kenya to Uganda in the hope of obtaining a permit to see the silverback gorillas of the Bwindi Impenetrable Forest. Unable to obtain a permit due to the popularity of the destination, I found myself "settling" for tracking the gorillas in the Volcano National Park of Ruhengeri, Rwanda. At that time, my understanding of Rwanda's history was based on a description from *Lonely Planet: East Africa*. I knew that a lot of people had been killed in the Rwanda genocide, but I was uninformed about the nature of the horror. The legacy of the genocide continues to haunt all aspects of daily life in Rwanda and after spending a few days there I all but forgot the original purpose of my trip. Inundated by stories about the genocide, I soon realized that I needed to learn more about it. I wondered how it was possible that so many people were tortured and massacred and I only had a vague understanding of what had happened.

I left Rwanda with the goal of reaching Goma in the Eastern Democratic Republic of the Congo (DRC),[1] by which the Bunagana border in Uganda was the shortest route. Captivated by a desire to learn more and somewhat comforted by the safety valve my fluency in Swahili could provide, I ignored the fact that the Congolese border was closed to foreigners; I ignored the potential danger of the environment; I ignored the fact that the Congo was out of my way. I knew that this might be my only chance to travel to the Congo and the fact that the border was less than 16km away made it difficult to resist the urge. After convincing a banana truck driver to hide me underneath the goods on his vehicle, I made it into Eastern Congo where I found myself face-to-face with members of the *Interahamwe*[2] who shared with me a completely different perspective from the one I heard in Rwanda. To have had the dual experience in the same few weeks of meeting victims of the genocide and perpetrators of the genocide made me want to learn more about the topic.

After returning home from the Great Lakes Region I began to read voraciously about the Rwanda genocide; in particular I developed a keen interest in the role that the United States played in the collective failure of the international community to intervene in the Rwanda genocide. This question arose as a result of the stories I heard from the victims of the genocide. In their view it would not have taken much for the international community to stop the genocide and in particular, they were in disbelief that the world's most powerful nation could not intervene to stop violence that was perpetrated with machetes.

I came across a number of explanations about why the United States and the international community chose not to intervene in Rwanda, who is to blame, and what mistakes were made. Scholars and journalists generally agree that the principal failures were a reluctance to accept the inevitable collapse of the Arusha Peace Process,[3] the UN reluctance to stop the violence, and most importantly, the withdrawal of the UN force from Rwanda after the ambush of ten Belgian peacekeepers during the second day of the genocide.

Three options were considered following the murder of the UN peacekeepers. The first option called for a reinforcement of the UN Assistance Mission for Rwanda (UNAMIR) to nearly 5,000 troops. The other two options considered were a complete and partial withdrawal, a distinction that was merely categorical because partial withdrawal meant all but a symbolic 270 troops. The literature describes a political environment in which the United States dominated the decision-making in an effort to downsize UN peacekeeping; the ambush of ten UN peacekeepers provided the perfect opportunity for the United States to advocate a position of withdrawal from Rwanda. While this position is clearly described by scholars on Rwanda, much of the existing literature does not delve into the reasons for U.S. opposition to peacekeeping in Rwanda and how that position developed.[4]

Samantha Power's *"A Problem from Hell": America and the Age of Genocide*, through a focus on the U.S. role, creates a compelling story of missed warning signs and bureaucratic failure. Power's work accurately captures the initial reaction of policymakers and the focus on the safety of Americans as the top priority. Her account of the U.S. response to the Rwanda genocide also presents a convincing argument that the lack of "noise" from the media and elsewhere placed policymakers in a position that did not compel them to make decisions or address the question of intervention.[5]

Bruce Jones, in *Peacemaking in Rwanda,* offers a different, but nonetheless also compelling case for why the U.S. government failed to intervene in the genocide. The Jones argument states that engagement in the peace process by the United States and the international community was less about solving Rwanda's problems and more about the fact that the situation in Rwanda was perceived to be easily remedied, resulting in the potential for a timely victory for both the UN and peacekeeping. Jones argues that the UN found itself in over its head as the situation deteriorated.[6]

While the Power and Jones accounts are important in that they question the approaches of the United States and the UN to atrocities prevention, their accounts leave several questions unanswered. In this book, I seek to expand on the existing literature by answering key questions that remain unanswered and by providing the crucial perspectives that are necessary to fully appreciate this historical tragedy. I capture the Rwandan perspectives, many of which have never been heard before; I look at why the warning signs in the years leading up to the genocide did not result in an alternative diplomatic approach that addressed these warnings, I look at the political context of decision-making in the spring of 1994, I delve into the nature of the bureaucratic decision-making process. In addition to delving into these vital aspects of the history, I seek to provide insights into why certain policymakers attempted to push for intervention despite the potential it had to impede their careers. In an effort to obtain this knowledge, I conducted interviews with policymakers and advisors from the Clinton administration both in person and over the phone, and I also traveled to Rwanda, where I interviewed senior officials from the genocidal government, Foreign Service Nationals (FSN) working for the U.S. embassy in 1994, and senior officials from the RPF.

At the same time that I conducted interviews with officials from the Clinton administration I was interning at the State Department in the Bureau of Democracy, Human Rights and Labor (DRL) under Assistant Secretary of State Lorne Craner. While working at the State Department, I obtained a better understanding of the nature of the bureaucracy and saw first-hand how and why some information never made it to senior officials, and the process by which the State Department uses an inter-bureau procedure to formulate a departmental decision. Furthermore, I had access to a number of policymakers from 1994 who still work for the State Department and as a result, I was able to arrange several of my interviews within the building. In many of these interviews, the informants were willing to answer all of my questions and to grant me extra time. Most of the interviewed were extremely regretful about what had happened in the spring of 1994 and critical of their own roles in contributing to the failure of U.S. foreign policy toward Rwanda. On several occasions, the informants stated that they were giving me information that they had never shared with any interviewer before, and when I asked why, they said that it was the angle that I approached the topic from, analyzing the process and context rather than blaming the individuals. That being said, it is impossible to fully separate a critique of the bureaucratic process from the culpability of individual policymakers.[7]

In these perspectives I learned why certain policymakers took a stand against the position of the administration, where different policymakers felt constrained, the prioritization crisis that confronted policymakers, and insight into the character of the interagency meetings. As a young scholar, having the chance to meet face to face with the individuals I had been reading about for more than a year made the work and research that I had done tangible. The accounts of the genocide became more than an abstract narrative as I had the unique opportunity of seeing their facial expressions and reactions to different questions that I was asking. I was surprised at the willingness of these individuals to share their perspectives, recollections, and critiques with me.

Beginning in June 2003, I worked a summer employment opportunity at the Pentagon in the Office of Stability Operations. Working under the direction of Vince Kern, who was the Director for Africa Region and head of the Rwanda Task Force during the genocide, I was able to gain an understanding of how the Pentagon bureaucracy functions.[8] Vince and I spoke on a daily basis about the Pentagon and Rwanda and the information I received from him was invaluable and never before documented. Vince Kern was the most senior official at the Pentagon working exclusively on Africa, yet he too had not been interviewed.

I left the State Department in December 2002 and within only a few weeks from the time I left Washington, DC, I flew to Kigali, Rwanda. The people I interviewed included the Foreign Minister, the Minister of Defense, the former President of the RPF, the former RPF spokesman, members of the RPF Executive Committee, and FSNs for the U.S. mission in Kigali. Not one person in this group had been questioned on their perspectives and interactions with the government of the United States before, during, and after Rwanda's genocide. Informants were more than willing to share information and as I listened to their stories, I could not understand how scholars and journalists had failed to capture these perspectives which are an integral component of the story.

In these perspectives I became aware of the Rwandan expectations for an international response to the genocide. For instance, to what extent did these expectations shape the RPF and the Rwandan government's objectives? Was the widespread civilian participation in the killing a result of low expectations for a potential U.S. or international response?

After conducting numerous interviews each day in Rwanda, I obtained data that I never expected to collect, such as the warnings provided by the RPF and the FSNs to the international community. Their perspectives shed new light on what the United States knew about the impending atrocities prior to the genocide. In addition to this, these perspectives enhance our understanding of some of the controversy surrounding the U.S. evacuation from Rwanda. For example, some diplomats misled the Rwandan employees at the U.S. embassy into believing that they would be evacuated with the American convoy. This was not the case and more than one-third of the employees lost their lives.

I spent the remainder of the field experience visiting some of the most horrific massacre sites—Nyamata, Ntarama, Murambi, and Rusatira. The massacre sites provided visual images for what I had been reading. As I began to write this book and reconstruct the story based on the new information that I obtained from interviews and documents, the pictures resonated in my mind. I view this written text as a way of creating awareness about how Rwanda was permitted to collapse, despite the fact that there were a wide range of interventions that could have been undertaken.

There are many obstacles that a researcher encounters when in Rwanda. The population has been traumatized by its recent history, there is an atmosphere of mistrust, and the government rules autocratically and blames it on a false claim that the ex-Rwandan Armed Forces (ex-FAR) rebels[9] and the *Interahamwe* militias continue to threaten Rwanda's border from inside the Democratic Republic of the Congo. There are mortar holes, skulls, and genocide memorials throughout the country that perpetually remind Rwandans of the genocide. The killers live among the victims because there are too many perpetrators to prosecute, and those who have gone to jail work within the communities and wear the pink clothes of the genocidaires.[10] To travel in Rwanda is an emotional experience and it is important to pace one's self. However, with only three weeks to conduct my interviews and see the important memorials that lay in each prefecture of Rwanda, pacing myself was not an option.

These questions of how the U.S. decision-making process can permit a genocide to take place and how a political context focuses foreign policy on national interest and away from morality are important because the U.S. government has a long history of repeatedly issuing the empty promise of "never again." Prior to the Rwanda genocide, this term was spoken in reference to the Armenian genocide, the Nazi Holocaust, and the genocide in Cambodia. In 1979, President Jimmy Carter issued a statement that "we must forge an unshakeable oath with all civilized people that never again will the world stand silent, never again will the world . . . fail to act in time to prevent this terrible crime of genocide. . . .we must harness the outrage of our own memories to stamp out oppression wherever it exists. We must understand that human rights and human dignity are indivisible."[11] Just a few years later, President

Ronald Reagan issued a similar statement that "Like the genocide of the Armenians before it, and the genocide of the Cambodians which followed it—and like too many other such persecutions of too many other peoples—the lessons of the Holocaust must never be forgotten."[12] Ten years later, Reagan's successor, President George Bush announced that "Each of us bears responsibility for our actions and for our failure to act . . . We must intervene when we see evil arise."[13]

As the Cold War began to wind down and the collapse of the Soviet Union meant there was no longer a bipolar threat, human rights emerged as a significant component of U.S. foreign policy. It appeared as though President Clinton, who had openly criticized his predecessor's human rights stance toward China, would be ready to act on the promises of never again by former Presidents Carter, Reagan, and Bush. However, Clinton did the opposite and his administration's failure to intervene in the Rwanda genocide reveals a need to reexamine the U.S. decision-making process to better understand how the gears of this mechanism do not cause a response to genocide.

—Jared Cohen,
Stanford, CA

NOTES

1. At the time of the Genocide, the Democratic Republic of Congo was known as Zaire. It was not until Mobutu Sese Seko fell in 1997 and Laurent Kabila changed the name to the DRC that it was no longer known as Zaire.

2. *Interahamwe,* the Kinyarwanda word for "those who work together," was the main civilian militia that carried out the killings during the Genocide.

3. The Arusha Peace Process emerged out of a series of failures to mediate conflict between the Rwanda Patriotic Front and the Government of Rwanda. The first of these attempts took place in Mwanza, Tanzania on October 17, 1990, two weeks after the RPF invasion of Rwanda. Following the Mwanza summit, there were five additional summits, most of which were held in Zaire and mediated by Zaire President Mobutu Sese Seko. These talks produced a loose ceasefire that eventually broke down in 1992. As a result, the Organization of African Unity (OAU) facilitated talks that began in 1992 under the leadership of Tanzanian President Ali Hassan Mwinyi. The series of talks in Tanzania became known as the Arusha Peace Process.

4. Scholars and journalists examine the role of the international community's role in the Rwanda genocide, however, Samantha Power's *"A Problem from Hell": America and the Age of Genocide* is the only account that focuses exclusively on the U.S. role. Peter Uvin's *Aiding Violence* argues that the international community not only failed to intervene, but also created a condition for genocide to take place through the character of development assistance, which Uvin argues further divided Rwandan so-

ciety. Most of the literature written on the failure of the international community to intervene focuses on the UN: Michael Barnett's *Eyewitness to a Genocide,* Bruce Jones' *Peacemaking in Rwanda*, and Alan Kuperman's *The Limits of Humanitarian Intervention*. Linda Melvern's *A People Betrayed: The Role of the West in Rwanda's Genocide* straddles an examination of the U.S. and European powers and the UN, but she makes a similar argument to Power. Gerard Prunier's *Rwanda Crisis* and Alison Des Forges' *Leave None to Tell the Story* offer the most significant objective accounts of the genocide's events, how they arose, and how early they could have been detected. Des Forges and Prunier's accounts are integral to determining which warning signs and events policymakers should have been expected to react to.

5. Samantha Power, *"A Problem from Hell:" America and the Age of Genocide*.

6. See Bruce Jones, *Peacemaking in Rwanda* (Boulder, CO: Lynne Rienner Publishers, Inc., 2001).

7. The views presented in this book do not necessarily reflect those of either the U.S. State Department or the U.S. Government.

8. A year before my arrival at the Pentagon, Vince had been working in another office with officials who were equally senior. However, under pressure from the media Secretary of Defense Donald Rumsfeld was forced to disband the office and Vince was placed temporarily as a special advisor to the Deputy Assistant Secretary of Defense for Stability Operations Joseph Collins. I was working in the Office of Peace Operations under Collins and Vince and I became the Africa team.

9. During the genocide, the Rwandan Armed Forces (FAR) were defending the genocidal government and fighting off the rebel RPF. However, once the RPF took control of the government in July 1994, the FAR fled to the Democratic Republic of Congo (DRC) and became the ex-FAR. This transformation marked the point at which the ex-FAR became a rebel group.

10. Genocidaires is the name given to the individuals, regardless of rank or position, who took part in the killings in 1994. Those who have been captured, arrested, and imprisoned, are forced to wear pink prison clothes and despite the fact that all criminals wear the pink attire, the genocidaires have become known as the "men in pink." Because the prisons are so overcrowded and such a great deal of community service needs to be done, they wander around the cities and towns under the escort of armed guards, performing various tasks and services.

11. Jimmy Carter, 39th President of the United States, Remarks at the Presentation of the Final Report of the President's Commission on the Holocaust, September 27, 1979, in http://library.ushmm.org/research.htm

12. Ronald Reagan, Proclamation 4838 of April 22, 1981, "Days of Remembrance of Victims of the Holocaust by the President of the United States of America," April 22, 1981, in Armenian National Institute archives, www.armeniangenocide.org/Affirmation.63/current_category.4/affirmation_detail.html

13. George Bush, 41st President of the United States, February 15, 1991, library.ushmm.org/research.htm

Acknowledgments

I am grateful to the Undergraduate Research Office at Stanford University for a generous grant that made it financially possible to travel to Rwanda in order to conduct interviews with senior officials in the government about their relationship with policymakers in Washington before and during the genocide. I would like to thank U.S. Embassy Kigali for arranging the majority of my interviews with top government officials and watching over my security while I was in Rwanda.

I would also like to thank Professors Stephen Stedman and Norman Naimark who advised me through the process of researching and writing. Their expertise proved invaluable and their support was energizing. I also offer a great deal of gratitude to Professor James Lowell Gibbs who advised me while in Rwanda. His anthropological expertise was integral in the development of my questions and methodology.

Jim Hogan, who assisted me in obtaining documents from the Department of Defense Freedom of Information Act Office (FOIA), made it possible to confirm testimonies of my informants and incorporate new information that I had not received from the oral histories.

There are a number of individuals who I would like to thank for offering their testimonies of the U.S. decision-making process during the genocide as well as thorough editing of the manuscript. First and foremost, Ambassador Prudence Bushnell has assisted me not only as an informant, but as an advisor. Her experience as Deputy Assistant Secretary of State for Africa during the genocide is an integral part of the history of the U.S. decision-making process toward Rwanda and her understanding of the decision-making process helped me to ensure that I captured the history in a fair and accurate manner.

I am grateful for the extensive meetings we had concerning drafts of my manuscript as well as the numerous phone calls in which I asked follow-up questions or obtained her guidance on pursuing this book. I am also grateful to Alison Des Forges, who not only serves as a senior analyst for Human Rights Watch, but is also considered by most scholars to be the world's expert on Rwanda. Des Forges, who became well-known in the spring of 1994 as a Rwanda expert, met with a number of senior officials in Washington, DC before and during the genocide. Her accounts of pressuring policymakers to take action are some of the most significant accounts of the role that the NGO community played in the U.S. decision-making process. In addition to permitting me to interview her on several occasions, Des Forges was also an important part of the editing process for this book. Her astuteness to Rwandan history ensured that the historical facts were in order and accurate. I also offer thanks to Vincent Kern, who I was fortunate to work with during my time in Stability Operations at the Pentagon. In addition to granting me his first interview ever on Rwanda, Vincent and I spoke on a daily basis about the history and he ensured that I understood the way in which Rwanda was addressed within the context of the Pentagon. The information offered from Vincent's expertise on Africa, in particular Rwanda, was a key component of my research. Former U.S. Senator Paul Simon's account of the Rwanda genocide was crucial in understanding the Congressional perspective on the genocide. Senator Simon offered me extensive feedback on the manuscript during the editing phase and I was honored to have had the opportunity to receive his input. He passed away just a week after I received his comments and I am saddened that I will not have the opportunity to share the completed version with him. Ambassador Joyce Leader, who was the Deputy Chief of Mission to the U.S. embassy in Kigali during the genocide was crucial to the materialization of this book. Ambassador Leader permitted me to interview her on several occasions and also offered important revisions to the manuscript, ensuring that the account of the years leading up to the genocide was accurate. As a policymaker on the ground in Kigali, the information offered by Ambassador Leader was invaluable.

There are a number of additional informants without whom this book could not have been possible. Former Secretary of Defense William Perry offered an important testimony about the perspectives of senior officials at the Pentagon during the genocide and the effect of Somalia on their decision-making. Former National Security Advisor Anthony Lake was also extremely helpful with his testimony about the approach from the White House. As the two most senior U.S. officials interviewed for this book, I am grateful for the time commitment and information provided by Perry and Lake. I would also like to thank former U.S. Ambassador to Rwanda David Rawson, former Assistant Secretary of State for Democracy, Human Rights and Labor (DRL) John Shattuck, and former Deputy Assistant Secretary of Defense (DASD) for Peacekeeping Sarah Sewall for agreeing to speak with me on the record about Rwanda and also for reading over the use of the interviews to ensure the utmost accuracy. I am grateful to former Commander in Chief of U.S. European Command General George Joulwan who provided a fascinating military perspective on the evacuation of Americans from Rwanda and the U.S. government's response to the cholera outbreak in Goma, Zaire. Former Under Secretary of Defense for Policy Walter Slocombe was also instrumental in the writing of this book. His account offered an important senior-level defense perspective on Rwanda.

There are also many State Department, Defense Department, and White House officials who spoke with me on the record but not for attribution by name. During the researching phase of this book I also came into contact with several officials who provided crucial information that was not for attribution.

Because a substantial amount of my research was conducted in Rwanda, there are also several Rwandan officials that I owe a great deal of gratitude. First, several senior Rwanda Patriotic Front (RPF) officials met with me extensively to talk about the political climate before the genocide, their perspectives on the Arusha Peace Process, and their contact with American officials and diplomats. I was fortunate to speak with former Chairman of the RPF Colonel Alexis Kanyarengwe, former RPF Executive Committee member Tito Rutaremara, former RPF Deputy Chairman and Spokesperson Denis Polisi, and former RPF Director of Intelligence Major General Kayumba Nyamwasa. I owe a most gracious thanks to Rwandan Foreign Minister Charles Murigande, who was in the United States during the genocide as an RPF liaison and offered one of the most important testimonies for this book.

I would also like to thank former Army Chief of Staff of the genocidal government, defector from that government, and present day Minister of Defense Major General Marcel Gatsinzi. I have interviewed Gatsinzi on several occasions and his testimonies have been the most important information I have received about what was occurring inside of the genocidal regime and what preparations were being made for genocide. When I worked for the Pentagon, I attended a July 2003 Ministers conference in Addis Ababa, Ethiopia at which Gatsinzi was present. We went over the manuscript together and he offered me extensive feedback on my analysis.

Finally, I am grateful to have had the opportunity to interview the Foreign Service Nationals (FSN) who worked for the U.S. embassy and USAID before the genocide and up until the U.S. mission was closed. These officials provided important perspectives on the U.S. decision not to evacuate its Rwandan employees and how they felt about what many of them have described as abandonment. The FSNs also had some of the most important information about what U.S. officials knew about the nature of the conflict before the genocide and many could offer specific accounts of personally giving information to diplomats.

PBS Frontline was also helpful to my research. While working as a consultant for the 10-year anniversary documentary of the Rwanda genocide, I worked with directors and producers to brainstorm on many of the questions I was looking at in my analysis. These conversations often assisted me in my own book.

Professor Lynn Eden at the Center for International Security and Cooperation and Professor Larry Diamond at the Hoover Institution were both instrumental in the final stages of this book. Dr. Eden met with me weekly for an extensive editing process and Dr. Diamond also guided me through this process. Their academic expertise proved to be invaluable in production of the final manuscript.

Finally, I would like to thank my friends and family for their support. My parents, grandparents, and sister were there for me to bounce ideas off of and to keep me motivated during points of frustration. I would like to thank my friends for casually copyediting my manuscript during their spare time.

I was fortunate to have had the opportunity to work with so many brilliant minds and distinguished officials both in the United States and Rwanda and to everybody involved I offer my appreciation.

Map of Rwanda

Introduction

"[The Rwanda genocide] is very sad, very sad indeed. It is unforgivable . . . I do not know how we could have sunken to that situation with the rest of the world watching and doing nothing about it. I think it is unforgivable. I do not know how we can ever explain that."

—Personal Interview with Former President
of the Republic of Zambia Kenneth Kaunda

"Never again," "always remember," and "we just did not know"—these are the phrases that have accompanied the aftermaths of holocausts, genocides, and other violations of human rights in the twentieth century. If the ideology behind these statements is to prevent future holocausts from occurring, how can one explain why in 1994, when the United States had extensive knowledge of a genocide taking place in Rwanda, it took no steps to stop the atrocities?

Beginning on April 6, 1994 and in just one hundred days, more than 800,000[1] people,[2] 11 percent of the total population, and 84 percent of the Rwandan Tutsi were brutally slaughtered.[3] In addition to these deaths, the *Interahamwe* militias raped 250,000 women and children, leaving more than 70 percent HIV positive.[4] This alarming number of deaths was accompanied by 4 million internally displaced persons and the 2.3 million refugees during the genocide that led to a temporary reduction of the population by 50 percent.[5] Millions more were traumatized, abused, branded, left orphaned, and had their limbs severed with machetes. The number of deaths was so high, and the remnants of corpses was so dense that "[humanitarian organizations] had to resort to using garbage trucks and by mid-May some 60,000 bodies had been picked up [in the cities alone] and summarily buried."[6] In the countryside, "the bodies of the victims . . . were often piled to a height of four or five feet, rotting for weeks and months since there was nobody to bury them." Over 40,000 bodies were tossed into the Kagera River, which resulted in the block-age of the river's flow at certain points, its pollution, and a massive outbreak of cholera.[7]

The manner in which the killers carried out the slaughter was extraordi-nary. Infants were picked up by their feet and thrown against walls,[8] others were thrown alive into latrines, pregnant women had the fetuses cut out of their stomachs, and mutilations were common with breasts and penises of-ten being chopped off.[9] The torture methods used to kill victims were so widely known amongst the population that individuals, if they had the money, often "paid their killers to be finished off quickly with a bullet rather than being slowly hacked to death with a [machete]."[10] *Interahamwe* militias forced parents to bury their children alive, and as the children tried to dig themselves out of the pit, the parents were forced to beat them with the shovels and continue covering them with dirt or risk the murder of the entire family.[11] The unending tales of brutality can themselves fill the pages of many volumes.

◆   ◆   ◆

The Rwanda genocide was one of humanity's greatest failures, with the U.S. government leading the charge for non-intervention. In seeking to understand how the world's most powerful nation turned a blind eye to genocide, one has to ask the questions of what the United States knew, and why, when the U.S. government had the capacity to end the atrocities, did it choose to not only play a bystander role, but also ensure that no other country or peacekeeping body could effectively intervene in Rwanda?

Despite playing a vital role, the United States was not alone in this com-placency. Both before and during the genocide, the French government pro-vided substantial weaponry, funding, and support to the government of Rwanda.[12] In fact, the role of the French became so suspicious that Rwandans came to refer to French President Francois Mitterand as "Mitterhamwe", an obvious insinuation that the French government was the financial life-line of the *Interhamwe* militias. In addition to the French, the Chinese government also served as a significant arms supplier to the Rwandan government. While not supplying arms to the Rwandan government, the Belgian and German governments—the only countries with colonial legacies in Rwanda—stood by as 800,000 Tutsis and Hutu sympathizers were brutally slaughtered and in particular, the Belgian withdrawal of its participation in UNAMIR served as the impetus for the Security Council's decision.

Despite the failures of other governments and the UN, the U.S. role warrants special attention. The U.S. role was monumental in the collective failure and its moral shortcoming was substantial. The U.S. role in this collective failure is essential to understanding why many of the world's other great powers and the United Nations did not attempt to stop the genocide. Had the United States taken the lead in, and advocated a strong international response to the genocide, there would have been an increase in the pressure placed on international organizations and other nations to take similar action. Instead, as the trend-setter for which international issues receive global attention, the U.S. government helped pave the way for non-intervention in Rwanda.

After conducting interviews with both American and Rwandan officials, I have concluded that the U.S. policy toward Rwanda during the genocide was nothing shy of 100 days of silence. Throughout the 100 days of genocide, senior officials at the White House, the State Department, and the Pentagon never sat down to formally discuss an intervention in Rwanda, deferred policymaking toward Rwanda to the lower ranks of government, avoided commitment of troops and resources, issued only sporadic diplomatic statements condemning the massacres, refused to use the term genocide to describe the killings, and did not consider the fact that the concept of intervention could include a variety of responses other than military commitment.

While the genocide began on April 6, 1994, the U.S. decision was not made on that day, nor was it made on any day that followed. Instead, the U.S. decision to not intervene in Rwanda was predetermined and made six months before the genocide began and before some of the principals even knew the location of Rwanda on a map. The metaphorical box for non-intervention in Rwanda and all other places like it was checked six months before the first machetes were drawn in Rwanda. Catastrophe in Somalia was the catalyst for this unspoken decision not to intervene in places like Rwanda. On October 3, 1993, the United States, in the midst of a humanitarian peacekeeping operation, lost eighteen American Army Rangers in Somalia and watched one being dragged through the streets of Mogadishu on international television. Peacekeeping became the scapegoat for their deaths.

As a result of this mentality, the Rwanda genocide began during a time when the United States was less than excited about the prospect of peacekeeping. It had drawn on lessons from Somalia and interventions in places like Rwanda were not in the cards. Perpetuating this mentality, the administration had come under a great deal of scrutiny from Republicans in Congress who were eager to criticize the Democratic President who they viewed as inexperienced in foreign policy.

By the time the genocide broke out in Rwanda, the Clinton administration had already begun shifting away from its earlier foreign policy of assertive multilateralism and began moving toward a new strategy in which U.S. involvement in peacekeeping would be based on a far more restrictive criteria that was much more selective and effective than the pre-Somalia Clinton policy. Given these factors, the Rwanda genocide broke out during a period of many global crises and policymakers, therefore, had to prioritize the numerous conflicts abroad within this new post-Somalia political context. At the time of the genocide, there was a political crisis in Haiti, a nuclear disarmament issue in North Korea, the violations of the safe havens in Bosnia, and great uncertainty as to whether or not the election in South Africa would result in a democratic transition or a violent confrontation between the Inkhata Freedom Party (IFP) and the African National Congress (ANC).

In addition to senior officials treating Rwanda as a low priority, many NGOs were not calling on the United States to intervene in Rwanda until at least two weeks into the crisis. Notable exceptions are Human Rights Watch and Oxfam, but even they did not initially label the violence in Rwanda a genocide. Even when the NGO community finally did issue serious pleas for intervention, the lack of exposure for the crisis removed any potential pressure on policymakers to take action. The media, which had the power to provide this exposure, was more focused on foreign policy issues like Bosnia, Haiti, North Korea, and South Africa, and domestic news such as the death of Jackie Onasis, the trial of Dr. Jack Kevorkian, the death of Richard Nixon, and the arrest of O.J. Simpson.

The genocide in Rwanda was preceded by four years of civil war, during which the UN, with the support of the United States, launched the Arusha Peace Process. As a result of negotiations and talks within the context of the peace process, diplomats and policymakers understood that there were human rights issues threatening the success of the talks, and that the distribution of arms and the training of civilian militias made some of the participants in the peace process uneasy. U.S. Ambassadors Robert Flaten and David Rawson, other American diplomats, and the international community, failed to recognize the Coalition for the Defense of the Republic (CDR) as the spoiler[13] to the talks, and as a result, the RPF began to lose faith in the Arusha Peace Process. This mistrust of the peace process, along with sporadic massacres of Tutsis, led the RPF to try and achieve peace on their own terms by breaking ceasefires and issuing demands. At the same time that the Arusha Peace Process was breaking down, the United States received additional warnings from Foreign Service Nationals (FSN), the RPF officials, secret informants, shared intelligence with other diplomatic missions, and their own observations and sources. Policymakers have insisted that they could not have predicted the genocide, and while this may be true, their witness to the same kind of killing and ethnically driven violence in the early 1990s, the known existence of lists for targeted ethnic assassinations, and the open extremism of hardliner Hutus, leads to a more plausible argument that they should have expected an unimaginable number of ethnically and politically driven murders, but were unlikely to proactively conclude that there was an impending genocide.[14] However, it is generally agreed upon that nobody, not even the RPF, could have predicted that the President would be assassinated on April 6, 1994, and up to 800,000 people would be killed in response.

When the Rwanda genocide began on April 6, 1994, Rwanda received some attention, but only in the sense that policymakers at all levels wanted to ensure that American diplomats and expatriates were safely evacuated out of Rwanda and into neighboring Burundi. The ambush of ten Belgian UNAMIR troops on April 7, led many in Washington to associate Rwanda with Somalia. By April 10, when the evacuation was complete, policymakers had the opportunity to use the evacuation procedure as a launching pad to intervene in the genocide, but remembering what had happened to the Belgian peacekeepers just three days earlier, senior officials in Washington gave a sigh of relief, praised the embassy staff for a job well done, and returned to issues that they deemed of greater importance to U.S. foreign policy.

Not only did the United States not advocate a response to the genocide, but the U.S. mission to the United Nations also, under orders from the Secretary of State, discouraged any international response by lobbying the Security Council for a withdrawal of all UNAMIR troops. After a few weeks of debate at the Security Council, the permanent members reached a compromise on April 21 that all but 270 troops should be withdrawn from Rwanda. The withdrawal of UNAMIR marked what Rwandans described as the departure of the international community,[15] resulting in the removal of the one arguably deterring force against the progression of the genocide. The withdrawal of UNAMIR was a decision made from the highest ranks of the government, and it was this crucial decision that created momentum for later decisions for inaction when confronted with the possibility of small-scale interventions.

More so than any officials in the U.S. government, President Clinton and National Security Advisor Anthony Lake had the power and influence to make Rwanda a priority. Had President Clinton or Anthony Lake deemed Rwanda a serious enough matter they could have used a principals meeting, memorandum, or direct phone call to inform the Secretary of State or the Secretary of Defense that Rwanda should be discussed and was considered an important issue by the White House. However, throughout the genocide neither President Clinton, nor Anthony Lake ever sat down to formally discuss Rwanda, and while it was occasionally covered in a briefing memorandum, no American response was ever discussed by either the President or the National Security Advisor.

With neither Anthony Lake, nor President Clinton taking the lead on Rwanda, responsibility over the issue fell into the hands of Dick Clarke who was the director of the peacekeeping desk at the National Security Council. As the overseer of the Presidential Directive Decision that outlined the Clinton administration's new post-Somalia approach to peacekeeping, Dick Clarke had a narrow focus of strategic interest as the determining factor for American foreign policy.[16] The apathy of the President and the National Security Advisor, led Clarke to believe that Rwanda was to be an early test case for the United States to say "no" to peacekeeping in areas that were not of strategic interest. As a result, Clarke dominated the interagency meetings and was successful in keeping Rwanda off the desks of the President, National Security Advisor, and senior officials.

Secretary of State Warren Christopher had his own list of interests and was unlikely to reprioritize without significant input from the White House. Secretary Christopher made the calculation that the environment on the ground had changed such that the UN Assistance Mission for Rwanda (UNAMIR) no longer possessed the mandate or the capability of performing effectively at low-risk. In Secretary Christopher's eyes, maintaining UNAMIR would have required a change in the mandate and objectives. Given the fact that this failed in Somalia, Secretary Christopher instructed the U.S. Mission to the United Nations to either remove or marginalize the existing UNAMIR force. With so many foreign policy issues confronting the administration in the spring of 1994, it is not surprising why Christopher did not red flag Rwanda. In addition to the President and the National Security Advisor demonstrating an apathetic stance on Rwanda, the Republicans in Congress were openly declaring that peacekeeping should be restricted, and as a result, Secretary Christopher was unlikely to support an American response to Rwanda that would create a firestorm in Congress, be difficult to obtain Congressional funding for, and was not even supported by the White House.

The only possible factor that could have changed the Secretary of State's position would have been if returning U.S. Ambassador to Rwanda David Rawson generated enough support for an intervention or firm response to the crisis. However, Ambassador Rawson's response to the genocide was hindered by the fact that he had a difficult time distinguishing between the different types of violence in Rwanda—civil war violence, political assassinations, and genocide. Even in his 2004 interview with PBS Frontline ten years after the Rwanda genocide, the former U.S. Ambassador continued to demonstrate an inability to separate the genocide violence from that of the civil war. Reflecting back on lessons learned from Rwanda, Ambassador Rawson stated, "We didn't understand the seriousness or the depth of the antagonism that was between the two sides."[17] Despite the Ambassador's statement, the genocide was not about antagonism between two sides, but instead a one-sided campaign by Hutu extremists to liquidate the Tutsi ethnic group and any Hutu who stood in their way.

The evacuation of diplomats from Rwanda within the first week of the genocide reduced the clout and influence of the officials working at U.S. Embassy Kigali. In Kigali they had a significant voice, but back at the State Department they served a similar role as action officers. Therefore, instead of pressuring the Secretary of State, or even the White House to respond to Rwanda, U.S. Ambassador David Rawson continued to advocate a return to the peace process, downplayed the nature of the conflict, and took the position of the administration. Even if Rawson had generated enough support and brought the issue before the Secretary of State, it is still unlikely that Christopher would have gone against Congress and the White House to respond to a conflict in Central Africa six months after Somalia amidst crises in Bosnia, Haiti, and North Korea.

The lack of concern over Rwanda at senior levels caused the crisis to fall down to the lower ranks of the bureaucracy, falling into the hands of the Deputy Assistant Secretary of State Prudence Bushnell. As a non-political appointment and a new face in Washington, Bushnell generated support among desk officers, regional officers, directors, and deputy directors, but even this sizable group was not influential enough to go against the NSC. Despite Bushnell's efforts, the voice of the White House could only be effectively challenged by an Assistant Secretary, Undersecretary, or the Secretary. The one political appointment in the State Department who voiced concern over Rwanda, Assistant Secretary of State for Democracy, Human Rights and Labor John Shattuck, was among the least influential in the bureaucracy because of his unpopular position of greater advocacy for human rights in China and his representation of a human rights bureau.

At the Pentagon, the absence of discussions concerning military force took the Secretary of Defense out of the equation, and because the Department of Defense was already arguing with Congress over defense spending, it would have been unlikely to expect the Secretary of Defense to argue for an intervention in Rwanda without an order from the White House. Responsibility for overseeing Rwanda at the Pentagon fell into the hands of two officials: Vince Kern, who was the Director for African Affairs and head of the Rwanda Task Force and Deputy Assistant Secretary of Defense for Peacekeeping Sarah Sewall. However, both Kern and Sewall were discouraged from arguing for a firm U.S. response by Congressional influence and open reluctance on the part of their superiors.

By mid-May, the bureaucracies received substantial evidence indicating hundreds of thousands of deaths and the mass migration of millions of refugees. Of course there was mass evidence of killings before mid-May, but most of the early intelligence focused on the civil war, the movement of rebel and government troops, and the status of the peace process. The transformation from an intelligence focus on these matters to the extraordinary humanitarian disaster was significant enough, and the pressure from the NGOs and the media was strong enough, that officials decided to at least entertain the idea of an American response. Officials spent the month of May determining which interventions were feasible within the context of committing no U.S. troops, spending no U.S. dollars, and placing nobody in harms way.[18] Proponents of intervention brought up the suggestion of jamming the extremist radio, but hardliners rebuffed this proposal by stating that it was a violation of Rwanda's sovereignty. There were other proposals for an airlift, announcing the killers' names over the radio, and a coalition of the willing. While discussions over these interventions persisted at the lower ranks of the government, the State Department's lawyers, under the direction of the Secretary of State, refused to call the crisis in Rwanda a genocide. They used a broad range of terms including "acts of genocide," "killings of mass scale," and "genocidal acts," but the fear that such a label could result in commitment or greater pressure on the administration, led senior policymakers to avoid use of the term genocide. Officials discussed the term genocide in the context of the Genocide Convention, and the symbolic nature of this treaty ensured that those who did not want to get involved in Rwanda could use terminology as a way of avoiding commitment. When the United States finally agreed to support a reinforced UN mission in mid-May 1994, the U.S. government delayed shipment of committed resources until one month after the genocide.

Experts suggest that full-scale military intervention would have been difficult if not impossible. By the third week of the genocide, the circumstances of the violence were such that the killing became decentralized. In particular, there were significant numbers of ordinary people (not employed by the government) who engaged in the killings and widespread dispersal of murder throughout the countryside. While the killing became decentralized, there seemed to be an endless supply of ordinary farming tools (machetes, hoes, axes, etc.) that were being used as murder weapons and the fact that victims and killers lived in close proximity made using them very easy. Even if these factors ruled out a commitment of military troops, they did not rule out intervention. Intervention is not synonymous with commitment of military force, yet if an administration is seeking to avoid intervention—as was the case with the Clinton administration—associating the two is an easy task.

The Clinton administration failed to blur the line between military commitment and other forms of intervention. In retrospect, there are a number of actions the United States could have done differently. Some of these included jamming hate radio and supporting a coalition of African troops from countries that had demonstrated an eagerness to resolve the conflict. However, more importantly than the interventions that could have been undertaken was the fact that senior officials in the U.S. government never acknowledged a need to explore solutions. The consequence of this was a weak U.S. posture vis-à-vis Rwanda. This weak posture, along with those of other nations, served as the impetus that the genocidaires needed to believe that they could get away with a liquidation campaign. Unfortunately for the Rwandan people, this was the green light to begin the genocide and to try and finish the job.

It is a shocking reality that senior officials never discussed the possibility of either military or non-military interventions in Rwanda. Even with all of the factors contributing to the marginalization of Rwanda, how could senior U.S. officials not at least discuss the possibility of action? With Presidential or Principal leadership, intervention in Rwanda might have become a reality, but even then it is not clear given the resource constraints and pressure on the Clinton administration. It is highly unlikely that Congress or the American public would have permitted a commitment of troops to Central Africa just six months after 18 Americans had been killed in Somalia and one dragged through the streets of Mogadishu on international television. Furthermore, the dismissal of Secretary of Defense Les Aspin after the Somalia debacle resulted in the Principals acting cautiously in regards to commitment of U.S. troops and resources to peacekeeping efforts. However, the power of diplomatic statements and small-scale interventions went incredibly underestimated and the U.S. government played the role of a reluctant superpower unwilling to assist in the facilitation of an end to the genocide. As a result, the small-scale interventions were often ignored or never proposed. Rwanda has become the quintessential example of what happens when the world turns a blind eye to genocide, and despite claims that this would not happen again after the Holocaust, and similar promises after Cambodia, the international community permitted one of humanity's greatest failures to occur in the spring of 1994.

The United States acknowledged its failure to intervene during the Rwandan genocide. The first statement came three and a half years later in December 1997, when Secretary of State Madeleine Albright said to the Organization of African Unity (OAU): "We, the international community, should have been more active in the early stages of atrocities in Rwanda in 1994, and called them what they were—genocide."[19] President Clinton, one year later on March 25, 1998, visited Rwanda and admitted that the 1994 Rwandan crisis was a genocide, not a civil war as the international community had viewed it: "It is important that the world know that these killings were not spontaneous or accidental. . . .These events grew from a policy aimed at the systematic destruction of a people."[20] The fact that two leading government figures offered a pained recognition of what had occurred during the months of

1994 is indicative of the fact that U.S. foreign policy had fallen short of its international responsibilities.

After the Holocaust ended in 1945, critics of U.S. foreign policy argued that more could have been done to halt the Nazi atrocities towards Jews, gypsies, and other minority groups by bombing railroad tracks and death camp gas chambers. Partly in reaction to these claims, the new United Nations pledged to ensure that such atrocities were never repeated by drafting the 1948 Convention on the Prevention and Punishment of the Crime of Genocide "Genocide Convention," a treaty that the United States refused to sign for almost forty years. Because the Cold War sparked rivalries between the Great Powers and politicized the Security Council, intervention became a tool for expanding influence rather than assisting those in need and resolving conflicts. From 1945 to 1992, there were 279 politically motivated vetoes related to peacekeeping operations in more than 100 major conflicts that left at least 20 million people dead.[21] The conclusion of the Cold War in 1989 brought hope that politics and humanitarian affairs had finally been separated.[22] The veto became less frequent and the UN involved itself in almost every conflict-stricken region of the world. The United States and the international community entered the final decade of the twentieth century with unprecedented ambition for peacekeeping, yet for Africa this ambition was more challenging than policymakers had expected.

◆ ◆ ◆

The Rwanda genocide was neither spontaneous, nor accidental. It was a deliberate campaign by Hutu extremists to liquidate the Tutsi population. Rwanda's history has been characterized by discrimination, violence, and ethnic division between the Hutus and Tutsis. While Rwanda experienced periodic phases of stability in its history, the ethnic tensions continued to exist both at home and abroad. The genocide in 1994 was the worst phase of Rwanda's volatile and bloody history[23] and before examining the role of the international community, it is necessary to understand the events that led to some of the world's greatest crimes against humanity.

FROM COLONIALISM TO INDEPENDENCE: A HISTORY OF ETHNIC DIVISION

The ethnic dimension of the Rwanda genocide was a result of a century of ethnic division, exacerbated by colonialism, and later used by the Hutu leadership to achieve independence on Hutu terms. Ethnic division was not inherently characteristic of Rwandan society and prior to colonial rule the countries' three ethnic groups coexisted peacefully. Rwanda is inhabited by three ethnic groups, the Hutu (84 percent), the Tutsi (15 percent), and the Twa (1 percent), who live among one another, speak the same language, and practice the same religion.[24] Historically, Rwanda was ruled by *mwamis* (Tutsi Chiefs) who oversaw the various kingdoms that made up Rwandan society, and despite the Tutsi control, Rwandan society was based on a highly mobile system where individuals could rise in status regardless of their ethnicity. When the Germans colonized Rwanda in 1897, their minimal presence and "style of indirect rule" permitted the Tutsis to retain control over the Rwandan kingdoms.[25] The Germans, while allowing the *mwamiship* system to continue, disrupted the mobility of Rwandan politics by declaring that the Tutsi, with their lighter skin, more pronounced facial features, impressive height, and supposed ancestral roots from Saharan Africa, were more intellectual and capable than the shorter, darker-skinned, Hutus.[26]

Following the First World War, the Belgians assumed control over the Rwandan colony and initially lent their support to the Tutsi minority, believing in the same Tutsi supremacy ideology as the Germans. Recognizing that they would receive overwhelming support from the Belgians, the Tutsi elite tightened their grip on Rwandan society, beginning what would become decades of mistreatment toward their Hutu subjects in the form of forced labor, irregular taxes, and unequal contractual law practices.[27] As a result, the majority Hutu population, found themselves racially discriminated against by both the Belgians and the Tutsis.[28] By the 1930s, the Belgians devised a system that required all Rwandans to carry an identity card indicating their name, location of residence, and ethnicity.[29] Ironically, the system that would later be used to round up Tutsis during the genocide was originally designed to more efficiently distinguish the Tutsi elite from the rest of the population.

At the conclusion of World War II, the Hutu sought to capitalize on the nationalist movements in neighboring countries by demanding that the Belgian favoritism of the Tutsi end, and independence be granted. The Belgians were exhausted from decades of colonialism and two World Wars. Faced with the difficult decision of granting independence or possibly suffering a military defeat, the Belgians decided that the risk of losing a war to their African subjects was far too great. Focusing on the most effective way to preserve their colonial ideology in the colonies, the Belgians recognized that by shifting their support to the Hutu majority, they could reconcile decades of oppressive rule and still salvage some influence in the region. As a result, the Belgians began to openly offer military and political support to

the Hutu majority while forcing the ruling Tutsis to devise less discrimina-
tory political and economic policies.[30]

With the understanding that Rwanda would gain independence, the Hutu
majority, with the help of the Belgians, launched the Hutu Revolution. The
Revolution began in response to a November 1959 Tutsi attack on a prominent Hutu sub-chief. The Hutus retaliated against the attack, resulting in violence from both sides that led to hundreds of casualties. The Belgians quickly
restored order and removed half of the Tutsi officials from their positions in
the government. The Belgian cooperation gave Hutu nationalists the confidence and support they needed to continue the transfer of power to a Hutu
majority. With the Hutus position solidified and hoards of refugees intimi-
dated into fleeing the country, Rwanda was granted independence under the
leadership of President Grégoire Kayibanda in 1961. In an effort to solidify
their power and seek retribution from years of oppression, the Hutu continued to attack their Tutsi "enemies" for another six years and while the violence temporarily subsided in 1967, the Hutu Revolution claimed more than
20,000 Tutsi lives and resulted in an additional 300,000 seeking refuge in
neighboring Burundi, Zaire, Tanzania, and Uganda.[31] The Kayibanda government promoted Hutu values and ruled with an authoritarian hand, however,
by the 1970s Rwanda suffered from government and military infighting,
harsh discrimination against Tutsis, and economic troubles. This unstable environment led many in Rwanda to grow restless over the deteriorating situation and in 1973, senior ranking General Juvenal Habyarimana overthrew
President Kayibanda in a non-violent coup d'etat.

The early Habyarimana years marked a dramatic change in Rwanda as the
violence subsided and society became more controlled. The fact that violence
against Tutsis came to a standstill with the emergence of the Habyarimana
regime overshadowed the authoritarian nature of his government. Habyarimana was viewed positively within the international community and as a result, attracted a great deal of foreign investment into Rwanda.[32] However, by
the late 1980s the prosperity of the Habyarimana years was interrupted by a
drop in coffee and tin prices that led to economic chaos in Rwanda. The economic crisis in Rwanda perpetuated political unrest, beginning with the assassination of the top prospect to succeed President Habyarimana, Colonel
Stanislas Mayuya,[33] and continuing with demands by dissidents for multipartyism and democratic reforms.

At this same time, Tutsi and moderate Hutu refugees living in Uganda
and calling themselves the Rwanda Patriotic Front (RPF), sought to capitalize on the weakened Habyarimana regime by using the discontent in
Rwanda as an opportunity to return home. The Ugandan government was
eager to rid itself of responsibility for hundreds of thousands of refugees

and thus encouraged the mobilization of the rebel RPF troops. Initially, the RPF and the Rwandan government opened negotiations for the repatriation of Tutsis living in exile; however, disconcerted with the government's conditions for repatriation, the RPF decided to return to Rwanda by force and on their own terms.[34] On October 1, 1990, the RPF invaded Rwanda from Uganda, driving Rwanda into further chaos and civil war. While the Rwandan Armed Forces (FAR) worked to defend Rwanda from the RPF invasion, an extremist faction of the Habyarimana government emerged in response to the civil war, arguing that the Tutsi planned to return Rwanda to the days of Tutsi supremacy. The extremists, led by an inner circle of radicals labeled *akazu*,[35] along with the Party for the Coalition for the Defense of the Republic (CDR), launched a propaganda campaign designed to manipulate the population into believing the extremist ideology.

Within a few days of the October 1, 1990, RPF invasion of Rwanda, the Belgian government dispatched its dignitaries to Kigali in order to work with President Habyarimana to find a solution to the civil war.[36] Following the Belgian visit to Rwanda, the Organization of African Unity (OAU), under the leadership of Mobutu Sese Seko, served as the principal mediator between the Rwanda government and the RPF. By the fall of 1991, general disapproval with Mobutu's role as the mediator coupled with the inefficiency of the talks, led the U.S. State Department and the French Ministry of Foreign Affairs to hold unofficial meetings with Habyarimana and the RPF leaders.[37] U.S. Embassy Kigali played an involved role in working with the two sides to broker a cease-fire and develop a solution. The unofficial talks by the United States and the French eventually escalated into the birth of the Arusha Peace Process in June 1992. Almost one year after launching the Arusha Peace Process, the UN deployed the United Nations Assistance Mission for Rwanda (UNAMIR) to maintain a ceasefire and monitor the Accords. After several rounds of deployments under a Chapter VI mandate,[38] UNAMIR's strength rose to 2,548 troops under the direction of Canadian General Romeo Dallaire.[39] The mission's Chapter VI mandate called upon the troops to oversee the security of Kigali, monitor the ceasefire, assist with de-mining, assist with humanitarian aid, and observe the repatriation of Rwandan refugees.[40] The mission, however, was relatively weak in that it did not have a sizable number of troops, lacked adequate supplies, and did not have an intelligence unit.[41] However, with a UN force supposedly offering greater stability to Kigali, both the RPF and the Habyarimana regime agreed to the Arusha Peace Process.

Working with the French and six additional African nations, the United States played the role of the "honest broker" in the Arusha Peace Process and looked to the peacemaking efforts in Angola and Namibia as a guide.[42] The official Arusha Peace Process lasted thirteen months and was facilitated by

Tanzania President Ali Hassan Mwinyi. Throughout the thirteen months, arguments persisted concerning who would be permitted to take part in the talks, the distribution of seats in the new parliament for the Broad Based Transitional Government (BBTG), and the composition of the armed forces.[43] After five rounds of talks between the RPF and the Rwandan government, President Habyarimana and RPF Chairman Alexis Kanyarengwe finally agreed on terms for the BBTG, reorganization of the armed forces, and repatriation rights for refugees and the Arusha Accords were signed on August 4, 1993. However, implementation of the Accords was a delayed process that never materialized before the genocide began. Eight months later, less than 24 hours after Habyarimana left Dar es Salaam for a meeting that was supposed to be about Burundi but focused on implementation of the Arusha Accords, his plane was shot down as it came into Kigali International Airport and the Accords that all parties involved had worked so feverishly to try and implement became little more than a dead letter. The genocide had begun.

NOTES

1. There has been controversy over the number of people killed in Rwanda. Estimates generally fall between 500,000 and 1 million people. There is uncertainty over the number of people killed because many historians argue that the number of Tutsi living in the country was documented incorrectly before the genocide. Given the fact that 800,000 is the most frequently cited statistic, I will use this figure throughout the book.

2. Michael Barnett, *Eyewitness to a Genocide,* Ithaca, New York: Cornell University Press, 2002, p. 1.

3. While the rate at which people were killed changed depending on the stage of the genocide, breaking down the rate at which people were killed (assuming equal pace) is still useful for demonstrating the magnitude of 800,000 deaths in 100 days. If one uses the figure 800,000 deaths, this also translates to 266,667 deaths per month, 66,667 deaths per week, 8,000 deaths per day, 333 deaths per hour, 6 deaths per minute, and 1 death per second. When I traveled with the Department of Defense to attend the Golden Spear Conference in Addis Ababa, Ethiopia, I showed this manuscript to the Rwandan Minister of Defense (I had interviewed him two years prior), the Rwanda Ambassador to Ethiopia, and the Army Chief of Staff of the Rwandan Armed Forces. When they saw the breakdown of how many people died per week, per hour, and per minute, and per second, they expressed great shock to one another and to me. They said that they had "never actually seen the figures broken down to the very minute," and they quietly shook their heads in disbelief.

4. Peter Landesman, "Minister of Rape", *New York Times Magazine*, September 15, 2002.

5. Bruce Jones, *Peacemaking in Rwanda*, Boulder, CO: Lynne Rienner Publishers, Inc., 2001, p. 1.

6. Medecins Sans Frontieres, *Bulletin* (April 1994) in Gerard Prunier, *The Rwanda Crisis: A History of a* Genocide, New York: Columbia University Press, 1995, p. 255

7. Ibid, p. 255.

8. I first heard of infants being thrown against walls during a formal dinner at the Joli Club in Kigali, Rwanda with two prominent members of the Kigali community. This atrocious method for killing off infants was confirmed by numerous victims and RPF officials during my discussions in the Kigali prefecture.

9. Stephen Smith, "Kigali livere a la fureur des tueurs Hutu," *Liberation* (11 April 1994) in Gerard Prunier, *The Rwanda Crisis: A History of a Genocide*, New York: Columbia University Press, 1995, p. 256.

10. United Nations, Commission des Droits de l'Homme, Rapport sur la situation des Droits d l'Homme au Rwanda soumis par Mr. Degni-Segui, Rapporteur Special de la Commission, 28 June 1994, p. 9, in Gerard Prunier, *The Rwanda Crisis: A History of a Genocide*, New York: Columbia University Press, 1995, p. 256.

11. UN Commission on Human Rights, Report of the Special Rapporteur on violence against women, its causes and consequences, Ms. Radhika Coomaraswamy (E/CN.4/1998/54/Add. 1) 4 February, 1998, p. 10, in Linda Melvern, *A People Betrayed: The Role of the West in Rwanda's Genocide,* New York: Zed Books, 2000, p. 158.

12. See Alison Des Forges, *Leave None to Tell the Story*, New York: Human Rights Watch, 1999.

13. Following Stephen John Stedman's definition of the CDR as a "spoiler" to the peace process in *Ending Civil Wars: The Implementation of Peace Agreements,* I will use this term throughout the book.

14. Some policymakers have explained that they were neither trained, nor were they prepared to look for genocide. They allege that they were more accustomed to look for signs of a return to violence, breakdown of a peace process, and ethnic violence, but they were not prepared to anticipate a genocide.

15. Personal Interview, Former RPF Chairman Colonel Alexis Kanyarengwe, Kigali, Rwanda, December 19, 2002.

16. PDD-25 was actually drafted by Susan Rice and Sara Sewall, while being guided by Dick Clarke.

17. PBS Frontline Interview, "Ghosts of Rwanda," Interview with Ambassador David Rawson, October 5, 2003.

18. Personal Interview, Former Assistant Secretary of State for Democracy, Human Rights and Labor John Shattuck, Via telephone to Boston, MA, February 24, 2003.

19. Philip Gourevitch, *We Wish to Inform You That Tomorrow We Will Be Killed With Our Families,* New York: Farrar, Straus and Giroux, 1998, p. 350.

20. Ibid, pp. 350–351.

21. Boutros-Ghali, Boutros. *An Agenda for Peace, Preventive Diplomacy, Peacemaking, and Peacekeeping, June 17, 1992.* A/47/277–S/24111.

22. 1989 is taken as the official year that the Cold War ended because it saw the collapse of Communism in Eastern Europe, the Berlin wall fell, the USSR withdrew

all of its troops from Afghanistan, and Gorbachev attempted to obtain support for his reforms.

23. Personal Interview, Former RPF Director of Intelligence Major General Kayumba Nyamwasa, Kigali, Rwanda, December 18, 2003.

24. Alison Des Forges, *Leave None to Tell the Story: Genocide in Rwanda*, New York: Human Rights Watch, 1999, p. 37.

25. Gerard Prunier, *The Rwanda Crisis: A History of a Genocide*, New York: Columbia University Press, 1995, p. 25.

26. Ibid, pp. 5–16; see also Alison Des Forges, *Leave None to Tell the Story: Genocide in Rwanda*, New York: Human Rights Watch, 1999, p. 37.

27. Gerard Prunier, *The Rwanda Crisis,* pp. 27–28.

28. Ibid, p. 39.

29. Alison Des Forges, *Leave None to Tell the Story*, p. 37.

30. Ibid, p. 39.

31. Alison Des Forges, *Leave None to Tell the Story: Genocide in Rwanda*, New York: Human Rights Watch, 1999, pp. 39–40.

32. Peter Uvin, *Aiding Violence: The Development Enterprise in Rwanda,* West Hartford, CT: Kumarian Press, 1998, p. 23.

33. Gerard Prunier, *The Rwanda Crisis: A History of a Genocide*, New York: Columbia University Press, 1995, p. 84.

34. Alison Des Forges, *Leave None to Tell the Story: Genocide in Rwanda*, New York: Human Rights Watch, 1999, p. 48.

35. Kinyarwanda for "little house," *akazu,* was a group of extremists led by President Habyarimana's wife. *Akazu* built a network of connections and acted as the eyes and ears of the authoritarian government. The group eventually determined that the President was becoming too moderate and looked for ways to undermine his authority.

36. Bruce Jones, *Peacemaking in Rwanda,* Boulder, CO: Lynne Rienner Publishers, Inc., 2001, p. 53.

37. Ibid, p. 57.

38. A Chapter VI mandate restricted the role of the UN troops to implementation. Under a Chapter VI mandate, UN troops do not play an enforcement role.

39. Adelman and Suhrke, *The International Response to Conflict and Genocide: Lessons from the Rwanda Experience,* New York: Steering Committee of the Joint Evaluation of Emergency Assistance to Rwanda, March 1996,p. 35.

40. Bruce Jones, *Peacemaking in Rwanda*, Boulder, CO: Lynne Rienner Publishers, Inc., 2001, pp. 105–106.

41. Ibid, pp. 107–108.

42. Ibid, *Peacemaking in Rwanda*, pp. 70–74.

43. Ibid, pp. 92–93.

1

Missed Opportunities

Something catastrophic was about to happen in Rwanda. Few policymakers who followed events in Central Africa during the early 1990s would dispute this. There were a plethora of sources indicating an impending disaster, yet there were few officials willing to accept this reality. Despite the fact that policymakers may not have been aware of plans for genocide, there was ample information to determine that ethnic violence was about to occur on an unparalleled level and this evidence alone, ought to have caused the humanitarian alarms to go off in Washington. Genocide was not something the policymakers working on Rwanda were trained or prepared to look for, but the concept of thousands of deaths was neither foreign to them, nor was it unimaginable in Rwanda's near future. However, their familiarity with the U.S. approach to Africa was not such to sound those alarms, but rather to seek solutions that did not fit the Rwandan political context, while attempting to play down warnings in the face of political solutions that they believed to be more viable.

Before examining the questions of what the United States knew about plans for a genocide and how it reacted to the various warnings it received, one must first examine the historical pattern of U.S. policy toward Africa, early policy toward Rwanda, and specific policy relations with Rwanda at the time that the most significant evidence of the genocide surfaced. Following World War II, U.S. policy toward Africa was heavily influenced by its Cold War policy of containment. In the Congo, the Central Intelligence Agency (CIA) supported the assassination of the Soviet-backed Prime Minister Patrice Lumumba and helped impose the initially western-friendly Joseph Mobutu Sese Seko. In Angola, the U.S. government backed the National Union for the

Total Independence of Angola (UNITA) rebel leader Jonas Savimbi, only halting aid in 1975 after the Clark Amendment prevented the United States from supporting rebel leaders in Africa. U.S. policy toward Africa changed once again with the election of Ronald Reagan in 1980. The Reagan administration nullified the Clark amendment and resumed support for the UNITA rebel leader through the late 1980s because, as then Assistant Secretary of State for African Affairs Chester Crocker argues, the United States viewed the Soviet and Cuban aggression as a "major obstacle . . . because they still thought they could find a way to win the war in Angola, which became their Vietnam."[1] In another example of containment in Africa, Crocker explains that the United States backed Eritrean rebel groups and the government of Somalia because "Ethiopia's government was caught up in a Soviet embrace, which militarized the country and led to huge domestic conflicts and human rights problems."[2] Rwanda, however, had a different place in the Cold War. Lacking major exports, minerals, and strategic location for the United States, Rwanda was neither an American, nor a Soviet priority. Because of these factors and the absence of an influential communist party in Rwanda, U.S. involvement in the small country in Central Africa never escalated beyond American funded development programs and friendly diplomatic relations.

After the stabilization of Rwandan society by the 1973 Habyarimana coup, donors and non-governmental organizations (NGO) flocked in large numbers to Rwanda, sparking a trend that by 1986 resulted in the presence of 200 donors in the country: about 20 bilateral ones, 30 multilateral ones, and 150 NGOs who managed more than 500 projects.[3] Despite the active role of international donors, the United States remained only a minor partner in the development of Rwanda, providing an average of $13 million in development aid from 1987 to 1990.[4] Despite the minimal role of the United States, the rise in development assistance from France, Belgium, and Germany continued to increase and by 1990, with the 210 volunteers and 453 technical assistants working as expatriates in Rwanda, NGO specialist Dr. Peter Uvin explains, "there was almost no corner of this small country where a four-wheel-drive vehicle with some technical assistant in it would not pass on a daily basis."[5]

Development assistance transformed the Rwandan economy as its country ranking among less developed countries (LDC) rose from the seventh poorest in 1976 to the nineteenth poorest in 1990. Compared to its neighbors, Burundi, Zaire, Uganda, and Tanzania, each of which was ranked higher in 1976, Rwanda rose dramatically by twelve spots in this LDC report and pulled ahead of each of the countries in the Great Lakes Region.[6] While this progress in development improved the Rwandan economy, the economic progress led many in the development community to ignore the autocratic nature and poor human rights record of the Habyarimana government.

As development organizations continued to tackle Rwanda's economic problems, many of the diplomatic missions in Kigali also pressed for democratization, working with the Rwandan leadership to ensure that the country moved toward a multiparty state. When President Juvenal Habyarimana announced multipartyism on June 10, 1991, permitting the formation of the Democratic Republican Movement (MDR),[7] the Christian Democrat Party (PDC), the Social Democratic Party (PSD), and the Liberal Party (PL), American diplomats felt optimistic that Rwanda was moving in the right direction. In an effort to warmly embrace this political change and democratic momentum, the United States Information Services (USIS) organized and facilitated a "study tour of the United States for a representative of each of the five registered parties—four from the opposition and one from the ruling party."[8] This initiative entailed a two-week program designed to acquaint the party leaders with the role parties play in a democratic process as well as to give the "participants a chance to get to know each other better."[9] Back in Kigali, Ambassador Robert Flaten and Deputy Chief of Mission (DCM) Joyce Leader divided up responsibility such that the Ambassador worked with the political parties and DCM Leader worked with civil society to "promote democracy." Leader recalls that she worked with Tutsi and Hutu groups that were advocating change openly by providing modest funding to support their activities.[10] She worked with several moderate Rwandan NGOs, mainly the Rwandan Human Rights Association (ARDHO), the Rwandan Association for the Defense of the Rights of the Person and of Public Liberties (ADL), the Christian League for the Defense of Human Rights (LICHREDOR), and the Association of Volunteers of Progress (AVP), to identify potential projects and eventually support them with equipment, funding for a conference, and offering them encouragement in strengthening their role by uniting together under an umbrella organization called the Liaison Committee of the Associations of the Defense of Human Rights in Rwanda (CLADHO).[11] The Embassy, through USIS, worked with civil society to run workshops for journalists with the objective of promoting responsible journalism.[12]

At the same time that USIS launched its initiatives, the U.S. Agency for International Development (USAID) launched a 5-year, $5 million project called Democracy in Governance (DIG) that covered a wide spectrum of democratic developments. DIG sought to "[establish] a training center that would lead to the expansion of media services" and to "develop a journalism association comprised of both government and independent journalists [where] printing presses and broadcast equipment would be made available."[13] In addition to promoting responsible journalism, DIG also sought to "strengthen the legislature," "decentralize the Kigali government in favor of local authorities," and "empower civil society by supporting and strengthening the skills of political and policy advocacy groups."[14] The Democracy in Governance project was ambitious and had a great deal of potential, but the project, which was just getting off the ground in early 1994, stalled as a result of the difficulty experienced with implementation of the Arusha Peace Accord.[15]

The launching of the Arusha Peace Process in 1992 led to a more active role by policymakers in Washington. Despite the fact that Tanzanian President Ali Hassan Mwinyi assumed the role of facilitator in the negotiations, the United States dispatched observers to the talks and worked with Rwandan officials on the ground in Kigali to promote the peace process.[16] From October 1990 up until two weeks before the genocide, there were four significant U.S. diplomatic visits to Rwanda. Most of these visits focused on encouraging the Habyarimana regime to pursue a negotiated peace with the RPF and to encourage its implementation. The first and most senior of these delegations came in May 1992, when Assistant Secretary of State for African Affairs Herman "Hank" J. Cohen traveled to Rwanda to stress what Deputy Chief of Mission Joyce Leader described as, "the importance of negotiations and highlight the readiness of the RPF to start talks, based on his discussion [with the RPF leadership] in Kampala."[17] In February and March 1994, the Assistant Secretary of State for International Organizations, Douglas Bennet, arrived in Rwanda "to discuss issues coming before the Security Council. [He] used this opportunity to stress to the Rwandans the importance of their success in implementing the peace process and thus the urgency of putting into place the transitional institutions."[18] The next diplomatic visit came in March 1994, when Deputy Assistant Secretary of Defense for Humanitarian Affairs Patricia Irvin traveled to Rwanda to discuss with the Foreign Minister and the Minister of Defense the pressing issue of "de-mining the countryside" and to identify "worthy humanitarian projects" that would become eligible for "DoD excess property, such as school desks for refugees."[19]

The final visit before the beginning of the genocide, and arguably the most important, was a trip taken by Deputy Assistant Secretary of State for African Affairs Prudence Bushnell. Prudence Bushnell recalls that in 1993, Assistant Secretary of State for African Affairs George Moose, Principal Deputy Assistant Secretary (PDAS) Ed Brynn, and she compiled a list of countries with particularly pressing issues in Africa and divided responsibility for them. As Bushnell explains, each of them "dedicated themselves to understanding their respective conflicts."[20] George Moose, Ed Brynn, and Prudence Bushnell did exactly that, with Bushnell taking Liberia, Burundi, and Rwanda.[21] Bushnell, who was accompanied by Director of the Office of Central Africa Affairs at the State Department, Arlene Render, left for Rwanda just two weeks before the genocide began.[22] Bushnell and Render set out with the objective of applying pressure on both sides to implement the transitional institutions and maintain a ceasefire. They warned the Rwandan leadership that the United Nations Assistance Mission for Rwanda (UNAMIR) was under review and that if they did not implement the interim government the Security Council could withdraw UNAMIR. She recalls, "I didn't exactly threaten them, I just warned them of this very harsh reality."[23] Bushnell had talking points regarding the establishment of the interim government and while she knew that the human rights situation required attention, senior officials in Washington expected her to maintain a narrow focus on the issue of transitional institutions.

When asked how soon she realized that the violence in Rwanda constituted genocide, Bushnell admits, "I knew that they had lists and that they were going down the list and killing the people on them, but, the first nauseating report of a systematic killing was when we heard about the Prime Minister Agathe Uliwingiyimana's [assassination on April 7].[24] That was awful."[25] Because she had overseen Rwanda in the Bureau of African Affairs and traveled to Rwanda just two weeks before the genocide, Bushnell knew more than most of the officials in Washington, yet even with her extensive background on the crisis, she explains that "Rwanda came out of the blue and I foresaw no explosion."[26]

THE WRONG KIND OF PEACE

The Arusha Peace Process proved more challenging than the Americans anticipated, and despite warnings from the involved parties that the Arusha Accords were likely to fail, the United States and the international community proceeded in hope that a diplomatic solution could end the civil war. At the forefront of the Arusha Accords is the question of whether or not the extremist Coalition for the Defense of the Republic (CDR) ought to have been included in the Arusha Peace Process. Negotiators initially raised this issue in the fall of 1992 during negotiations over the composition and responsibilities of the Cabinet and the National Assembly. These negotiations eventually culminated in the Arusha Accord Protocol on Political Power Sharing, which was signed on January 9, 1993, and granted the CDR one seat in the Transitional National Assembly. However, the CDR did not sign the peace accord until August 4, 1993 and therefore, did not subscribe to the Code of Conduct for political parties written into the accord, a document that included the renunciation of violence. Without signing the Code of Conduct, the CDR was not permitted to take up its one seat in the Transitional National Assembly.[27]

By January 1994 the political context changed and hard-line Hutu-Power[28] factions tried to gather as many votes in the Transitional National Assembly as possible in order to keep the President in power. According to Human Rights Watch senior consultant and Rwanda expert Alison Des Forges, President Habyarimana needed the CDR vote to fight off impeachment by the National Assembly.[29] When the CDR asked to sign the Accord in January 1994, the RPF refused and insisted that it would block any implementation of Accords that wrote the CDR into the peace process. Diplomats from the United States, Europe, and the UN were trying to unblock the implementation, arguing to the RPF that it would be better to have the extremist CDR held responsible by the terms of the Accords and have a stake in the future of the country than to leave them out in the cold to play a spoiler role. This was the stance held by diplomats and as one State Department official argued, "If you don't bring [the CDR] into the tent, they're going to burn the tent down."[30] During her meeting with the Rwanda Patriotic Front (RPF) on March 25, 1994, Director for Central Africa at the State Department, Arlene Render, "strongly defended the principle of inclusion [of the CDR]." She explained that "parties could not be denied a seat in the National Assembly just because the Front [RPF] did not happen to like them."[31] According to U.S. officials, the U.S. suggestion that the CDR be included in a power-sharing government was not out of a belief that the CDR platform was acceptable, but rather in the interest of breaking the deadlock and moving forward on implementation of the Arusha Accords. In a confidential March 25, 1994 State Department cable from U.S. Embassy Kigali, policymakers were informed that "The CDR issue remains the major stumbling block to setting up institutions. The observer group is agreed that CDR has duly indicated its intention to abide by the Arusha Accord and should be seated in the Assembly."[32]

The RPF continued to block implementation of a Broad Based Transitional Government (BBTG) that included the CDR through the beginning of the genocide. According to former Army Chief of Staff of the Genocidal Government (defector to the RPF after ten days of genocide), "When the members of parliament had to swear in there were always delays and the political parties were always telling the international community that the government does not want the BBTG to be settled, so the Ambassadors here, especially the U.S. knew that the government did not want to implement the Arusha Accords."[33] The RPF position was the strongest of all parties and the most serious obstacle to the success of Arusha in the weeks before the genocide and it is therefore important to analyze why the RPF, who initially joined the Arusha Peace Process in hope that a power sharing government would end the violence, chose to take a firm position against inclusion of the CDR.

According to a number of senior RPF officials on the RPF Executive Committee, the CDR's initial failure to sign the Code of Conduct destroyed their credibility as a potential partner in the peace process. RPF officials argue that the CDR's initial failure to discontinue messages that called for expulsion of *inyenzi* (Tutsi)[34] and open discrimination through the media against all Rwandan Tutsis, illuminated their unwillingness to remove themselves from an extremist platform.[35] In an illustration of this position, Deputy RPF Chairman Denis Polisi, who also served as RPF Spokesman, recalls being present at a meeting with Ambassador Rawson, Deputy Chief of Mission Joyce Leader, Deputy Assistant Secretary of State Prudence Bushnell, State Department Director for Central Africa Arlene Render, and other RPF diplomats, in which he remembers that Bushnell asked the RPF leadership "if [they] would agree for the CDR to be part of the new institution." According to Polisi, the RPF delegation responded that "the RPF [was] convinced that national reconciliation was the ultimate objective and associating that kind of extremist party into a transitional institution would mean that Rwanda is going nowhere."[36] From the time the CDR was formed in March 1992,[37] Ambassador Flaten and his successor David Rawson,[38] debated with the RPF leadership over its inclusion in the Arusha Peace Process and the new transitional institutions.[39] While the RPF successfully blocked the CDR from taking up the seat assigned to it in the Transitional National Assembly, it never prevailed in the debate over whether the CDR should be written into the transitional institutions.

According to RPF officials, they were not opposed to bringing opposition parties into the Arusha Peace Process, but they indicated that they would only consider inclusion of the CDR after its leaders "signed a Code of Conduct, which of course the CDR would always refuse [until January 1994]. This Code of Conduct included basic elements such as 'no systematic violence against Tutsi'."[40] RPF Executive Committee member and current President of the Legal and Constitutional Commission, Tito Rutaremara, stated that the American stance on the CDR infuriated the RPF delegation and made them question "how the United States Ambassador would advocate inclusion of an extremist party that refuses to sign a Code of Conduct that includes elements such as 'no systematic violence against Tutsi'? We had signed the Code of Conduct, others had signed it, but the CDR would not sign."[41] Even though the CDR eventually agreed to sign the Code of Conduct in January 1994, Rutaremara argues that the CDR's initial unwillingness to sign a code of ethics was an indication of what they stood for and that "Those ambassadors just didn't have it right, they wanted these extremist people included."[42] According to Rutaremara, the CDR intended to disrupt the Arusha Process and RPF officials allegedly told Americans on numerous occasions that "the CDR was not going to allow for implementation of the transitional government."[43] RPF Deputy Chairman Denis Polisi recalls that in the winter of 1994, the Americans warned the RPF that "[they] would have problems if [they] did not accept inclusion of the CDR in the Arusha Process."[44] Ironically, when the

CDR eventually signed the Code of Conduct, it was the RPF who blocked implementation of the transitional government, not the CDR.

By the time Deputy Assistant Secretary of State Bushnell and Arlene Render came to meet with the RPF and Rwandan leadership in March 1994, massacres of Tutsis and moderate Hutus had already occurred in Mutara in October 1990, Bagogwe between 1991 and 1993, Murambi in November 1991, and Bugesera in March 1992.[45] There were additional massacres in August 1992, followed by massacres from December 1992 to January 1993, and then by late January there was a brief hiatus in the violence that lasted until the genocide. However, the violence against civilians that ceased during this brief period was merely replaced by systematic political assassinations of prominent politicians, both Hutu and Tutsi. While historians argue that these early massacres were an attempt by some political parties and factions to manipulate democratic change,[46] the RPF have their own theory about the meaning of the small-scale massacres between 1990 and 1994. In an interview for this book, Rwandan Foreign Minister Charles Murigande, who served as an RPF liaison to the United States before and during the genocide, shared this theory:

> We would argue with [U.S. officials and the diplomatic community] that the killings of Tutsi in Bugesera, Bagogwe, and elsewhere was a pilot project. They were just testing to see the resolve of the international community and they were trying to determine whether or not the foreign powers were ready to accommodate this catastrophe or whether they would sit idle.[47]

In the absence of documents proving or disproving the RPF theory, one can only view Foreign Minister Murigande's assessment as speculation. Therefore, while the RPF may offer an interesting and perhaps convincing perspective, the true purpose of these massacres still remains uncertain. However, one can also make the argument that extremists used the massacres of Tutsis as part of a bargaining game designed to force the RPF to either make concessions, or break the ceasefire and taint their international image.

INSIDE THE AMERICAN EMBASSY

The American Embassy had a familiarity with the autocratic nature of the Habyarimana regime and recognized that the human rights situation was deteriorating in the early 1990s. However, despite this familiarity, diplomats remained focused on democratization and the peace process and tended to avoid reports that indicated the possibility of failure. The Arusha Peace Process was one of the defining events for those posted in Rwanda and their success, in part, rested on their ability to help broker peace between the Habyarimana government and the RPF. The embassy officials were concerned with human rights issues, but they did not entertain the possibility that the deteriorating human rights situation could lead to the failure of the Arusha Peace Process. Because human rights violations occurred within the context of a civil war, diplomats tended to view them as political violence associated with this war and as such, they failed to realize that addressing the human rights situation, in particular the small-scale massacres of Tutsis, was a prerequisite for discussions about transitional institutions and a ceasefire. Diplomats and policymakers believed that if the ceasefire could hold and transitional institutions could be implemented, the result would be an end to the human rights violations. They did not, however, think that addressing these violations as the primary strategy would lead to a ceasefire and the cooperation of all parties for the transitional institutions. In hindsight, these massacres, perpetrated by extremists who did not want a power sharing government, foreshadowed and eventually characterized the spoiler role that the CDR would play throughout the Arusha Peace Process.

While the extremists rarely made references to a final solution to exterminate the Tutsi ethnic group (most statements called for violence and discrimination against Tutsis), there were some instances in which they transparently advocated liquidation of the Tutsis. One of the clearest declarations of extremist plans occurred as early as November 1992 when Leon Mugesera, a senior affiliate of President Habyarimana, addressed a National Republican Movement for Development and Democracy (MRND) party rally announcing: "The fatal mistake we made in 1959 was to let [the Tutsi] get out. . . . They belong in Ethiopia and we are going to find them a shortcut to get there by throwing them into the Nyabarongo River. I must insist on this point. We have to act. Wipe them all out!"[48] On April 4, 1994, in an equally alarming declaration, Colonel Bagosora, at a dinner hosted by the Senegalese, announced what he perceived to be the best way forward for Rwanda: "The only plausible solution for Rwanda would be elimination of Tutsi." UNAMIR General Dallaire, UN Secretary General Special Representative General Booh-Booh,[49] and Commander of UNAMIR's Belgian contingent Colonel Luc Marchal[50] attended the same dinner and Colonel Luc Marchal recalls being so shocked by the bluntness of the statement that he "'had no doubt' what was being prepared and expected 'tens of thousands of deaths'."[51]

Despite RPF concerns, open calls for extremism, and the occurrence of ethnically motivated massacres, American diplomats in Rwanda sent few cables concerning human rights to their counterparts at the State Department and no cables that indicated a fear of genocide. According to Deputy Chief of Mission Joyce Leader, both Ambassador Flaten and later Ambassador Rawson focused on encouraging participation of rival political parties in a democratic process and, later, their adherence to the Arusha Accords. As a result, the majority of the cables reported on the progress of democratization and the Arusha Peace Process. While there were sporadic cables concerning human rights abuses, those cables that were not about the implementation of the Arusha Accords, focused on UNAMIR, efforts to get people on both sides to work toward peace, and the status of the ceasefire. There were cables that focused on the security situation, but by in large, these focused on the safety of Americans living in Rwanda or the RPF's commitment to the ceasefire.[52]

Alarmed by the lack of human rights reporting in the early 1990s, Kevin Aiston, the State Department's Rwanda desk officer, cabled the U.S. Embassy in Kigali with a request for more information on human rights issues in Rwanda. He informed the embassy that Human Rights Watch and other NGOs had come by the State Department to brief desk officers and regional officers on the deteriorating human rights situation in Rwanda. He wanted to know why the cables did not mesh with their concerns. Deputy Chief of Mission Leader recalls that, while the embassy viewed human rights as a major issue in Rwanda and was in constant touch with local human rights activists, these activists often took their concerns directly to counterpart organizations in the United States before coming to the American embassy.[53] In an interview for this book, Leader highlighted this phenomenon:

> Believe it or not, we were behind the Rwanda desk. We were right there in Kigali and they knew more than we did. People were not going through the U.S. embassy. Often times when the desk would tell us about what was going on in Rwanda regarding human rights it was the first we heard of it.[54]

Diplomats at the U.S. mission in Kigali had the information and contacts necessary to grasp the human rights situation in Rwanda. They were in direct contact with CDR leader Jean-Bosco Barayagwiza, who Leader explains "was well-known to the Embassy because he was the director of political affairs at the Ministry of Foreign Affairs."[55] While Barayagwiza's extremist ideology could not necessarily be connected to human rights violations, his leadership of the *Impuzamugambi*,[56] the youth wing of the CDR that was very similar in structure to the *Interahamwe*, could connect him to the violent anti-Tutsi demonstrations of his militia group.[57]

Outside of the official meetings, cables, and intelligence reports, each of the American diplomats in Rwanda had their contacts and sources who provided them with information from the street. As the situation grew worse in 1993, Leader recalls a Tutsi friend of hers failing to show up for their tennis date and "dropping out of sight." The next week, Leader remembers receiving a phone call in which this friend informed her that, "he had fled to the southern town of Butare and taken a room at a hotel for the weekend because friends had told him they had seen his name on a 'list'."[58] In hindsight Leader recalls this event as evidence that lists of Tutsis and moderate Hutus who should be assassinated may already have been compiled by January 1993 and understood that "these lists were infamous and having one's name on a list was ominous."[59] She recalls that, "there were always persistent rumors of lists of people, Hutu as well as Tutsi, who were marked for death."[60] This knowledge aroused suspicion for Leader, but the focus still remained predominantly on the implementation of the transitional institutions.

The Foreign Service Nationals (FSNs) working for the U.S. mission in Kigali (these included Rwandans working for the American Embassy and USAID in positions that ranged from receptionists to high-level procurement officers) understood the culture, the history, and the politics in Rwanda. While diplomats went about their daily business, uncomfortable tensions existed between the FSNs at the U.S. Mission in Kigali. The FSNs belonged to different political parties, some from the extremist CDR and MRND, and others from the PL or the RPF. For the most part, FSNs recall the political tensions creating a work environment that was awkward and uncomfortable, but there were, however, some instances where the political tensions between FSNs escalated to confrontation. On one of these occasions, a Tutsi FSN for USAID recalled an instance in early 1994 when the entire staff, both Rwandan and American, met for an informal lunch meeting around the outdoor dining table on the grounds of Kigali's USAID office. According to this FSN, a grenade exploded at a nearby location during the meeting, causing one American official to ask "what was happening?" The FSN answered the U.S. official's question, explaining that the political climate had become dangerous and the extremist parties wanted to prevent the democratization of the country. According to this same FSN, when the U.S. officials left the lunch table and only Rwandans remained, one FSN who was affiliated with the CDR stood up and yelled at his Tutsi colleague for his comments to their American colleagues. According to this Tutsi FSN, his CDR colleague exploded at him and yelled "what are you doing! . . . if you people [Tutsi] keep this up, we are just going to get rid of all of you!"[61]

Deputy Chief of Mission Leader recognized this tension, but understood that it was something the FSNs wished to keep private from their American counterparts. She explained that "most of the FSNs did not talk openly about politics because the FSNs were both Hutu and Tutsi and there were definite tensions between them."[62] She explained that Americans did not push their staff for information because it "would have been very uncomfortable for them and even put their lives at risk."[63] There were, of course, exceptions to this. According to Leader, there was one FSN whom she trusted and "knew [that he] was very well-informed and bright" and could provide her with "a useful analysis."[64] Throughout the civil war, they had informal lunches from time to time and Leader discussed with him the political climate of Rwanda.[65] In March 1993, another luncheon companion "suggested elements on the right might be moved to mount a coup . . . perhaps [because] the hard-liners did not believe the president was moving firmly enough against the RPF or objectionable parts of the peace agreement."[66]

WHAT THE INTELLIGENCE COMMUNITY KNEW

The United States intelligence capabilities in Rwanda were minimal. There was only one "human intelligence asset in the region . . . a U.S. defense attaché based in Cameroon."[67] Despite this minimal presence, by chance, the attaché was present in Rwanda as the genocide broke out and provided the Defense Intelligence Agency (DIA) with "valuable information."[68] The DIA, more than any other intelligence agency, had information that "permitted it to comprehend the progression of events somewhat sooner and more accurately than other government agencies or non-governmental organizations."[69] The Central Intelligence Agency (CIA) had similar information to that of the DIA, but because the CIA analyst on Rwanda was new, the information and estimates she provided tended to be more conservative.[70] In January 1993, the "CIA warned of a likelihood of large-scale ethnic violence" and in an even more significant report in December 1993, the CIA found information indicating that "some 40 million tons of small arms had been transferred from Poland to Rwanda, via Belgium, an extraordinary quantity for a government allegedly committed to a peace process."[71] The State Department Bureau of Intelligence and Research (INR) received similar information to that of the CIA. It had capable and knowledgeable analysts documenting the events and distributing information throughout the lower ranks of the State Department. INR received numerous reports concerning small-scale massacres and as the reports became more pessimistic, analysts "fully expected a return to war and a return to violence by February 1994."[72]

While many of the CIA, DIA, and INR reports warned of a return to violence, none of them predicted that the resumption of the civil war could escalate to a genocide.[73] Furthermore, the CIA, DIA, and INR wrote numerous reports on a daily basis and these reports, for the most part, were read by desk officers and regional officers. On rare occasions they were passed to a deputy director, director, or DAS, but unless intelligence is requested by the Assistant Secretary or other senior officials, it is unlikely that they would see a report on Rwanda. There were, however, some executive level reports prepared, or references to Rwanda in the daily intelligence brief that was circulated throughout the various government agencies, but even so, with so many other pressing issues, there was little time for policymakers to read about the problems in Rwanda.

The CIA produces reports that get distributed throughout the bureaucracies and it also distributes separate executive level reports. During the civil war, the CIA generated a total of 147 reports on Rwanda, ten of which were at the executive level. There was one report in particular that stands out to historians as a possible prediction of genocide. On March 15, 1994, the CIA prepared a report indicating that if the situation in Rwanda worsened, as many as 300,000–500,000 people could be killed. However, this report was not written by anyone from the Asia, Pacific, Latin America, and Africa (APLA) office, nor was it shared with any analysts. Instead, this document was an executive report, written by an intelligence official who specialized in matters other than Africa, and it was designed to go to the National Security Advisor. Sources reveal that the document was seen by a number of CIA officials simply because the cover sheet stated the "300–500,000 potential deaths" figure. There was a fear at the CIA that Dick Clarke and officials from the NSC would want to scapegoat the intelligence community if things in Rwanda turned out to be worse than expected. Illuminating this fear, CIA Director James Woolsey read the subject of the report and according to sources responded, "We are out of the frying pan on this one." What Woolsey appears to have meant by this is that if the U.S. government underestimated the potential for violence in Rwanda, the CIA would have covered its basis and avoided accountability. It is not surprising that a report designed for this purpose did not catch the attention of senior policymakers.

Given their limited capacity in Rwanda, U.S. intelligence agencies looked to Rwanda's former colonial powers for vital information. In 1992, the Belgian Ambassador to Rwanda, Johan Swinnen, received leaked information which indicated that the "secret group [akazu][74] is planning the extermination of the Tutsi of Rwanda to resolve once and for all, in their own way, the ethnic problem and to crush the internal Hutu opposition."[75] Swinnen claimed he shared this intelligence with the American embassy. When asked about this alleged information, Joyce Leader recalled, "If Ambassador Swinnen passed such information to the American Embassy, it did not reach me. It is possible that he shared something of this sort with Ambassador Robert Flaten who may have shared it with the Desk in Washington or elsewhere. But I was not aware of it."[76] A year later in December 1993, a group of senior officials in the Rwandan army, apparently uneasy over the rise in extremism, wrote an anonymous letter "copied to all diplomatic missions [in Rwanda] . . . [warning that] massacres would spread throughout Rwanda, starting in those areas where there were large concentrations of Tutsi. Opposition politicians were going to be assassinated and names were specified."[77]

Throughout the civil war, the RPF had a very capable intelligence unit, and according to one State Department official, the United States, despite some wariness over biased information, occasionally consulted the RPF for intelligence.[78] Led by Major General Kayumba Nyamwasa, the RPF intelligence unit used its own men and agents from the RPF to spy on the Rwandan Army (FAR), interrogated enemy captives and deserters, and used individuals from within the President's National Revolutionary Movement for Development and Democracy (MRND) and the FAR to act as double agents.[79]

In addition to consultations with the RPF intelligence units, Africa regional offices in the U.S. intelligence agencies also utilized the RPF liaisons present in the United States Dr. Charles Murigande, who served on the RPF Executive Committee, was one of these liaisons while simultaneously working as a professor of mathematics at Howard University in Maryland. As one of the most educated members of the rebel movement, Charles Murigande acted as an RPF liaison to the United States throughout the civil war and the genocide. Murigande began his campaign of awareness in the first year of the civil war. In response to the 1990 massacres of Tutsis at Mutara, Murigande describes this campaign of awareness as one that involved speaking to the press, conveying information about the massacres to officials at the State Department, Congress, think tanks, and a number of lobbyists.[80] However, Murigande felt frustrated by the inability of those he was pleading with to pledge action. He recalls having met with the International Republican Institute (IRI), the National Democratic Institute (NDI), the Center for Strategic International Studies (CSIS), the Brookings Institute, and the Heritage Foundation, and despite the think tankers responding "that they were going to share the information with people they were in contact with," there was no follow-up on their part, revealing that there was no interest beyond humoring the RPF's claims.[81] Murigande also met with a number of U.S. policymakers to discuss the RPF knowledge of the situation as it prevailed in Rwanda.[82]

Despite Murigande's recollection of the events, one must examine the context of the situation before passing judgment on those he met with. Think tanks, the State Department, and intelligence agencies grew accustomed to meeting with representatives from rebel groups and they had no reasons to believe that the RPF was any different from the dozens of other rebel groups claiming to be shortchanged by their respective governments. It is important to note that at the time Murigande began appealing to people in Washington, the RPF had just invaded Rwanda and sparked a civil war. Furthermore, the international community viewed President Habyarimana as the Rwandan leader who ended the violence in Rwanda and some viewed the RPF as the spoiler to this peace. Because nobody in Washington could have predicted that a genocide would occur just four years later, it is not surprising why think tankers and government officials received the RPF as just another rebel group attempting to make its appeal to the international community.

AVAILABILITY OF ARMS

The most significant evidence that extremists were planning a genocide came with the distribution of arms to civilians and the training of extremist militias. However, the fact that planning for the genocide began in the context of a civil war, this evidence was overshadowed by the militarization that is common to any sovereign nation engulfed in a civil war. This militarization began in 1990 and lasted until 1994. From 1991 to 1992, France sent more than $6 million worth of mortars, light artillery, armored cars, and helicopters, and in 1993 Rwanda increased their imports dramatically.[83] Similar imports came from China between 1992 and 1994 when the Oriental Machinery Company sent $4.6 million worth of goods, including 581,000[84] machetes and hundreds of thousands of axes, hoes, and maize cutters to "companies not usually concerned with agricultural tools."[85] In addition to the importation of massive amounts of arms into Rwanda, the army increased dramatically from 3,000 to 40,000 soldiers between 1990 and 1992.[86] Because of the launching of civil war in 1990, and because policymakers and diplomats were unlikely to take the time to examine importation records, it is unlikely that any of these imports and increases in the army would have resulted in speculation by diplomatic missions in Kigali that a genocide was being planned. However, while the quantity of arms flowing into Rwanda was in and of itself alarming, the officials in the embassy should have paid greater attention to the manner in which the Rwandan military handled and delivered these arms, which was a more suspicious matter. The United States also should have treated the influx of arms differently during periods of ceasefire than during the numerous returns to violence.

In interviews for this book, I learned that policymakers received information from a variety of sources, both Rwandan and UN, concerning arms caches, distribution of arms to civilians, and the existence of extremist anti-Tutsi militias. Nonetheless, diplomats and even visiting policymakers from Washington, ensured that the focus remained on the success of the peace process. When U.S. Ambassador Robert Flaten and later U.S. Ambassador David Rawson and Deputy Chief of Mission Joyce Leader met with members of the RPF Executive Committee, RPF leadership argued that something had to be done to halt the distribution of arms, but the focus on the Arusha Accords detracted from this pressing issue.[87] RPF Deputy Chairman Denis Polisi claims to have given Ambassador Rawson evidence that there were cars and trucks carrying weapons for the *Interahamwe.* According to Polisi, he provided the specifics, including the "date and brand of the vehicles carrying them," as well as the "license plate numbers and final destinations." Denis Polisi recalls taking "every opportunity we had to share the evidence of distribution of arms and training of civilian militias with the US ambassador. He had all of this information. In fact, the U.S. Ambassador was the most informed person in the entire country about what was happening."[88] While there is truth in this statement that Ambassador Rawson knew more about Rwanda than any other official, knowledge of the language and the culture did not, in Rawson's case, translate into the political astuteness in 1994 that would have enabled him to use his understanding of Rwanda to determine that there were two separate conflicts brewing—civil war and genocide.

As early as August 1992, Joyce Leader, learned from an early leader of the *Interahamwe* about "the creation of the *Interahamwe* . . . its transformation into a militia . . . [and] the training at camps outside of Kigali."[89] Inside of these camps, "individuals were taught to kill, with emphasis on killing at speed, cutting the achilles heel in order to prevent escape. One of the men who ran the camps was the American-trained Lieutenant-Colonel Innocent Nzabanita, who was nicknamed *Gisimba* [wild animal]."[90] The Belgians verified the organized distribution of arms to the civilian population and "reported that a meeting chaired by Habyarimana on November 5, 1993 at the Hotel Rebero decided 'to distribute grenades, machetes and other weapons to the *Interahamwe* and to CDR youth. The objective is to kill Tutsi and other Rwandans who are in the cities and who do not support them.'"[91]

While it seems that the distribution of arms should have provided clear warning of what was to come, policymakers and diplomats have defended their inability to appreciate the meaning of this influx of arms. According to Joyce Leader, the U.S. embassy had knowledge of the *Interahamwe* and the distribution of arms, but the connections were not made in such a way that they added up to genocide. She explains:

> Guns were being handed out to local communities, ostensibly for "self-defense". And there were rumors of clandestine meetings of Interahamwe. Did these bits and pieces add up to a concerted strategy to "exterminate" Tutsi and Hutu opposition? If they did, we did not see it at the time. In hindsight, I believe planning for such an eventuality may well have been underway in 1992, and I believe it crystallized in early 1993, but I had at the time no evidence to support such a contention.[92]

Why did Leader and other diplomats not see the plans for genocide at the time? Why did the pieces not add up? It seems that the answer is two-fold.

First, diplomats and policymakers focused first and foremost on the Arusha Peace Process and the civil war. Viewing the violence through a civil war lens, they tended to accept the explanation that the distribution of arms was for defensive purposes. Second, these policymakers and diplomats were not accustomed to look for genocide. After all, genocide is a rare occurrence and policymakers working on Rwanda had never worked in policy during such an event. However, the fact remains that there was ample evidence that there was potential for widespread killing and whether or not this would be termed genocide should not have mattered given the fact that both labels would result in an unimaginable number of deaths. Even if one is to make the argument that the distribution of arms was for defensive purposes, the trend of ethnic violence that, in particular, Ambassador Rawson was familiar with, should have aroused great suspicion about extremist plans.

On January 11, 1994, Major General Romeo Dallaire, Force Commander for UNAMIR, sent a cable to Major General Maurice Baril concerning an insider in the FAR who was ready to disclose revelatory information about the extremist plans. The informant claimed that he was "paid RF 150,000 a month to train the *Interahamwe* by the MRND" and that the *Interahamwe* have, on their own, "trained 1,700 men in the FAR military camps outside of the capital." The informant acknowledged his own role and admitted to having "trained 300 personnel in three week training sessions at the RGF camps" since the deployment of UNAMIR. He also admitted that, "since the UNAMIR mandate he has been ordered to register all Tutsi in Kigali. He suspects it is for their extermination." The informant presented the shocking capacity of the *Interahamwe* to carry out a plan of extermination by killing 1000 Tutsis every twenty minutes. He was willing to come clean and disclose all information, including the "location of major weapons cache with at least 135 weapons" and details of where 110 G3s and AK47s were already distributed. All that the informant requested was protection for him and his family outside of Rwanda in exchange for immediate release of all information. Colonel Luc Marchal, second-in-command for UNAMIR, sent a Senegalese troop along with an additional UNAMIR troop to go "with [the informant] to the basement of the MRND headquarters where there were 137 Kalashnikov assault rifles and ammunition. He showed them more arms caches hidden in bushes and undergrowth at strategic cross-road sites in Kigali."[93] The information was alarming.

Dallaire cabled New York to "[recommend] that the informant be granted protection and evacuated out of Rwanda."[94] However, despite the information provided in the memorandum, Dallaire concluded with the possibility that, "The force commander does have certain reservations on the suddenness of the change of heart of the informant. . . . Possibility of a trap not

fully excluded, as this may be a set-up against the very very important political person."[95] Dallaire's disclaimer at the end of the memorandum made
it possible for officials in New York and Washington to justify their dis-
couragement of an escalation of UNAMIR's role that would permit Dallaire
to seize the arms caches.

Major General Dallaire then met with the U.S. Ambassador David Rawson,
the French Ambassador, and the Belgian Ambassador, in an effort to convey
the importance and validity of the information provided by the "informant."
All three ambassadors were shocked by the information and "expressed serious concern," pledging to consult their respective capitals.[96] Rawson passed
the cable to Washington. A Political Military Advisor for the U.S. Department
of State, Tony Marley, remembers either seeing the cable sent by General
Dallaire or reading talking points on it. Despite his assertion that he shared
and distributed the cable throughout the Africa Bureau of the State Department, neither Deputy Assistant Secretary of State Prudence Bushnell, nor Assistant Secretary of State George Moose ever received a copy of General Dallaire's cable. According to officials inside of the Africa Bureau, it does not
appear that even the Africa analysts at the State Department's Bureau of Intelligence and Research had the opportunity to see General Dallaire's cable.
It is not clear who saw the cable and as a result, it is difficult to determine
who or what was responsible for this important piece of intelligence slipping
through the cracks of the bureaucracy. According to Marley, the failure of
those who saw the cable to take it seriously was a result of "[having] heard
allegations of genocide [from Rwandans], or warnings of genocide, pertaining to Rwanda dating back at least to 1992. . . . We had heard them cry wolf
so many times that we failed to react to this claim of genocidal planning."[97]

Dallaire had all of the information he needed to be certain that the claims of
the distribution of arms and the widespread existence of weapons caches were
valid. As a result, he appealed to New York to permit him to seize the arms:

> We can expect more frequent and more violent demonstrations, more grenade
> and armed attacks on ethnic and political groups, more assassinations and quite
> possibly outright attacks on UNAMIR installations. Each day of delay in au-
> thorizing deterrent arms recovery operations will result in an ever deteriorating
> security situation and may, if the arms continue to be distributed, result in an in-
> ability of UNAMIR to carry out its mandate in all aspects.[98]

Both the United States and the UN received the message, but perhaps because
Dallaire indicated in the January 11 memorandum that he could not guarantee the validity of the informant's claims, they forbade him from acting. According to U.S. Ambassador to the UN Madeleine Albright, UN officials in
New York "instructed Dallaire to inform the Rwandan president of the alle-

gations and urge him to investigate." Albright recalls that Ambassador Rawson relayed his impression to Washington that "President Habyarimana had seemed to 'get the message.'"[99] Frustrated by the restrictions placed on him from the UN, Dallaire continued to cable New York and inform them that "weapons distribution, death squad target lists, planning and civil unrest and demonstrations abound . . . could have catastrophic consequences."[100]

THE RWANDAN MEDIA PROVIDED CLEAR WARNING

The Rwandan media, most notably *Kangura* and by August 1993, Radio Television Mille Collines (RTLM), openly advocated discrimination, persecution, and even extermination of Tutsis. Radio Rwanda also contributed to the anti-Tutsi propaganda, but after a change in its management in April 1992, the broadcasts were significantly more low-key than their counterpart RTLM.[101] At the U.S. Embassy and USAID, the State Department employed dozens of Foreign Service Nationals, all of whom spoke the country's main language of Kinyarwanda and could comprehensibly translate the extremist broadcasts and publications. When asked whether or not she had any of her FSNs perform this task, Joyce Leader answered,

> I tried to get some of the FSNs to listen to RTLM Radio and their reply to me was, "Madaam Leader we don't listen to that stuff (sarcastic tone)." Of course they did listen to it, they just didn't want to admit it to any of us. So it was very difficult to get any of them to translate the propaganda for us.[102]

Leader's FSNs openly disagree with this statement. Seven FSNs who worked for the U.S. mission from 1990–1994 recall a position created in the early 1990s specifically for the purpose of translating the radio and publications. According to FSNs, the U.S. embassy paid Dieudonne Habimana,[103] the FSN appointed to this position, to translate extremist articles from *Kangura* and later broadcasts from Radio Rwanda and RTLM.[104] Every day, he provided summary reports for Ambassador Rawson and FSNs argue that if he did not know what the content of the propaganda was, than it is because he chose to ignore the information that was given to him.[105] In addition to Habimana's transcriptions, Charles Murigande claims that he engaged in similar tactics with officials in Washington and recalls:

> The U.S. cannot claim they didn't know, especially since we were drawing their attention on these, why did they decide not to know, when RPF, MDR, when PL, when all these political forces were telling them there is a dangerous radio here? You should not take their word for it, especially when the genocide started. The

U.S. officials in the embassy had the translation in front of them and they were sending it back to the U.S.[106]

In fact, Ambassador Rawson did not need anybody to translate the media for him. Having grown up in Burundi and having been posted in Rwanda in the mid-1970s, the Ambassador was fluent in Kirundi; which according to Kinyarwanda speakers, Kirundi is similar enough to understand Kinyarwanda with accuracy.[107] RTLM, which was the most extremist media organization in Rwanda, broadcasted out of a studio near the U.S. embassy. When a bomb explosion later destroyed the RTLM office, its owners, anxious to continue the transmission, began to broadcast out of the back of trucks. These trucks drove throughout Rwanda's prefectures and even broadcast on the same street as the U.S. embassy in Kigali. FSNs recall the mobility and frequency of RTLM forced people to hear the broadcasts and as a result, it was almost impossible for Rawson to avoid the extremist messages "even if he had tried to."[108] Rawson, however, explains that while he could follow a formal speech fairly closely, he had difficulty understanding the everyday radio broadcasts and informal delivery of the Kinyarwanda messages.[109] Even if he could not understand them clearly, the anti-Tutsi messages were loud and clear. Given the volatile environment in Rwanda at the time, it would have seemed appropriate for the Ambassador to seek clarification from his Rwandan colleagues on parts of the broadcasts that he did not understand.

FSNs assert that diplomats were given translations of the extremist messages propagated over the radio and in the newspapers; however, how much of that information they passed to Washington is unclear. Even if the diplomats working at the U.S. embassy decided not to forward the information to Washington, RPF Executive Committee members claim to have shared the information about hate propaganda with the various U.S. delegations that came to visit Rwanda throughout the civil war. Frustrated by the response from diplomats in Kigali, the RPF sent a delegation to the United States in order to push the issue of hate propaganda. During this trip, the RPF representatives claim that they provided individuals in Washington and New York with both radio frequencies and locations of the mobile RTLM.[110]

Despite the overwhelming amount of evidence proving the existence of the dangerous hate propaganda, the U.S. mission focused its attention on condemning press censorship and irresponsible journalism. Diplomats were used to confronting these more standard human rights violations and, as a result, focused on what was familiar rather than the pressing issue of extremism. Wanting to share their stories about being abused for writing articles that the government deemed "political" or controversial, journalists who were victimized by these harsh censorship policies often made the rounds to the diplomatic missions scattered throughout Kigali. One such journalist was Boniface Ntawuyirushintege who was "beaten on his feet until he couldn't walk."[111] The U.S. embassy listened to Ntawuyirushintege's story and denounced such treatment and restriction of civil liberties.

THE WARNINGS BECOME A REALITY

On April 6, 1994, a plane carrying Rwanda President Juvenal Habyarimana and Burundi President Cyprien Ntaryamira was shot down as it made its way into Kigali International Airport. U.S. Ambassador David Rawson and his wife heard the explosion from their residence. Almost immediately, the Ambassador received a phone call from the President's Director of the Cabinet informing him that the President's plane had been shot down. Later in the evening, Rawson received an additional phone call from Commander of the UN Mission in Rwanda (UNAMIR) Romeo Dallaire confirming that the plane had been shot down. Ambassador Rawson immediately sought to alert everybody in the embassy circles of the President's death. Rawson recalls that the UN had also hoped to bring western ambassadors together for a meeting with remaining members of the government; however, such a meeting never occurred because the potential attendees could not make it across the barriers that had been erected throughout Kigali.[112]

A few days before the crash of the Presidential plane Linda Thomas Greenfield, the regional refugee officer for the Great Lakes at the State Department, flew from Nairobi to Kigali to monitor the situation of Burundian refugees from the Burundian civil war, a situation that had grown significantly worse since the 1993 assassination of Burundi's first democratically elected President, Melchior Ndadaye. While she came to inquire about the situation of Burundian refugees in Butare,[113] Greenfield found herself present for the beginning of the genocide. At the time of the crash, Linda Greenfield and Carlos Rodriguez, a representative for the UN High Commission on Refugees (UNHCR), were at Deputy Chief of Mission Joyce Leader's home. As Leader recalls, they heard a distant explosion, and Ambassador Rawson's phone call confirmed that the President's plane had crashed. They later learned all aboard had been killed, including the President of Rwanda and the President of Burundi. She recalls waking up at 5:00am on the morning of April 7 to the sound of gunshots and within 3 hours had reports that the violence was not a war, but a systematic slaughter:

> I knew that a systematic killing was taking place almost immediately. My friends were calling and telling me that people were being systematically

killed, people I didn't know were calling and telling us how the armed men were going from door to door looking for Tutsi and killing them simply because they were Tutsi. We shared this information with Arlene Render who was the director at AF/C [State Department's Bureau of African Affairs—Central Africa Office].[114]

In addition to the inundation of phone calls, Leader also witnessed the systematic nature of the violence first-hand. Soldiers came to the gate at her residence looking for the Prime Minister. Armed men spotted preparations for the Prime Minister to scale the wall that separated her residence from that of Joyce Leader. The Prime Minister had to abort these preparations and fled elsewhere. Nonetheless, she was captured, tortured, killed, and then displayed with "her dressing gown thrown up over her upper body and a beer bottle shoved into her vagina."[115] Leader did not witness the ambush, but she heard the shots that killed the Prime Minister.

Shortly after, armed men arrived at the gate to Deputy Chief of Mission Leader's residence and demanded entry. She permitted them to enter her compound where they approached Ms. Greenfield, a tall African-American woman, and accused her of being Tutsi. After pressure from Joyce Leader and proof of her American citizenship with the presentation of her passport, the soldiers left Greenfield alone. On their way out of the compound they beat the gardener who was the only staff person present and who was also a Tutsi.

That same day, Leader heard from American staff members of the Seventh Day Adventist School, most notably Carl Wilkens,[116] that "civilians, probably *Interahamwe* militia, had come on the campus that morning and begun killing Tutsi." The reports she received in the first days of the genocide were enough to convince Leader that this was carefully planned and systematic.[117] Leader spent the majority of her time on April 7–8 on the phone with the State Department discussing what was happening in Rwanda and assessing the next steps for diplomacy and for the Americans. Leader recalls that Washington was privy to all that the U.S. embassy knew about what was occurring; and the fear that Americans could get mixed up in the violence, convinced all involved that an evacuation would be necessary. The conversations continued into the evening and kept Leader so consumed that she only returned to the U.S. embassy to lock the doors.[118]

Leader observed that there were three types of killings occurring in Rwanda following the plane crash: There were Hutus killing Tutsis and moderate Hutu civilians, radical Hutus assassinating moderate politicians, and there were the killings on both sides that were taking place within the context of the civil war.[119] Leader knew the severity of the situation. She heard rumors that the RPF commanders were sending orders to Ruhengeri and directing troops to move south and take Kigali. This was the revolutionary moment for the RPF, who had waited long enough and viewed the chaos as their best opportunity to try and take Kigali. With the prospect of an invasion of Kigali, Leader was certain that "Kigali was going to turn into a bloodbath."[120] She was right. After two days of discussion on procedure and the events in Rwanda, the State Department made the decision to evacuate.

NOTES

1. Assistant Secretary of State for African Affairs Chester Crocker, CNN Interview with Senior Editor John Hashimoto, "Cold War Chat," February 14, 1999. www.cnn.com/SPECIALS/cold.war/guides/debate/chats/crocker/

2. Assistant Secretary of State for African Affairs Chester Crocker, CNN Interview with Senior Editor John Hashimoto, "Cold War Chat," February 14, 1999. www.cnn.com/SPECIALS/cold.war/guides/debate/chats/crocker/

3. Peter Uvin, *Aiding Violence,* West Hartford, CT: Kumarian Press, Inc., 1998, p. 41.

4. Ibid, p. 91f.

5. Ibid, p. 42.

6. World Bank Yearly Developments Reports, compiled by Filip Reynjens in *L'Afrique des Grands Lacs en crise,* Paris: Karthala, 1994, p. 35, in Gerard Prunier, *The Rwanda Crisis,* p. 78.

7. The predecessor of the MDR was the Democratic Republican Movement for the Emancipation of the Bahutu (MDR-PARMEHUTU), formed in 1991. "Parmehutu" was deliberately dropped to overcome ethnic association. As events unfolded the MDR became associated with the "Hutu Power" movement.

8. Joyce E. Leader, *Rwanda's Struggle for Democracy and Peace, 1991–1994,* Washington, DC: The Fund for Peace, 2001, p. 4.

9. Ibid.

10. Personal Interview, Former Deputy Chief of Mission Joyce E. Leader, Washington, DC, November 18, 2002.

11. Joyce Leader, *Rwanda's Struggle for Democracy and Peace, 1991–1994,* pp. 6–7. While the U.S. supported the formation of CLADHO, this was something that Rwandan parties took upon themselves.

12. Ibid.

13. Joyce Leader, *Rwanda's Struggle for Democracy and Peace, 1991–1994,* p. 50.

14. Ibid.

15. Ibid.

16. Tony Marley, who was the U.S. government's fourth U.S. observer at the Arusha Peace Talks will be spoken about in the later chapters; however, it is important to note that prior to the arrival of Tony Marley, there were several other observers.

17. Joyce Leader, *Rwanda's Struggle for Democracy and Peace, 1991–1994,* p. 13.

18. Joyce Leader, *Rwanda's Struggle for Democracy and Peace, 1991–1994,* pp. 58–59.

19. Ibid, p. 59.

20. Personal Interview, Former Deputy Assistant Secretary of State for African Affairs Prudence Bushnell, Washington, DC, December 9, 2002.

21. Ibid.

22. Personal Interview, Former Deputy Assistant Secretary of State for African Affairs Prudence Bushnell, Washington, DC, December 9, 2002; see also Samantha Power, "*A Problem from Hell:*" *America and the Age of Genocide,* p. 345.

23. Personal Interview, Former Deputy Assistant Secretary of State for African Affairs Prudence Bushnell, Washington, DC, December 9, 2002.

24. After the assassination of President Habyarimana, Prime Minister Uliwingiyimana attempted to appeal to the people to remain calm, but before she could arrive at the radio station, the Presidential Guard, who viewed the Prime Minister as a moderate, discovered her in a neighboring UN staff house and murdered her.

25. Personal Interview, Former Deputy Assistant Secretary of State for African Affairs Prudence Bushnell, Washington, DC, December 9, 2002.

26. Personal Interview, Former Deputy Assistant Secretary of State for African Affairs Prudence Bushnell, Washington, DC, December 9, 2002.

27. Personal Interview, Former Deputy Chief of Mission Joyce Leader, Via email, September 26, 2003.

28. "Hutu Power" was the slogan of the most extremist members of the CDR and the MRND whose anti-Tutsi platforms called for harsh discrimination of Tutsis and expulsion of the ethnic group.

29. Personal Interview, Human Rights Watch Consultant Alison Des Forges, Via telephone to Buffalo, NY, October 22, 2003.

30. State Department official, confidential Bruce Jones interview, Washington, DC, June 1995, in Bruce Jones, *Peacemaking in Rwanda,* p. 82.

31. Confidential State Department cable #01316 from Kigali, Rwanda. Subject: DAS Bushnell Meets Habyarimana and RPF, March 25, 1994.

32. Ibid.

33. Personal Interview, Former Army Chief of Staff of the Genocidal Government Major General Marcel Gatsinzi, Kigali, Rwanda, December 24, 2002. It is important to note that Gatsinzi defected as the Army Chief of Staff of the Genocidal Government ten days into the genocide. He later joined the RPF and currently serves as Minister of Defense of Rwanda.

34. "Inyenzi" is the Kinyarwanda word for "cockroach" and the term used by extremists to describe the RPF and the Tutsi population that they associated with the rebels.

35. Bruce Jones, *Peacemaking in Rwanda,* p. 32; see also Michael Barnett, *Eyewitness to a Genocide,* p. 54; see also Adelman and Suhrke, *The International Response to Conflict and Genocide: Lessons from the Rwanda Experience,* March 1996, Chapter 2, p. 4.

36. Personal Interview, Deputy RPF Chairman and RPF Spokesman Denis Polisi, Kigali, Rwanda, December 20, 2002.

37. Michael Barnett, *Eyewitness to a Genocide,* p. 54.

38. Robert Flaten served as the U.S. Ambassador to Rwanda until November 23, 1993 when he was replaced by David Rawson, who arrived January 6, 1994.

39. State Department official, Confidential Bruce Jones interview, Washington, DC, June 1995; in Bruce Jones, *Peacemaking in Rwanda,* p. 82.

40. Personal Interview, The Honorable President of the Judicial and Constitutional Commission Tito Rutaremara, Kigali, Rwanda, December 20, 2002.

41. Personal Interview, The Honorable President of the Judicial and Constitutional Commission Tito Rutaremara, Kigali, Rwanda, December 20, 2002.

42. Personal Interview, The Honorable President of the Judicial and Constitutional Commission Tito Rutaremara, Kigali, Rwanda, December 20, 2002.

43. Ibid; see also Stephen John Stedman, Donald Rothchild, and Elizabeth M. Cousens, *Ending Civil Wars: The Implementation of Peace Agreements,* Boulder, CO: Lynne Rienner Publishers, Inc., 2002, p. 93; see also Stephen John Stedman, "Spoiler Problems in Peace Processes," *International Security* 22, 2 (Fall 1997), pp. 5–53, in Michael Barnett, *Eyewitness to a Genocide,* p. 75.

44. Personal Interview, Deputy RPF Chairman and RPF Spokesman Denis Polisi, Kigali, Rwanda, December 20, 2002.

45. Gerard Prunier, *The Rwanda Crisis,* p. 139.

46. Ibid, p. 143.

47. Personal Interview, Foreign Minister of the Republic of Rwanda Dr. Charles Murigande, Kigali, Rwanda, December 20, 2002.

48. Organization for African Union, *Rwanda: The Preventable Genocide*, p. 4, citing Federation Internationale des Ligues des Droties de l'Homme, Rwanda Report of March 1993, pp. 24–25, in Samantha Power, *"A Problem from Hell:" America and the Age of Genocide,* pp. 339–340.

49. Jaques-Roger Booh-Booh served as the UN Secretary General's special representative to Rwanda.

50. Colonel Luc Marchal headed the Belgian contingent of UNAMIR and was considered to be Belgium's top peacekeeper.

51. *Lettre ouverte aux parlementaires: Le texte du rapport du groupe "Rwanda" du Senat* (Brussels: Editions Luc Pire, 1997), p. 134; Commission d'enquete parlementaire concernant concernant les evenements du Rwanda, *Rapport* (Brussels: Senat de Belgique, December 6, 1997) (www.senate.be/docs), section 3.6.4.5, quoting Astri Suhrke, in Alan Kuperman, *Limits of Humanitarian Intervention,* p. 81–84; see also Alison Des Forges, *Leave None to Tell the Story*, p. 172.

52. Personal Interview, Former Deputy Chief of Mission Joyce E. Leader, Washington, DC, November 18, 2002.

53. Personal Interview, Former Deputy Chief of Mission Joyce E. Leader, Washington, DC, November 18, 2002.

54. Ibid.

55. Joyce Leader, *Rwanda's Struggle for Democracy and Peace, 1991–1994*, p. 11; see also Des Forges, p. 228.

56. *Impuzamugambi* is Kinyarwanda for "those who have the same goal."

57. Alison Des Forges, *Leave None to Tell the Story,* p. 228.

58. Joyce Leader, *Rwanda's Struggle for Democracy and Peace, 1991–1994*, p. 23.

59. Ibid.

60. Personal Interview, Former Deputy Chief of Mission Joyce Leader, Via e-mail to Washington, DC, May 11, 2003.

61. Personal Interview, Foreign Service National USAID [D], Kigali, Rwanda, December 19, 2002.

62. Joyce Leader, *Rwanda's Struggle for Democracy and Peace, 1991–1994*, p. 23.

63. Personal Interview, Former Deputy Chief of Mission Joyce E. Leader, Washington, DC, November 18, 2002.

64. Ibid.

65. Personal Interview, Former Deputy Chief of Mission Joyce E. Leader, Washington, DC, November 18, 2002; see also, personal interview, Foreign Service National USAID [B], Kigali, Rwanda, December 19, 2002.

66. Joyce Leader, *Rwanda's Struggle for Democracy and Peace, 1991–1994*, p. 30.

67. Alan Kuperman, *The Limits of Humanitarian Intervention*, p. 32.

68. Ibid.

69. Ibid, p. 24.

70. Personal Interview, State Department Official [A], Via telephone to Washington, DC, February 25, 2003.

71. Organization for African Unity, *Rwanda: The Preventable Genocide*, OAU, chap. 9, p. 5, in Samantha Power, *"A Problem From Hell:" America and the Age of Genocide,* p. 338.

72. Personal Interview, State Department Official [A], Via telephone to Washington, DC, February 25, 2003.

73. Scholars have repeatedly cited a January 1994 CIA report in which it was predicted that as many as half a million people could die if there was a return to violence in Rwanda. No January report existed. The report was written in March and was not written for the reasons that scholars such as Samantha Power and Howard Adelman and Astri Suhrke suggest. These scholars argue that the report was written as a prediction for a possible outcome. In response to their conclusions, I inquired about this report in interviews with State Department Officials, Intelligence Officials, Defense Department Officials, and White House Officials. After asking more than 7 officials who claim they would have seen the report if it was written, not one recalled its existence. In an interview with State Department Official [A] on February 25, 2003, I was informed that even if such a report did exist and was seen, the prediction would have been so preposterous that they would have "rolled their eyes at it."

74. The Kinyarwanda word for 'little house', *akazu* was the secret society of hardliner Hutus, led by the President's wife and advocated the most overt platform of extremism, while criticizing the President and the soft-liners for selling the Hutu government out to the RPF.

75. Belgian Senate, *Commission d'enquete parlementaire concernant les evenements du Rwanda,* Report, 6 December 1997, p. 82, in Linda Melvern, *A People Betrayed: The Role of the West in Rwanda's Genocide,* p. 43.

76. Personal Interview, Former Deputy Chief of Mission Joyce Leader, Via e-mail to Washington, DC, May 11, 2003.

77. Cuichaoua (ed.), *Les Crises Politiques au Burundi et au Rwanda*, pp. 653–654, in Linda Melvern, *A People Betrayed: The Role of the West in Rwanda's Genocide*, p. 89.

78. Personal Interview, State Department Official [A], Via telephone to Washington, DC, February 25, 2003.

79. Personal Interview, Former RPF Director of Intelligence Major General Kayumba Nyamwasa, Kigali, Rwanda, December 18, 2002.

80. Personal Interview, Foreign Minister of Rwanda Dr. Charles Murigande, Kigali, Rwanda, December 20, 2002.

81. Ibid.

82. Ibid. A/S for DRL John Shattuck and State Department Official [A], verified that Murigande obtained meetings with them.

83. Linda Melvern, *A People Betrayed: The Role of the West in Rwanda's Genocide*, p. 78

84. Ibid, p. 64

85. Pierre Galand and Michel Choussudovsky, L'Usage de la Dette Exterieure du Rwanda (1990/1994) La Responsabilite des Bailleurs de Fonds. Analyse et Recommandations. Preliminary Report. Brussels and Ottawa, November 1996, unpublished, in Linda Melvern, *A People Betrayed: The Role of the West in Rwanda's Genocide*, p. 65.

86. Colette Braeckman, *1994 Genocide au Rwanda*. Paris: Fayart, p. 154 ff.; Human Rights Watch 1994a, in Peter Uvin, *Aiding Violence*, p. 65.

87. The RPF had no base in Rwanda until after its June 1992 offensive. At that time, Ambassador Flaten did meet with RPF officials, but only in the north. In late December 1993, when the RPF brought a battalion to Kigali, Ambassador Rawson and Deputy Chief of Mission Leader had more frequent contact with the RPF leaders. Rawson met with the RPF on an almost daily basis in connection with the Arusha implementation negotiations.

88. Personal Interview, Former RPF Deputy Chairman and RPF Spokesman Denis Polisi, Kigali, Rwanda, December 20, 2002.

89. Joyce E. Leader, *Rwanda's Struggle for Democracy and Peace, 1991–1994*, Washington, DC: The Fund for Peace, 2001, p. 16.

90. Linda Melvern, *A People Betrayed: The Role of the West in Rwanda's Genocide*, p. 45. Melvern initially cited the word "Gisinda" for "wild animal," however, after consultation with senior consultant for Human Rights Watch and Rwanda expert Alison Des Forges, I learned that Melvern's spelling of the Kinyarwanda word was incorrect.

91. Walter de Bock and Gert Van Langendonck, "Legerstaf wist alles over nakende genocide Rwanda," *De Morgen*, November 4, 1995, p. 1, in Alison Des Forges, *Leave None to Tell the Story*, p. 143.

92. Personal Interview, Former Deputy Chief of Mission Joyce Leader, Via e-mail to Washington, DC, May 11, 2003.

93. Linda Melvern, *A People Betrayed: The Role of the West in Rwanda's Genocide*, p. 95.

94. Facsimile from Major General Romeo Dallaire, Force Commander, United Nations Assistance Mission for Rwanda, to Major General Maurice Baril, United

Nations Department of Peacekeeping Operations, "Request for Protection of the Informant," January 11, 1994, Source: US House of Representatives, Committee on International Relations, Subcommittee on International Operations and Human Rights, "Hearing: Rwanda: Genocide and the Continuing Cycle of Violence", May 5, 1998, in William Ferroggiaro, *A National Security Archive Briefing Book,* August 20, 2001, found in www.gwu.edu/~nsarchiv/NSAEBB/NSAEBB53/press.html.

95. Ibid.

96. Linda Melvern, *A People Betrayed: The Role of the West in Rwanda's Genocide,* pp. 94–95.

97. Tony Marley, interview, "The Triumph of Evil," *Frontline,* PBS, January 26, 1999; available at PBS Online: www.pbs.org/wgbh/pages/frontline/shows/evil/interviews/marley.html

98. Colin Keating, Linda Melvern Interview, New York, 13 September, 1994, in Linda Melvern, *A People Betrayed: The Role of the West in Rwanda's Genocide,* p. 99. While this is Dallaire's quote, it is paraphrased by Colin Keating.

99. Madeleine Albright, *Madam Secretary: A Memoir*, New York: Easton Press, 2003, p. 148.

100. UN Security Council, *Report of the Independent Inquiry into the Actions of the UN during the 1994 Genocide in Rwanda*, 15 December 1999, p. 12, in Linda Melvern, *A People Betrayed: The Role of the West in Rwanda's Genocide*, p. 101.

101. Personal Interview, Human Rights Watch Consultant Alison Des Forges, October 22, 2003, via telephone to Buffalo, NY.

102. Personal Interview, Former Deputy Chief of Mission Joyce E. Leader, Washington, DC, November 18, 2002.

103. This FSN's name is used because he is currently living abroad and because he has yet to be cited or referred to in any sources on Rwanda, it is a necessary contribution.

104. This testimony was verified by interviews with 7 FSNs who worked for USAID or the U.S. embassy during the Rwanda crisis.

105. Personal Interview, Foreign Service National USAID [C], Kigali, Rwanda, November 23, 2002, verified by an additional six FSNs, Foreign Minister Charles Murigande, Denis Polisi, Alexis Kanyarengwe, Tito Rutaremara, and Major General Kayumba Nyamwasa

106. Personal Interview, Foreign Minister of Rwanda Dr. Charles Murigande, Kigali, Rwanda, December 20, 2002.

107. Personal Interview, Foreign Service National USAID [A], Kigali, Rwanda, December 19, 2002.

108. Personal Interview, RPF Deputy Chairman and RPF Spokesman Denis Polisi, Kigali, Rwanda, December 20, 2002.

109. Personal Interview, Former U.S. Ambassador to Rwanda David Rawson, Via telephone to Michigan, September 26, 2003.

110. Ibid.

111. Joyce E. Leader, *Rwanda's Struggle for Democracy and Peace, 1991–1994,* Washington, DC: The Fund for Peace, 2001, p. 9.

112. Personal Interview, Former U.S. Ambassador to Rwanda David Rawson, Via telephone to Michigan, September 26, 2003.

113. Butare is a southern prefecture in Rwanda that houses one of the main border crossings with Burundi in Kanyaru-Haut.

114. Personal Interview, Deputy Chief of Mission Joyce E. Leader, Washington, DC, November 18, 2002. Policymakers were taken back by this information, but more preoccupied with the urgency of deciding what to do about the embassy. Would they evacuate? If they did, would it be safe? What was the best way to ensure the safety of Americans living in Rwanda?

115. Alison Des Forges, *Leave None to Tell the Story,* p. 190.

116. Carl Wilkens was the only American to remain in Rwanda throughout the genocide. In a November 19, 2003 interview with PBS Frontline for the documentary "Ghosts of Rwanda," on which I worked as a consultant, Wilkens was asked why he did not leave with the American convoy. He responded: "Sometimes the hardest questions almost have the simplest answers, and yet in their simplicity, we almost don't believe it. For a while, when people would ask me why [I] choose to stay, I would try to go into some detail [about] that Tutsi young lady and that Tutsi young man [who worked for me]. [They] were [the] faces [of the victims of the genocide], representing the country and I felt if I left, they were going to be killed. . . . The first three weeks, I never left my house, and I was wondering, why did I stay? What am I doing? [Then I realized] the two people in my house [were] still alive, and I [was] very grateful for that. . . ."

117. Joyce E. Leader, *Rwanda's Struggle for Democracy and Peace, 1991–1994,* Washington, DC: The Fund for Peace, 2001, p. 61–62.

118. Personal Interview, Deputy Chief of Mission Joyce E. Leader, Washington, DC, November 18, 2002.

119. Joyce E. Leader, *Rwanda's Struggle for Democracy and Peace, 1991–1994,* Washington, DC: The Fund for Peace, 2001, p. 61–62.

120. Ibid.

2

The "Somalia Hangover": Peacekeeping Reformed

"In my mind [Rwanda] is still one of the big regrets that I have from my time as Secretary of Defense. While it might not have been politically possible, we could have at least tried harder, and I feel guilty about that."

—Personal Interview with Former Secretary
of Defense William Perry, February 10, 2003

In August 1992, President George H. Bush launched "Operation Provide Relief" in Somalia in response to a famine that had already claimed the lives of 300,000 Somalis by March 1992, and threatened the lives of seventy percent of the population with malnutrition.[1] The operation was designed to airlift food relief to the starving populations of Somalia and Northern Kenya,[2] but in the initial stages the airlift failed to alleviate the famine in several key southern areas. Eager to increase the effectiveness of the mission by providing a more secure environment for the airlifts, President Bush deployed 25,426 American Marines and soldiers by January 1993 to lead the multinational Unified Task Force (UNITAF).[3]

When Bill Clinton arrived on the presidential scene in 1992, the U.S. was still formulating its post-Cold War foreign policy. Despite campaign speeches declaring Clinton's plans to bring the United States out of an economic recession, eradicate unemployment, and work to pass a new health care plan,[4] Clinton also stressed the importance of humanitarian intervention and peacekeeping through a policy of assertive multilateralism. With Clinton's election to the White House, the partnership between the United Nations and the United States strengthened and it appeared as though the improved cooperation between the United States and the UN would result in unprecedented ambition for peacekeeping. While Clinton's first two foreign

47

policy issues were the instructions for the National Security Council to draft a peacekeeping strategy and review Bosnia, Somalia became President Clinton's first foreign policy initiative. Clinton planned to continue and expand on what President Bush had already begun.[5] At the same time that Clinton assumed control over Somalia from President Bush, the date of the March 1993 UN Security Council Resolution 814 calling for a handover of UNITAF to the UN by May 1993, was only four months away. On March 23, 1993, Ambassador Albright praised the new ambition of the Somalia mission and pledged full American support for the effort:

> [By moving from] feeding starving people to establishing security in the region . . . we will embark on an unprecedented enterprise aimed at nothing less than restoration of an entire country as a proud, functioning and viable member of the community of nations . . . We will vigorously support it.[6]

On May 4, 1993, the transfer to the UN was complete and the American led UNITAF became the United Nations Operation in Somalia II (UNOSOM II). Differently than George Bush who did not advocate interference in Somalia's political situation, President Clinton urged the Secretary General to order the UN to "seek, as appropriate, pledges and contributions from states and others to assist in financing the rehabilitation of the political institutions and economy of Somalia."[7]

The U.S. government and the UN worked to re-define new objectives for the post-Cold War world that extended beyond standard humanitarian assistance. These objectives included protecting human rights and using peacekeeping to bring stability to regions where political conflict prevented the success of humanitarian intervention. On June 24, 1993, in a speech given before the Subcommittee on International Security, International Organizations, and Human Rights of the House Committee on Foreign Affairs, U.S. Ambassador to the United Nations Madeleine Albright stressed the importance of addressing the "new platter of issues [that] confronts contributing nations, including deployments into internal conflicts and to protect humanitarian aid convoys." She emphasized that UN peacekeeping was in "U.S. national interest . . . economically, politically, and humanitarian."[8] Just eleven days before 18 American rangers were killed in Mogadishu, Madeleine Albright addressed the National War College and reaffirmed the U.S. commitment to "[containing] the chaos" in countries threatened with crisis "and [easing] the suffering in regions of greatest humanitarian concern."[9] According to Deputy Assistant Secretary of Defense for Peacekeeping Sarah Sewall, the Clinton administration had "high hopes for what UN peace operations would be able to do . . . and it was believed that as an international community [the U.S.] would be able to conduct a wide range of operations under a UN umbrella.

There was a lot of effort on the part of the NSC that [the U.S.] should be able to do more."[10]

SHIFT IN POLICY—THE EMERGENCE OF PDD-25

While President Clinton was encouraging the Secretary General to promote nation building in Somalia, he also instructed senior officials at the National Security Council to draft a presidential review decision (PRD-13) that would outline the future of the U.S. role in peacekeeping.[11] The unreleased PRD-13 expanded the criteria for how the administration defined "national interest" by arguing that a humanitarian threat abroad "constitutes a threat to international peace and security."[12]

In a September 1993 keynote address to the National War College, Ambassador Albright summarized the content of PRD-13 by explaining the new, more ambitious role that the U.S. would play in peacekeeping:

> The Clinton Administration is fashioning a new framework that is more diverse and flexible than an old—a framework that will advance American interests, promote American values, and preserve American leadership . . . If American servicemen and servicewomen are sent into combat, they will go with the training, the equipment, the support, and the leadership they need to get the job done.[13]

Albright's speech to the National War College, while reflecting the administration's interventionist approach to peacekeeping, revealed the importance of prioritization. She asserted that "the U.S. will also consider voting against renewal of certain long-standing peace operations that are failing to meet established objectives in order to free military and financial resources for more pressing UN missions."[14]

WHAT DID SOMALIA MEAN FOR PEACEKEEPING?

Initially, Somalia illuminated America's new peacekeeping strategy. The United States was responsible for feeding hundreds of thousands of Somalis under UNITAF, and the UNOSOM II mission that followed had a Chapter VII mandate to carry out its mission. However, on June 5, 1993, just one month after the deployment of UNOSOM II, General Mohammed Farah Aideed's militia ambushed 24 Pakistani peacekeepers. The murder of UN troops led to an emergency session of the Security Council that, with strong U.S. support, decided for "all necessary measures to be used to apprehend and punish those responsible for the attacks."[15] However, on August 5 the *Washington Post* received a leaked draft of PRD-13 which expressed concerns that Somalia and the potential deployment of troops to Bosnia "were causing a great deal of anxiety in Congress . . . forcing senior officials to reconsider their earlier plans to allow U.S. troops to be placed under UN command."[16] Just three days later, the number of American casualties in Somalia reached double digits when a remote controlled land mine killed four American troops. After the death toll increased to twelve, Senator Robert Byrd, the Chairman of the Senate Appropriations Committee, spoke before the Senate, attacking the Clinton administration for its increased involvement in Somalia. This harsh criticism from a member of the President's own political party led to a number of other condemnations of the policy shift in Somalia. Both House Speaker Thomas Foley and Minority Leader Bob Dole declared that the United States needed to pull out of Somalia and that Congress would examine the role of the United States' involvement in Somalia's civil war.[17] Despite the growing number of casualties and opposition from Republicans in Congress, Clinton insisted that UNOSOM II "was well-conceived and properly undertaken."[18]

The escalation of violence and the Security Council's decision to punish those responsible for the murder of the Pakistani peacekeepers, led to an October 3, 1993, American Army Ranger mission to capture the senior officials in the Somali National Alliance (NSA). The operation was a failure and the downing of two Blackhawk helicopters led to the deaths of 18 Americans, the injury of 78 others, and one American Ranger being dragged through the streets of Mogadishu. After seeing these images on television, then Deputy Secretary of Defense William Perry, who would later replace Les Aspin as Secretary of Defense, recalls a number of officials and critics asking the "question of why we were sending a military force over to a nation that didn't want them."[19] The disaster brought immediate criticism of the Clinton administration and this "negative residue from Somalia" became the Congressional basis for opposition to the Clinton administration's foreign policy, which according to Perry "had a profound affect on [The Pentagon's] thinking on Rwanda."[20] There was neither a meeting, nor was there a decision that because of Somalia, the United States would not intervene in Rwanda. The voice of criticism over the Somalia debacle was so overwhelming that such a meeting would not have been necessary to determine that Rwanda, six months after Somalia, was a political non-starter. The criticism unleashed on the administration made opposition from outside the foreign policy apparatus so widespread that few policymakers wanted to challenge this criticism. Furthermore, Somalia gave Republicans in Congress another excuse to criticize the President for his foreign policy and to argue that the President was not giving enough attention to domestic issues.

Prior to the October 3 firefight in Mogadishu, Republicans in Congress criticized the Clinton administration for the cost of Somalia and the risk to Amer-

By yielding to Congressional pressure and portraying himself as an ally to Congress, Clinton appeared to respond to public opinion, which in the end was more helpful to his image than it was embarrassing.[33] The administration could afford to swallow some of its pride because blame was easily shared with the past Bush administration and could also be placed on the UN.[34] The next election was two years away, and a vibrant return to domestic issues would be a popular rebound from the heavily criticized events in Somalia. In this case, Somalia served as an important context when viewing future peacekeeping challenges.

While the events in Somalia reinforced existing opposition to intervention in Africa, the possibility of future interventions was never ruled out. General George Joulwan, who served as the Commander in Chief (CINC) of United States European Command (USEUCOM), understood this possibility and wanted to be prepared. As CINC for USEUCOM, he had 83 nations in his region, most of which were located in Africa. He recalls that after Somalia, "I wanted to get my arms around the situation. We had a disaster in Somalia and, in my view that would not be our last military operation in Africa. What concerned me about Africa was the way we seemed to view operations there. It was almost as if you made it up as you went along because we were busy planning for 'the big one' somewhere else. To me it was backwards." General Joulwan suggested that "we had to be able to give clear, candid military advice about whether or not we should conduct operations there but, if we get told to do it, we better be prepared to execute in a professional way."[35]

AND THEN CAME RWANDA

In response to the unexpected speed at which a force was authorized following the signing of the Arusha Accords,[36] Secretary General Boutros Boutros-Ghali sent a reconnaissance mission to Kigali on August 19, 1993, to assess the progress of its implementation. Upon their return, one member of the mission recalled, "our report was that this was a winner mission, where the UN can redeem itself, that there is a peace agreement with some holes but that everyone is behind it. . . . We knew that the UN badly wanted a wink, and we told them that this was it."[37] The reconnaissance mission suggested that the UN deploy a force of 5,000 troops, but the United States was unwilling to cover the costs of a force size greater than 2,548.[38] On September 24, Boutros-Ghali presented a report to the Security Council proposing a compromised UN force in Rwanda of 2,548 troops under a Chapter VI Mandate calling on the force to ensure the security of Kigali, monitor the ceasefire, assist with de-mining, assist with humanitarian relief, and monitor the repatriation of Rwandan refugees.[39] The mission, however, was relatively weak in that it did not have a sizable number of troops, lacked adequate supplies, and did not have an intelligence unit.[40]

Ten days later, the Security Council authorized the deployment of UNAMIR; however, the October 3 firefight in Mogadishu and a fatal American helicopter crash just two days after the Security Council vote, resulted in America's skepticism over this new UN peacekeeping mission.[41] This anxiety grew worse on October 21, 1993 just one month before the first UNAMIR troops arrived in Kigali with the assassination of Burundian President Melchior Ndadaye.[42] The fact that a Hutu President was killed in neighboring Burundi led to a Coalition for the Defense of the Republic (CDR) response that encompassed the murdering of RPF sympathizers, killing of Tutsis near the Burundian border with the Rwandan Gikongoro prefecture, and also the elimination of dissidents from within their own party.[43] By the time the first UNAMIR troops arrived in Kigali in early November,[44] temporary order had been restored to Kigali and despite RPF threats to break the ceasefire if the Habyarimana government did not implement the transitional institutions, there were almost four months of calm. However, the extremists used the unstable environment as an opportunity to assassinate PSD executive secretary Felicien Gatabazi.[45] Tutsi members of the PSD responded to the assassination by lynching the CDR Chairman, resulting in too volatile a situation for Habyarimana to inaugurate the BBTG on February 22, 1994. Demonstrations followed the assassinations and as the violence escalated, the UN mission that appeared "winnable" in August 1993 seemed to be hanging on to its objectives by a thread.

THE RPF, UNAMIR, AND THE ARUSHA PEACE PROCESS

The Rwanda Patriotic Front was a vital player in the Arusha Peace Process and they had a serious stake in the continuation of a UN presence in Rwanda. However, the RPF was hesitant to enter the Arusha Peace Process during a period in which they had the upper hand in the civil war. RPF Executive Committee members believed that "[they] were dealing with a government that never wanted to sign the accords . . . the most influential members of government did not want it . . . and it was a way for them to stall RPF victory . . . and hold on to power."[46] Foreign Minister Charles Murigande argues that the RPF continuously resumed violence against the Rwandan Armed Forces (FAR) in order to "show the Rwandan government that the killing of Tutsi for no other reason than them being Tutsi" was unacceptable.[47] He suggests that they could have continued moving south and taken Kigali in these efforts of "self-defense," but they "stopped and went back in order to give negotiations a chance."[48] According to RPF Director of Intelligence Kayumba Nyamwasa, the RPF agreed to commit to the Arusha Peace Process for two reasons: 1) To gain more credibility, legitimacy, and support from the international community; and 2) Because they were assured that a UN force would be deployed to reduce the risk to the 600 RPF soldiers and officials in Kigali.[49] However, as consultant for Human Rights Watch Alison Des Forges explains, the RPF's intentions were more self-serving than in adherence to the international community's wishes. She argues that their forces were spread more than they would have liked and strategically it left them disadvantaged.[50] They needed to return to the Peace Process in order to recollect their forces.

The UN Assistance Mission for Rwanda (UNAMIR) had a number of problems in addition to those previously mentioned. The RPF had higher expectations for the mission than the international community, in that they expected the force to protect them against violence committed by Hutu extremists. RPF Executive Committee Member Tito Rutaremara argues that because of UNAMIR, Tutsis and moderate Hutus chose not to flee the civil war and instead, chose to seek refuge in facilities and areas under UNAMIR vigilance. As a result, Rutaremara suggests that, "We would have been better off without the UN because all they did was provide false hope and demonstrate that the international community was not going to do anything to protect people."[51]

NOTES

1. Clement E. Adibe, *Managing Arms in Peace Processes: Somalia*, New York: United Nations Institute for Disarmament Research, 1995, p. 17, in Stephen John Stedman, *Restore Hope: The United States in Somalia*, Background Paper for Session 4, June 18, 1996, pp. 1–2.

2. Stephen John Stedman, *Restore Hope: The United States in Somalia*, Background Paper for Session 4, June 18, 1996, pp. 2–3.

3. John L. Hirsch and Robert B. Oakley, *Somalia and Operation Restore Hope: Reflections on Peacekmaking and Peacekeeping,* Washington DC: United States Institute of Peace Press, 1995, p. 63, in Michael Mackinnon, *The Evolution of U.S. Peacekeeping Policy Under Clinton,* p. 17. UNITAF was comprised of a force of 38,301 troops, of which 25,426 troops were American. The first American troops arrived in Somalia on December 7, 1992.

4. Donald C.F. Daniel, "The United States," in Trevor Findley (ed.), *Challenges for the New Peacekeepers,* SIPRI Research Report #12, Oxford: Oxford University Press, 1996, pp. 89–90, in Michael Mackinnon, *The Evolution of U.S. Peacekeeping Policy Under Clinton,* p. 19.

5. Michael Mackinnon, *The Evolution of U.S. Peacekeeping Policy Under Clinton,* p. 20.

6. UN Document, Provisional Verbatim, S/PV.3188, in Ibid, p. 42.

7. United Nations, *The United Nations and Somalia, 1992–1995,* Document 52, Resolution 814, pp. 261–263, in Michael Mackinnon, *The Evolution of U.S. Peacekeeping Policy Under Clinton,* p. 21.

8. Madeleine Albright, *Myths of Peacekeeping,* Address before the Subcommittee on International Security, International Organizations, and Human Rights of the House Committee on Foreign Affairs, June 24, 1993.

9. Madeleine Albright, *Use of Force in a Post-Cold War World,* Address at the National War College, National Defense University, Fort McNair, Washington DC, 23 September 1993.

10. Personal Interview, Deputy Assistant Secretary of Defense for Peacekeeping Sarah Sewall, Via telephone to Boston, MA, February 13, 2003.

11. Michael MacKinnon, *The Evolution of U.S. Peacekeeping Policy Under Clinton,* p. 31. The PRD-13 process lasted 14 months.

12. Michael MacKinnon, *The Evolution of U.S. Peacekeeping Policy Under Clinton,* p. 22.

13. Madeleine Albright, *Use of Force in a Post-Cold War World,* Address at the National War College, National Defense University, Fort McNair, Washington DC, 23 September 1993, in Ibid, p. 167.

14. Ibid.

15. Michael Barnett, *Eyewitness to a Genocide,* p. 36.

16. Michael MacKinnon, *The Evolution of U.S. Peacekeeping Policy Under Clinton,* p. 23.

17. Ibid.

18. Keith B. Richburg, "4 US Soldiers Killed in Somalia; UN Blames Land-mine on Warlord," *Washington Post,* 9 August 1993, p. A1, in Michael Mackinnon, *The Evolution of U.S. Peacekeeping Policy Under Clinton,* p. 22.

19. Personal Interview, Former Secretary of Defense Dr. William Perry, Stanford, CA, February 10, 2003.

20. Ibid.

21. Michael Mackinnon, *The Evolution of U.S. Peacekeeping Policy Under Clinton,* p. 100.

22. Michael Barnett, *Eyewitness to a Genocide,* p. 38.

23. Michael MacKinnon, *The Evolution of U.S. Peacekeeping Policy Under Clinton,* p. 78 in footnote on p. 89, footnote 18.

24. Ibid, pp. 92–93.

25. Personal Interview, Former National Security Advisor Anthony Lake, Georgetown, MD, November 20, 2002.

26. Michael MacKinnon, *The Evolution of U.S. Peacekeeping Policy Under Clinton,* p. 24.

27. White paper, Department of State, "The Clinton Administration's Policy on Reforming Multilateral Peace Operations," May 1994. Non-classified; see also, Memorandum for the Vice President, et al., "PDD 25: U.S. Policy on Reforming Mul-

tilateral Peace Operations," May 3, 1994. Confidential with Secret attachment, in William Ferroggiaro, *A National Security Archive Briefing Book,* August 20, 2001, found at: www.gwu.edu/~nsarchiv/NSAEBB/NSAEBB53/press.html.

28. Ibid.

29. Ibid.

30. Michael MacKinnon, *The Evolution of U.S. Peacekeeping Policy Under Clinton,* p. 67

31. Elaine Sciolino, "New US Peacekeeping Policy De-emphasizes Role of the UN," *New York Times,* 6 May 1994, p. A2, in Michael Mackinnon, *The Evolution of U.S. Peacekeeping Policy Under Clinton,* p. 30.

32. Personal Interview, National Security Advisor Anthony Lake, Georgetown, MD, November 20, 2002.

33. Michael Barnett, *Eyewitness to a Genocide,* p. 41.

34. For details of how Clinton used the UN as a scapegoat for Somalia, see Michael Barnett, *Eyewitness to a Genocide,* pp. 38–48.

35. Personal Interview, Former Commander in Chief of U.S. European Command General George Joulwan, *Washington, DC,* September 7, 2004.

36. Michael Barnett, *Eyewitness to a Genocide,* p. 64.

37. Brent Beardsley, Michael Barnett interview, October 17, 2000, in Michael Barnett, *Eyewitness to a Genocide,* p. 65.

38. Michael Barnett, *Eyewitness to a Genocide,* p. 67.

39. Bruce Jones, *Peacemaking in Rwanda,* pp. 105–106.

40. Ibid, pp. 107–108.

41. Bruce Jones, *Peacemaking in Rwanda,* p. 68.

42. Differently than Rwanda, Burundi had always been controlled by the Tutsi minority. However, on June 1, 1993, in Burundi's first free and fair election, Melchior Ndadaye was elected as the President of Burundi by 64.8 percent. At first, the election appeared to be a success and the runner-up, Tutsi General Pierre Buyoya, gracefully accepted defeat. His assassination just four months later sparked ethnic violence in Burundi, but it also became the justification that the CDR used for a fabricated Tutsi plan to take over Rwanda and liquidate the Hutus.

43. Gerard Prunier, *The Rwanda Crisis,* p. 203.

44. Ibid, pp. 203–204.

45. Ibid, p. 206.

46. Personal Interview, Former RPF Director of Intelligence Major General Kayumba Nyamwasa, Kigali, Rwanda, December 18, 2002.

47. Personal Interview, Foreign Minister of Rwanda Dr. Charles Murigande, Kigali, Rwanda, December 20, 2002.

48. Ibid.

49. Personal Interview, Foreign Minister of Rwanda Dr. Charles Murigande, Kigali, Rwanda, December 20, 2002.

50. Personal Interview, Human Rights Watch Consultant Alison Des Forges, Via telephone to Buffalo, NY, October 22, 2003.

51. Personal Interview, President of the Judicial and Constitutional Commission Tito Rutaremara, Kigali, Rwanda, December 20, 2002.

3

The "Dangerous Spring of 1994"

"If Bosnia is a testing ground for post-Cold War morality, Rwanda is a horror of even greater dimensions, not only because the scale of the violations of basic humanitarian law is so great, but also because the world's response is being tested under the added weight of racism. If our response to Bosnia has been grossly inadequate, an even greater evil in Rwanda is eliciting an even weaker response."

—Former Assistant Secretary of State John Shattuck

Rwanda was one of many trouble spots in the spring of 1994, and compared to regions of economic, political, and strategic importance, Rwanda ranked as a low priority for most policymakers in Washington, DC. The administration faced the possibility of being drawn into crises in Bosnia, Haiti, and North Korea, as well as an uncertain situation in South Africa. In addition to an array of international crises and events, the administration was also preoccupied with its foreign policy objectives, one of which was reaching an agreement on free trade with China. Each of these issues ranked higher on the list of priorities than the conflict in Rwanda. North Korea was on its way to becoming a nuclear power, Bosnia was located in a strategic region of the world, Haiti was a conflict close to American borders, and Clinton had an invested interest in South Africa, which was one of Africa's only industrialized countries. If the administration was reluctant to intervene in these prioritized crises, it is not surprising that policymakers did not want to intervene in a low-priority conflict like Rwanda. According to National Security Advisor Anthony Lake and one of his White House colleagues, Rwanda suffered from a "chronology problem,"[1] in that "[intervention] just wasn't going to happen in Rwanda. It was a period of a lot of international threats, and Rwanda just didn't seem like it was that important compared to these."[2]

AN OVEREXTENDED UNITED NATIONS

The events of October 3, 1993 resulted in a feud between President Clinton and Secretary General Boutros-Ghali over who bore the responsibility for the failure of UNOSOM II. Clinton blamed the UN for the American casualties in Somalia, arguing that the UN needed to act more rationally and discontinue missions that were destined for failure and likely to marginalize the organization. Clinton blamed the UN as a way of saving face, but in actuality, the October 3 operation was American proposed, American planned, and American led.[3] The shift in blame to the UN enabled the Clinton administration to provide Congress and America with an excuse for why Somalia went from humanitarian relief to nation building with catastrophic consequences. Clinton argued that the UN had overextended itself and therefore, forced the United States into commitment of resources, funds, and troops in regions that were not of strategic interest. Between 1989 and 1993, the UN had deployed new forces in Angola, Mozambique, Western Sahara, Somalia, El Salvador, Cambodia, Haiti, and the former Yugoslavia. Furthermore, the United States was responsible for thirty percent of the UN fees, and the UN Transitional Authority in Cambodia (UNTAC) was the most expensive mission in UN history.[4] According to the Clinton administration, the UN managed too many conflicts, the UN spent money unnecessarily, and the UN failed to distinguish between missions that were achievable and those that would force the organization to send troops into harms way. By April 6, 1994, the United Nations had 71,543 deployed troops in seventeen global hot spots, nearly half of which were in Africa, as seen in Table 3.1.[5]

The Bush administration supported UN deployments in Angola, Western Sahara, Somalia, and Mozambique, and the Clinton administration, in addition

Table 3.1.   United Nations Deployments in Africa (March 1994)[6]

Country	Number of Troops	Annual Cost of the Mission	Date of Deployment
Liberia	374	$70 million	September 1993
Rwanda	2,206	$98 million	June 1993
Mozambique	6,754	$329 million	December 1992
Somalia	22,289	$1 billion	April 1992
Western Sahara	336	$40 million	September 1991
Angola	81	$25 million	June 1991

to the mission in Rwanda, supported the deployment of troops to Liberia in September 1993. The Clinton administration, arguing that six missions in Africa was far too many given the fact that many of the countries were not vital to American interests, looked to cut costs and reduce the presence of UN troops. The UNOMOZ mission in Mozambique, alone cost $329 million and UNOSOM II in Somalia, in addition to its unpopularity, cost $1 billion annually. These missions convinced the Clinton administration and critics of the UN that the United States was spending far too much money on peacekeeping.

THE ELECTIONS IN SOUTH AFRICA

The United States took an immediate interest in South Africa during the spring of 1994. The Clinton administration viewed South Africa as a country of national interest because, as the most industrialized country in Africa, South Africa served as significant ally and trading partner to the United States. More importantly, it was the U.S. government's hope that a stabilized and industrialized South Africa could serve as the engine of Africa and lead the continent to greater prosperity. The U.S. government had for decades viewed South Africa as a strategic country, voting in favor of a mandatory UN embargo on the apartheid regime in 1976 and encouraging the fall of the apartheid system.

When Mandela was released from prison, it appeared as though the U.S. hope for South Africa to become Africa's leader could finally seem a viable option. At the same time that the genocide was taking place in Rwanda, South Africa held a landmark election between April 26 and April 29 that led to the fall of apartheid and the creation of a Government of National Unity. In part, because the issue in South Africa was related to racial equality, the United States made the calculation that election monitoring and open diplomatic support for the transition was in American interest. The lead up to the election jeopardized the end of apartheid and as a result, prior to April 26, there was great uncertainty surrounding the events leading up to the election. The fighting between the Inkatha Freedom Party (IFP) and the African National Congress (ANC) led many in Washington to question whether or not the election in South Africa would lead to democratic transition or a violent confrontation. Initially, IFP leader Mangosuthu Buthelezi refused to enter the election, and the White House feared a violent IFP boycott could disrupt the elections and destabilize the country. Officials in Washington wanted to ensure that they would not have to confront such events. With tensions at their height in South Africa, one White House official argues that government officials working on Africa were distracted from many of the other pressing African issues such as the violence in Rwanda and Burundi.[7] As one senior policy advisor at the White House recalls:

> The question you may ask is whether the African followers were sufficiently attentive to what was going on in Rwanda because we were so concerned with South Africa. It was all about preparing for the elections in South Africa, and we were not watching the conflict in Rwanda closely enough. . . . We did not monitor the events leading up to the genocide closely, in part, because of South Africa.[8]

It is understandable why policymakers prioritized South Africa as there was incentive provided by the President, a strong South African lobby, significant attention given to the election in the media, and Congressional support. According to Senator Paul Simon, he and other members of the Africa Sub-committee spoke to the President about South African issues, and as a result, hesitated to bring other pressing issues in Africa. Simon alleges that he thought about making a plea for Rwanda in the midst of the South Africa events, but he claimed that with the administration's Africa focus centered on South Africa, he "just didn't think [his] plea would have resonated."[9] He recalls few members of Congress being concerned with African issues and explained that the majority of discussions taking place on the Congressional floor were over "which members of Congress were going to get invitations to Nelson Mandela's inauguration, and then by the way here is what is happening in Rwanda . . . they didn't care about Rwanda."[10]

INSTABILITY IN HAITI, BOSNIA, AND NORTH KOREA

The collapse of the Duvalier regime and the ascendance of the democratically elected Jean-Bertrand Aristide led many American policymakers to believe that Haiti could become a functional democracy. Only months after his victory in 1991, General Raoul Cedras led an army coup to overthrow Aristide. The United States reacted swiftly and worked with the Organization of American States (OAS) and the UN to draft the Governor's Island Accords. The Accords called for the reinstatement of President Aristide, the discontinuation of the embargo, and the disarming of the military junta. One week after the October 3 firefight in Mogadishu, the UN deployed a task force of American and Canadian military advisors to assist in implementation of the Governor's Island Accords. The task force set out for Port-au-Prince on the U.S.S. *Harlan*, but upon arrival, a group of armed rebels who opposed the U.S. presence in Haiti challenged their entrance into the harbor, forcing the U.S.S. *Harlan* to back down and returned to the United States without a fight.

According to one senior official at the White House, the United States backed away from Haiti because of the freshness of the Somalia experience.[11] Despite the fact that the initiative in Haiti was relatively well-organized, Republicans used the U.S.S. *Harlan* as a way to chastise the administration and label the mission an "embarrassing retreat." Because Republicans popularized this perspective, Haiti came to reinforce the legacy of Somalia and served as the first example of how the administration was no longer willing to commit soldiers to peacekeeping, regardless of proximity to the United States. The hesitancy in response to a country of close proximity to the United States proved that crises abroad, particularly those in regions of marginal importance to the United States, were unlikely to receive attention, let alone intervention.

At the same time that the Haiti crisis lingered, Serbian President Slobodon Milosavic, who had begun a campaign of ethnic cleansing in the spring of 1992, continued to promote violence against Albanians in Bosnia. In an effort to stabilize the region, the UN created safe havens to protect potential victims and warned the Bosnian Serbs that their ambush of the UN-created safe havens would result in a swift and forceful response from the United Nations. Four days before the beginning of the genocide in Rwanda, and just two days after the Security Council extended the UNPROFOR mandate for an additional six months, Serbian militias called the UN bluff and attacked the Gorazde safe haven in the former Yugoslavia. This was a worst nightmare for Anthony Lake, who alleges that he had been preoccupied with Bosnia since January 1993, but never expected it to deteriorate to such conditions.[12]

In addition to the ethnic cleansing in Bosnia and the instability in Haiti, the United States also faced a great dilemma in North Korea. In late 1993 and even more so early 1994, North Korean nuclear program increased its activity in what came to be known as the defueling crisis. The spring of 1994 saw the first time in decades that policymakers thought there would be war on the Korean peninsula. The history of the nuclear crisis is far too extensive to cover in the pages of this book, but the immediate crisis of the spring of 1994 began as a result of the North Korean decision to unload irradiated fuel rods from the 5-megawatt reactor at Yongbyon.[13] Korean scholar Don Oberdorfer explains that the "Unloading of the reactor in 1994 was of great importance . . . because this entire load of rods could be converted into enough plutonium for four or five nuclear weapons."[14]

It was amidst the worsening conflict in Rwanda that North Korea began to defuel its nuclear reactor. As a potential nuclear power and grave threat to the United States, North Korea required serious attention. Because of its history as an enemy of the United States, along with the fear invoked by the possibility that they could possess one or more atomic bombs and long range missiles capable of hitting the United States, North Korea received a barrage of media attention, pressure from various lobby groups, and discussion in Congress. As former Secretary of Defense William Perry recalls, "The defueling of the North Korean reactor was the turning point, when it appeared that dialogue and preventive diplomacy had failed and when U.S. strategy shifted to coercive diplomacy involving sanctions."[15]

By May 1994, the nuclear crisis grew more serious and the Pentagon began to speak increasingly about the possibility of war, presenting their contingency plans to President Clinton. The Pentagon responded to the crisis by gathering "every active four-star general and admiral in the U.S. military, including several brought from commands across the world, to a Pentagon conference room on May 18. The subject was how the entire U.S. military would support . . . war plans for Korea, with troops, materiel, and logistics."[16] These plans were so serious that Secretary Perry, and Chairman of the Joint Chiefs of Staff General John "Shali" Shalikashvili informed President Clinton that in the event of war there would be "52,000 U.S. military casualties . . . and 490,000 South Korean military casualties in the first ninety days, plus an enormous number of North Korean and civilian lives, at a financial outlay exceeding $61 billion."[17] This was a crisis of great urgency for the administration and it was not until a visit by President Carter that coincided with the conclusion of the genocide in Rwanda that the crisis began to stabilize.

HOW THE MEDIA MANAGED THE "DANGEROUS SPRING OF 1994"

The media and crisis management are not mutually exclusive. With the power to influence hundreds of millions of people, the media have the ability to generate concern about virtually unknown crises, while at the same time possessing the ability to magnify what is already high-profile. The sequential crises of Somalia and Rwanda illustrate this.

Just a few years before the genocide in Rwanda, the media helped bring to light the suffering of the Somali people. During the George H. Bush administration, images of starving children in Somalia filled the pages of newspapers and magazines. These images had a profound effect on the administration, which felt compelled to intervene for humanitarian reasons.

The Rwanda genocide was not given this same coverage. While hundreds of thousands of Rwandans were slaughtered by the blades of machetes, the pages of newspapers and magazines were filled with stories and photographs related to international crises such as North Korea, Bosnia, Haiti, and South Africa; and domestic issues like the death of Richard Nixon, the death of Jackie Onassis, and the arrest of O.J. Simpson.

In order to determine why there was no significant media pressure in the spring of 1994, it is important to understand why Rwanda was not a story. Prior to April 6, 1994, the international media did not cover the deteriorating situation in Rwanda, and even the small-scale massacres and the neighboring mini-genocide in Burundi did not result in much media attention. African coverage has been historically less appealing to media organizations unless the particular crises involves western expatriates, diplomats, or floods of refugees. The initial coverage on Rwanda focused on the body count and as one journalist recalls, "neglected the part that power and money had played in the calculations of those who launched the genocide."

Where television is concerned, African news is generally only big news when it involves a lot of bodies. The higher the mound, the greater the possibility that the world will, however briefly, send its camera teams and correspondents."[18] While there is some truth to this argument, the United States has historically sent cameras into areas that are vital to American interests. During the Cold War, both Angola and Rhodesia received media attention, and throughout the first half the 1990s, South Africa and the crumbling of apartheid were frequently covered by media organizations.

The April 6, 1994 dual assassination of two heads of state, along with members of their cabinet, should have made the front page of newspapers and magazines, but instead it received one-minute time slots on the news broadcasts and was not even mentioned by many popular magazines in the United States. The massacres and assassinations received very little media attention and it was not until the massive flow of refugees into neighboring Zaire and Tanzania that the media covered Rwanda at length. The worst wave of massacres occurred in the first three weeks, but the media's focus on the presidential election in South Africa, the Serbian attack on the safe havens in Gorazde, and the political crisis in Haiti, led to a cloud over the most severe phase of the genocide. Officials at the White House do not recall media pressure and argue that the first significant effect of the media came three weeks into the genocide when CNN depicted the "bodies going down the river into Lake Victoria."[19] As Fergal Keane, a journalist in the spring of 1994 and author of *Season of Blood* explains:

The world's attention was focused on the elections [in South Africa] and, having spent four years preparing for that moment, I was in no mood to head for Rwanda. In the second week of April film began to arrive in Johannesburg for transmission to British and American television networks. Much of the material seemed to be coming from the border between Rwanda and Tanzania, the Rusomo Falls Bridge, across which tens of thousands of refugees were pouring each day.[20]

When the media finally took an interest in Rwanda, they chose to focus on the bodies and the horror, rather than the details of the conflict. Given the fact that the journalists covering the genocide were not Rwanda experts and were likely working on tight deadlines, they were quick to categorize the killing as tribal violence. The media continuously misportrayed the violence in Rwanda as a civil war, tribal conflict, ethnic strife, and other stereotypical classifications of African conflicts. In the minimal media coverage during the month of April, journalists portrayed Rwanda as a civil war rather than a genocide. The attempts by Rwandan experts to publish op-eds on Rwanda were rebuffed. Roger Winter, the director of the U.S. Committee for Refugees, wrote an op-ed describing what he saw in his early April trip to Rwanda, but both the *New York Times* and the *Washington Post* rejected the article. Winter had to settle for publication in the *Toronto Globe and Mail* on April 14.[21] Alison Des Forges took part in hundreds of interviews after April 6, 1994 but found them "totally unsatisfactory in that the journalists cared only abut sensationalism." It is surprising that journalists felt the need to dramatize the conflict, when the sheer fact that genocide was occurring was sensational in and of itself. In one instance recalled by Des Forges, she was interviewed at length about the history of the conflict in Rwanda, but the producers of the network ended up omitting the broadcast because "they just got in the most wonderful footage of a decapitation." Des Forges argues that the media wanted to portray the genocide with "the old clichés of tribalism, or at best, the 'failed state' explanation."[22] On April 16, 1994, the *New York Times* published an article entitled "Tribes Battle for Rwandan Capital: New Massacres Reported," in which it described events where "[one tribe] attacked defenseless people with knives, bats and spears, and that there were 1,180 bodies in the [Musha Parish] including 650 children."[23] The article portrayed the inhumane nature of the violence but failed to explain the systematic characteristic of the atrocities. According to Special BBC Correspondent Fergal Keane, most reporters, particularly those viewing Rwanda from the outside, reached a consensus that "Rwanda was a madhouse, a primitive torture chamber where rival tribes were busy settling ancient scores."[24]

RWANDA WAS NOT THE STORY

The media clearly missed covering Rwanda during the most horrific phase of the genocide. Given this fact, one has to ask the question of what stories preoccupied their attention. An examination of *Time, Newsweek,* and *U.S. News & World Report* from April to August 1994 demonstrates where the focus of the media was during the one hundred days of genocide in Rwanda.

In the first week of the genocide, not one of the three magazines even mentioned the assassinations of the two African Presidents—Rwanda President Juvenal Habyarimana and Burundi President Cyprien Ntaryamira. Instead, the April 11 issues carried cover stories on the economic recession, Wall Street, and a home guide for buyers, sellers, and owners. *U.S. News & World Report* published three articles in its World Report for April 11, "In South Africa: bullets before ballots, The demise of COCOM, and Russians flee the old empire."[25] In the same week's issue, *Time* magazine focused its international attention on four articles: "South Africa: Emergency in Zululand, Haiti: Still Punishing the Victims, Mexico: The Ruling Party's New Man, and Italy: Victory to the Knight from the Right."[26] *Newsweek* also failed to cover the dual assassination and the beginning of genocide in its April 11 issue. Editors chose six articles on international affairs that they felt were more news worthy than the events in Rwanda: "South Africa: Ballots or Bullets, Middle East: Does Peace have a Prayer? Japan: An L.A. Killing Hurts the Trade Talks, Singapore: Justice in Six Lashes, Serial Killings London's House of Horror," and a final article on Henry Kissinger's new book on the uses of power.[27] The lack of coverage of the assassination and the first week of violence that took nearly 100,000 lives foreshadowed the role that the media would play in covering the Rwanda genocide.

The first mention of Rwanda came in the April 18 issues of *Newsweek* and *Time*. *Newsweek* published an article entitled "Corpses Everywhere" in which it explained the deaths of the two presidents and the resulting "tribal war death toll."[28] *Time* Magazine included a similar issue entitled "Descent into Mayhem," describing the "tribal slaughter [that] erupts in Rwanda, trapping foreigners and forcing the U.S. to send troops to the region."[29] It took two weeks of genocide and the assassination of two African presidents for editors to decide to include stories on Rwanda, and even then the focus remained on American expatriates and the UN. The following week, *Time* magazine published a more detailed, three-page article entitled "Streets of Slaughter," describing the "tribal bloodlust and political rivalry [that turned] the country into an unimaginable hell of killing, looting and anarchy."[30] *Newsweek* also published a lengthier article than in its April 11 issue. In an article entitled "Deeper Into the Abyss," journalist Joshua Hammer describes the killings in Rwanda as "an orgy of tribal slaughter [killing] thousands as most of the foreigners flee for their lives."[31] *U.S. News & World Report* did not mention Rwanda in the month of April, and neither *Time* nor *Newsweek* chose to give Rwanda a cover story. True, there were other pressing events going on at the same time, but *Time* featured two consecutive health related covers in April, the first on smoking and the second on cancer. *U.S. News & World Report* was more focused on the trial of Jack Kevorkian and the Paula Jones sexual harassment suit than it was on Rwanda, and *Newsweek* chose to give cover stories to antioxidants and the suicide of Nirvana's lead singer Kurt Cobain.

The May 2 issues marked the first week since April 18 where Rwanda was left out of all three magazines altogether. Richard Nixon died in the last week of April, and as a result, all three cover stories paid tribute to the late President. The inauguration of Nelson Mandela took place during the first week of May, marking the official end of apartheid and transition to a government of national unity. All three magazines featured this landmark event on the cover during their May 9 issues and only *Newsweek* magazine published an article that week on Rwanda. In the first photo journal of the Genocide, Patrick Robert wrote a brief article in *Newsweek* entitled "Mass Murder" with two pages of graphic photos from Rwanda. The week of May 16 marked the turning point for coverage on the Rwanda crisis as it reached its peak in popular magazine coverage. In this previous week, 250,000 Rwandan refugees fled to western Tanzania, capturing the attention of the media and the international community. *U.S. News & World Report*, a month and a half after the start of genocide, finally published its first article on Rwanda entitled "Rwanda's Trail of Tears."[32] However, this article focused on the flood of refugees into Tanzania and how Rwanda can find hope because of what has happened in South Africa, rather than on the massacres. *U.S. News & World Report* did not publish another article on Rwanda until July 4. In its May 16 issue, *Time* featured Rwanda as its cover story with the quotation "There are no devils left in Hell . . . They are all in Rwanda."[33] The eight-page spread was the first cover story on Rwanda and the most detailed and lengthy article published on Rwanda in the three magazines throughout the genocide. *Newsweek*'s May 16 issue featured an article on Rwanda entitled "Escape from Hell,"[34] featuring the refugee crisis rather than the massacres. During the week of May 23, both *Time* and *Newsweek* published articles on Rwanda, depicting the massacres in the churches and the growing refugee crisis. That same week Jackie Kennedy Onassis died and as a result, the May 30 issues all featured a tribute to the late first lady on their covers and did not publish articles on Rwanda. The death of Jackie Kennedy Onassis temporarily halted coverage of Rwanda in *Newsweek*, but *Time* magazine persisted with its weekly articles on the genocide. The following week, *Time* included a one-page critique of the international community in an article on Rwanda entitled "Sorry, Wrong Country: Despite its outrage, the international community has neither the will nor the way to stop the slaughter."[35] During the week of June 13, *Time* magazine was, for the second straight week, the only magazine out of the three to publish an article on Rwanda. The week of June 20 marked a switch between *Newsweek* covering Rwanda, while *Time* magazine focused on other issues.

The week of June 27 changed coverage on Rwanda significantly. Football Hall of Famer O.J. Simpson caught the media's attention in a high-speed chase following the double murder of Ron Goldman and Nicole Brown-Simpson. *Newsweek* gave the O.J. Simpson story three covers in a row, despite the fact that it had never featured the Rwanda genocide on its cover. *Time* magazine also gave O.J. Simpson several covers in the final weeks of the Rwanda genocide. *U.S. News & World Report*, which had only written one story on Rwanda throughout the genocide, also covered the O.J. Simpson events in several cover stories and even more articles.

NOTES

1. Personal Interview, National Security Advisor Anthony Lake, Georgetown, MD, November 20, 2002.

2. Personal Interview, White House Official [A], Washington, DC, November 21, 2002.

3. Michael Barnett, *Eyewitness to a Genocide,* pp. 38–39.

4. Linda Melvern, *A People Betrayed: The Role of the West in Rwanda's Genocide,* p. 77.

5. Ibid, p. 235.

6. United Nations Statistic.

7. This was not the case at the State Department or the Pentagon because there were desk officers, diplomats, and regional officers who had specific countries in their portfolio. At the NSC, Susan Rice and Donald Steinberg managed Africa.

8. Personal Interview, Former White House Official [A], Washington, DC, November 21, 2002.

9. Personal Interview, Former Senator Paul Simon, Via telephone to Illinois, December 9, 2002.

10. Personal Interview, Former White House Official [A], Washington, DC, November 21, 2002.

11. Personal Interview, Former White House Official [A], Washington, DC, November 21, 2002.

12. Personal Interview, Former National Security Advisor Anthony Lake, Washington, DC, November 20, 2002.

13. Don Oberdorfer, *The Two Koreas*, Basic Books, 2001, p. 306. The danger of unloading irradiated fuel rods lay in the fact that the North Koreans could chemically treat the plant in order to separate plutonium for atomic weapons from other radioactive material.

14. Don Oberdorfer, *The Two Koreas*, Basic Books, 2001, p. 308.

15. Ibid, p. 316.

16. Ibid, p. 315.

17. Ibid.

18. Fergal Keane, *Season of Blood*, London: Penguin Books, 1995, p. 7.

19. Personal Interview, Former White House Official [A], Washington, DC, November 21, 2002.

20. Fergal Keane, *Season of Blood*, pp. 5–6.

21. Roger Winter, 'Power, not tribalism, strokes Rwanda's Slaughter', *Globe and Mail*, Toronto, 14 April 1994. *The New York Times* that day published: Frank Smyth, "French Guns, Rwandan Blood," in Linda Melvern, *A People Betrayed: The Role of the West in Rwanda's Genocide,* p. 138.

22. Personal e-mail correspondence with Alison Des Forges, May 18, 2002.

23. Associated Press, Nairobi, 'Tribes Battle for Rwandan Capital: New Massacres Reported', *New York Times*, 16 April 1994, in Linda Melvern, *A People Betrayed: The Role of the West in Rwanda's Genocide,* p. 161.

24. Fergal Keane, *Season of Blood*, p. 6.

25. *U.S. News & World Report*, April 11, 1994, Vol. 116, No. 14.

26. *Time Magazine*, April 11, 1994, Vol. 143, No. 15.

27. *Newsweek*, April 11, 1994.

28. Tom Masland with Joshua Hammer, *Corpses Everywhere, Newsweek*, April 18, 1994.

29. Marguerite Michaels, *Time Magazine*, April 18, 1994, Vol. 143, No. 16.

30. Marguerite Michaels, *Time Magazine*, April 25, 1994, Vol. 143, No. 17.

31. Joshua Hammer, "Deeper Into the Abyss," *Newsweek*, April 25, 1994.

32. Jeremiah Kamau, "Rwanda's Trail of Tears," *U.S. News & World Report*, May 16, 1994, Vol. 116, No. 19.

33. Nancy Gibbs, "Why? The Killing Fields of Rwanda," *Time Magazine*, May 16, 1994, Vol. 143, No. 20.

34. Joshua Hammer, "Escape From Hell," *Newsweek*, May 16, 1994.

35. Marguerite Michaels, "Sorry, Wrong Country," *Time Magazine*, June 6, 1994, Vol. 143, No. 23.

4

Getting Out

"U.S. Foreign Service Officials said that according to the U.S. government law and policy, they were not allowed to evacuate any Foreign Service Nationals, it was something prohibited by law. We called them, they said we are very sorry we cannot do anything . . . I saw that we were abandoned and I said to God, it was very critical to see the international community and then UNAMIR leave while people were being butchered, this was a shame for me."

— Personal Interview, Foreign Service National USAID [D], December 19, 2002

When President Habyarimana's plane was shot down on April 6, 1994, diplomats in Kigali and officials in Washington immediately assessed the situation. Senior officials wanted to know the locations of Americans and whether or not they were safe. While this was the primary concern of American policymakers, those who followed Africa more closely in the U.S. government also wanted to know whether there would be a return to violence and who would fill the power vacuums left by the assassinations of the Rwandan and Burundian presidents.

While U.S. officials worked feverishly to find answers to these questions, the situation in Rwanda took a turn for the worse. The day after the assassinations, extremists ambushed ten Belgian UN Assistance Mission for Rwanda (UNAMIR) peacekeepers in hope that it would provoke an international withdrawal from Rwanda. The ambush of UN peacekeepers was all too familiar to the black hawk down incident in Mogadishu six months earlier. This event underscored the decision to evacuate.

As the United States began its evacuation of its expatriates and closed its embassy, UNAMIR was losing key support from the victimized Belgians. Despite the fact that discussions over the withdrawal of UNAMIR began at the same time as the American evacuation, the two warrant separate analysis.

The evacuation of American diplomats and expatriates from Rwanda raised several questions for policymakers. How would the evacuation take place to ensure that no American lives were lost? How would the United States treat the Foreign Service Nationals (FSNs) who worked for the U.S. embassy?

The decision to withdraw UNAMIR was a turning point for Rwanda. The impact of the April 7 ambush caused the main contingents of the mission to pull out. At this time, the United States was anxious to cut peacekeeping missions, did not want another Somalia, and believed the mission had changed. As a result, UNAMIR was partially withdrawn and left with a mere symbolic force. While this was ultimately a decision of the UN Security Council, the U.S. government was the principal advocate among countries with a seat on the Security Council for a UN withdrawal from Rwanda. This decision marked the turning point for Rwanda and those who claim that U.S. policy during the genocide was characterized by an absence of decision-making, are proven wrong by this very clear and consequential choice. The withdrawal of UNAMIR was a sign to the extremists that the international community would not stop them from carrying out a final solution and it was a sign to the Tutsi that the international community was not interested in protecting them.

IN THE GREAT TRADITION

After the April 6, 1994 dual assassination of Rwandan President Juvenal Habyarimana and Burundian President Cyprien Ntaryamira, policymakers in Washington focused immediately on the safety of American expatriates.[1] That same day, Deputy Assistant Secretary of State for African Affairs Prudence Bushnell sent a memorandum to Secretary of State Warren Christopher, in which she predicted that "if, as it appears, both Presidents have been killed, there is a strong likelihood that widespread violence could break out in either or both countries, particularly if it is confirmed that the plane was shot down. Our strategy is to appeal for calm in both countries, both through public statements and in other ways."[2] In the memorandum, Deputy Assistant Secretary Bushnell noted that "all Americans are believed to be safe" and she explained that there was a high likelihood that they would have to evacuate American expatriates out of Rwanda.[3] After notifying the Secretary of State, Deputy Assistant Secretary Bushnell organized a task force to meet in the Operations Center on the seventh floor of the State Department. The first question she asked pertained to the location of American diplomats, the status of the U.S. mission, and the safety of American expatriates. At this meeting, it was collectively decided that "State would send a formal request to DoD requesting planning begin for a possible Non-combatant Evacuation Order (NEO) from Kigali that examined both permissive and non-permissive environments." State indicated that it would send directives to the American Embassies in Brussels, Paris, and the U.S. Mission to the United Nations to actively work this issue with their counterparts. U.S. European Command (EUCOM), along with Joint Staff J-3 (Directorate of Operations), was designated as the points of contact for military cooperation and planning with the Belgians and French for the evacuation procedures.[4] Officials believed that coordination with the Europeans was essential because as the experienced nations in the region, they would help ensure that the NEO ran smoothly. After the decision was made to evacuate and close the U.S. mission in Kigali, senior officials delegated responsibility to the embassy staff and hoped that they would not have to react to the dangerous prospect of American lives being lost in the midst of a Central African war.[5]

Commander in Chief of U.S. European Command, General George Joulwan, recalls that in April 1994, just a few months after he had assumed command, "we got the mission to evacuate the American ambassador out of Rwanda, when the civil war between the Hutus and Tutsis broke out." His response was rapid, he "found out where Rwanda was, drew a circle around it, and had the staff find out what forces were available in the region. It was not easy, especially when you look at the time needed to get assets there and the poor infrastructure of the country."[6]

In preparation for the evacuation, the Pentagon looked for forces to deploy to Bujumbura as an added insurance should an attack occur on the American convoy that was driving south from Kigali to Burundi. According to General Joulwan, this effort required coordination between EUCOM and Central Command (CENTCOM) that would slow the process. In an effort to overcome this obstacle, General Joulwan requested permission from CENTCOM Commander in Chief General Binford "Binnie" Peay to "place a Marine force in CENTCOM under the operational control of EUCOM." Not only did General Peay obtain approval from the Joint Chiefs of Staff for this operation, but he also arranged for a "C130 [aircraft] to support and serve as a radio relay with the Ambassador's evacuation party."[7] While these served as minor victories, there were several other obstacles that the Pentagon needed to overcome in order to ensure a safe, efficient, and casualty free evacuation. As Vince Kern, who was serving as Director of African Affairs at the Pentagon explains, just getting the quick reaction force (QRF) to Burundi was a challenge in and of itself. Kern argues that, "it would have been completely out of the question to expect those troops to be used for anything other than a re-action to potential attacks on the U.S. convoy." He recalls that, "those troops came off of an Amphibious Readiness Group (ARG) that had been stationed off the coast of Somalia to provide a quick reaction force to American marines who were protecting the embassy in Mogadishu." Deploying those small forces to Burundi presented a problem because, as Kern explains, "the situation in Somalia was so bad that we had to have a detachment of Marines protecting the embassy and then we had to have marines offshore to come to the rescue of marines at the embassy should they be overwhelmed . . . but we essentially uncovered the marines by moving that ARG south so they could fly helicopters into Bujumbura." Kern argues that it was nerve-racking to have those soldiers in Bujumbura because "the main interest in the Depart-ment of Defense and elsewhere was getting those marines back onto the ARG and getting the ARG back to Somalia so more American lives would not be lost in Mogadishu."[8]

Ambassador Rawson recalls that the decision to evacuate by land instead of by air came as a result of their inability to safely reach the airport. General Joulwan describes this in greater detail:

> There was good intelligence about what was happening on the ground from the Belgians . . . The road between the embassy and the airfield, which was con-trolled by the Hutus who had killed so many people, was probably about two miles long. The trip to the airport would be like running the gauntlet. So the ad-vice we gave the ambassador was to drive south and come into Burundi and we would meet them there.[9]

Ambassador Rawson explained that they were cut off from the airport be-cause the RPF who had been positioned in the National Assembly building had moved out against the government forces in two places, cutting off any kind of safe route to the airport in Kigali and making it so that the Ambas-sador could not guarantee the safety of the American convoy.[10]

On the morning of April 8, President Clinton called Secretary of State War-ren Christopher "to express his concern about the safety of Americans in Rwanda in light of the deteriorating situation there, and also just concern about the general status of fighting and the status of UN personnel and oth-ers, not to mention the hostilities going on involving the citizens in Rwanda." In response to the President's phone call, Secretary Christopher "assured the President that the Department [of State] and the Pentagon have been working very closely together to assure the safety of Americans in Rwanda and to get the best available information about the conditions that do exist there."[11] That same day, President Clinton issued a statement in which he said "I mention [Rwanda] only because there are a sizable number of Americans there and it is a very tense situation. And I just want to assure the families of those who are there that we are doing everything we possibly can to be on top of the situation to take all the appropriate steps to try to assure the safety of our citizens there."[12]

In a secret memorandum later that day, the Assistant Secretary of Defense for Special Operations and Low-intensity Conflict (SO/LIC) informed Under Secretary of Defense for Policy Frank Wisner of the evacuation plans and briefed him on the current situation. The Assistant Secretary of Defense explained that "There is a glimmer of hope that this crisis is waning . . . Although there is still some gunfire between the RPF forces and the Hutu-extremists, [there are discussions] that are trying to install a ceasefire, return the forces to their respective camps, and return the city to civilian government control."[13] While this perception of the situation on the ground was severely off-base, the focus of the intelligence concerning the violence centered around the possible influence it could have on the evacuation. It is therefore, likely that the "glimmer of hope" referred more to the situation growing secure enough to conduct a successful evacuation.

The State Department's first responsibility is always to Americans living abroad and as Deputy Assistant Secretary Bushnell explains, "we had to put our blinders on and I do not apologize for that because we had to address our primary responsibility—American citizens . . . If Rwandans were being killed I'm sorry, but I had an obligation to get Americans out."[14] The National Security Council held the same position as the State Department. As National Security Advisor Anthony Lake remembers, "When the president's plane was shot down and all hell broke loose . . . we [at the NSC] were concerned, but we needed to evacuate the Americans out of Rwanda."[15] Secretary of Defense William Perry argues that the Pentagon shared the anxiety of the White House and the State Department. He remembers being concerned over the fact that this was going to be a "close one and it was quite possible that we could have lost a couple of those people."[16]

Deputy Assistant Secretary Bushnell recalls that in the midst of the evacuation procedure, an abundance of information concerning systematic killings became readily available through reports from American diplomats, intelligence agencies, and American expatriates in Rwanda. However, much of this information came in the midst of what she called a very "nerve-racking evacuation process; it was second-rate info to our primary concern which was getting our people out of there."[17]

By April 10 the 258 Americans[18] were out of Rwanda and the doors to the U.S. embassy in Kigali had been closed. The convoy consisted of "about 300 cars and trucks" and was monitored using a C130 aircraft to gather intelligence along the route. The C130 proved to be useful in helping "the convoy avoid some ambushes and get safely into Burundi." After the convoy reached Bujumbura, Burundi, the "Marines secured the airfield and flew the Ambassador and other Americans out." General Joulwan, who oversaw this operation, recalls "I'll never forget the praise the Ambassador had for the professionalism and response from the troops and the support he got from EUCOM. He came to EUCOM headquarters in Stuttgart to personally thank the command."[19] The Ambassador was not the only senior U.S. official to praise the operation. That same day, Secretary of State Warren Christopher appeared on NBC's *Meet the Press* where he discussed how the United States had no intention of going into Rwanda and how "in the great tradition, the Ambassador was in the last car."

It may be in a great tradition that the Ambassador was in the last car, but there were many who were not accompanying the Ambassador at all. More than one-third of the Foreign Service Nationals (FSNs) working for the U.S. embassy in Kigali were killed in the genocide. These were officials who worked in the embassy, at USAID, at embassy warehouses, and who were employees of the U.S. Department of State. Some of these FSNs had worked for the U.S. embassy for close to a decade. Of the survivors I spoke with, many of them were bitter and all of them explained that they were surprised by the U.S. decision not to evacuate them out of Rwanda.

When the evacuation plans began, FSNs thought that they would be evacuated with the Americans because they knew, and the Americans knew, that the FSNs were facing certain death. In some cases, FSNs returned to their homes and waited for phone calls from the embassy that never came. These phone calls were in some cases promised by embassy officials, but more often than not, FSNs expected to be evacuated and thus awaited instructions. Tragically, this waiting period and these expectations resulted in a delayed attempt to hide from extremists. As a result, the consequences of waiting were in some cases fatal.

The questions of why we did not evacuate our FSNs and whether it was even possible are questions that warrant an in-depth discussion. There are a lot of reasons, looking at it retrospectively, that contributed to the omission of FSNs from the evacuation: It could have been dangerous to the Americans, the Ambassador created additional chaos by arriving late for the evacuation, and Congress was only concerned with the Americans. Nonetheless, it was understood that these people were going to certain deaths.

In order to examine the question of why the United States did not evacuate the FSNs, it is important to first look at how embassy officials explain their decision not to evacuate FSNs out of Rwanda. According to Ambassador Rawson, numerous individuals, some of whom were embassy employees sought refuge in the embassy compound immediately after the downing of the President's plane. He recalls that "people from the surrounding area . . . gathered at [the] gate [and] asked if they could come in and stay inside." Rawson remembers telling them "Well, you have to understand this is the American residence, the American Embassy. This is not necessarily a safe place for you." He suggested that they "go to the church," but the individuals who pleaded with him explained "Oh, if we go in the church, they will come there and find us and kill us." After hearing these pleas, Rawson conceded and told the "300 people" waiting outside of the gate "OK, come on in." Despite providing sanctuary for these 300 people, Rawson recalls that "even the compound was obviously not secure." He remembers "at one point in time, somebody from one of the attacking forces got up in a tree and shot down into the compound and killed a baby, and wounded a couple of people." With the embassy no longer safe for the 300 people seeking refuge in it and the evacuation plans ready for implementation, Rawson "went out and told [them] that we weren't going to be there any longer; that when we left, the United States flag would come down, and they were going to have to make their own decisions about what to do."[20]

When one looks at the efforts made by the expatriates protecting Tutsis in the Hotel Milles Collines and the Seventh Day Adventist Church, it appears that if extremist leaders were pressured by foreigners, in particular Americans, certain safe havens could be guaranteed. While it would have been unrealistic for Rawson to save every Rwandan Tutsi, he could have demanded that the American embassy not be touched, that the individuals seeking sanctuary on the compound be left alone, and that they consider the individuals inside, friends of the embassy.

Instead of undertaking these creatively heroic acts, Ambassador Rawson followed protocol and returned to his residence while the remaining officials (Deputy Chief of Mission Joyce Leader, Consular Officer Laura Lane,[21] Intelligence Operative Lieutenant Colonel Chuck Vuckovic, and a communicator named Walt Meyers) worked on the logistics of the evacuation. Conversations with RPF officials, FSNs, and journalists reveal that the U.S. Ambassador seemed indecisive, panicked, and unsure of how to handle the evacuation. In an interview with PBS Frontline, Laura Lane offers a recollection that is harmonious with this characterization of the Ambassador's actions. According to Lane, getting the Ambassador on board for the evacuation was a difficult and strange experience. She explains:

We were ordered to leave, and so we're like, "OK, we're going to organize this last convoy," and we said, "OK, Mr. Ambassador, we're ready to go," and he wasn't leaving. Walt [Meyers] got back from his last mission of mercy, so to speak, around town, and we said, "Walt, the ambassador was supposed to be here at the embassy." There was a cease-fire. He should have been able to make it through. He said he was going to come, but then he didn't show up. We called back over the radio, and I can't remember the conversation, but I didn't get the sense he was going to get in the car and come. . . . By that time, the cease-fire in that area had obviously lapsed, and so Walt grabbed the gendarme and then they went to the ambassador's house and brought the ambassador [back].[22]

Lane explains that she "had been four days without sleep. [She] hadn't showered. [She was] eating MREs." While she and her colleagues were trying to organize the evacuation amidst these difficult conditions, she recalls that "[Ambassador Rawson] arrived, just having taken a shower, in a suit." Lane "was struck by that, because [she] was like, 'Wow, after all of us have been through, this AID work, we're having the prime minister killed at the house next door . . . It just seemed so [inconsistent] with the whole situation."[23] This story is consistent with claims that the Ambassador was so taken back by the events in Rwanda that he was too confused and panicked to devise anything extraordinary to try and save some Rwandan lives. Instead, his indecisiveness made it difficult to save even American lives. This recollection raises an important issue: Had Rawson been more engaged, it is not inconceivable that he could have used his clout as the American Ambassador to devise some way to either save the FSNs or those seeking refuge in the U.S. embassy. After all, other foreigners living in Rwanda who did not have the clout of an American Ambassador found success in their endeavors.

Ambassador Rawson is not the only embassy official who was confronted with the FSN question. Laura Lane recalls the difficulty of not being able to evacuate her Rwandan colleagues in great detail. One of her major responsibilities at the embassy was visas and she had an FSN named Ricimbi who she worked very close with. Lane "remembers talking to him, and he'd tell [her over the phone, 'They've come by my house twice now. Is there anything you can do? Can you send an embassy vehicle?'" For Lane this was particularly difficult because she knew that "he had six children and his wife." She recalls saying "Ricimbi, I'm going to try to figure out a way to get to you," but also remembers vividly her fruitless efforts: "I never did [get them], I never could . . . which was hard, because here I was worrying about the 258 Americans. But there were so many other people there that, just because they weren't American, they still mattered. I wanted to stay."[24]

To embassy officials, evacuating non-Americans seemed to contradict their mission of prioritizing Americans. Laura Lane remembers this sad dilemma all too clearly:

We could have [provided an effective sanctuary at the embassy], and I felt like we had an obligation to do that, particularly for the Foreign Service Nationals. These were people that worked right by my side, and just because I was born in the United States of America, I got to get in a car and leave; and they were born in Rwanda, and they had to stay. That wasn't right, and so in the end, I followed the order. [My husband] and I were the last car out, and there was a very, very sad moment. . . .[25]

Ambassador Rawson offers an explanation that is seemingly more consequential in logic. In an interview for this book, he explained that the embassy already had an evacuation plan and even if they had tried to evacuate FSNs or other Rwandans, there is a strong likelihood that they would have been removed from the convoys at the various check points between Kigali and the border to Burundi, possibly jeopardizing the lives of Americans and running contrary to the State Department's primary obligation. He asserts that "there was no way that we could have gotten any Rwandans out of the country without [the Rwandan Army] knowing. People were scattered all over town and there was no gathering of all employees. We had some telephone conversations, but there was nothing we could do. The orders were to close down the embassy and evacuate the Americans and that is what we did."[26]

It is in response to this explanation that I would like to once again draw on the fact that had the Ambassador been more engaged, it might have been possible to negotiate the safe passage of FSNs back to the embassy for evacuation. Second, the evacuation marked a departure from on-the-ground diplomatic efforts, but Secretary of State Christopher, whose knowledge of Rwanda was so limited that he had to look up where Rwanda was in an atlas, viewed the evacuation as a success and as if a great tragedy had been averted.[27] In his eyes it had—the Americans had been rescued.

Throughout the evacuation process, Congress kept a close watch on the Clinton administration to ensure that its objectives did not extend beyond evacuation of American nationals to Burundi. Congress was extremely nervous that the evacuation could escalate to another Somalia. In response to the evacuation, Senator Bob Dole issued a statement on CBS's April 10 broadcast of *Face the Nation* saying "I don't think we have any national interest there . . . The Americans are out, and as far as I'm concerned, in Rwanda, that ought to be the end of it."[28]

On April 11, exactly one day after the successful evacuation of American expatriates, Deputy Assistant Secretary of Defense for Middle East and Africa Molly Williamson sent a memorandum to Under Secretary of Defense Wisner providing talking points on Rwanda and Burundi. The memorandum explained that the Rwanda Patriotic Front (RPF) would observe a 48-hour ceasefire to allow for the completion of expatriate departures from Kigali, that little should be expected from the State Department beyond diplomatic statements, and that the government of Burundi would probably fall.[29] In an attached options paper on Rwanda, the Under Secretary of Defense was warned that "Unless both sides can be convinced to return to the peace process, a massive (hundreds of thousands of deaths) bloodbath will ensue that would likely spill over into Burundi. In addition, millions of refugees will flee into neighboring Uganda, Tanzania, and Zaire, far exceeding the absorptive capacity of those nations."[30]

That same day, Michael McCurry, the State Department spokesman, responded to the question of "whether or not the USA, the only super-power, had a responsibility to lead an international effort to restore order in Rwanda," by explaining that Rwanda "would be under review at the UN, the appropriate place for such discussions."[31]

Later that evening, President Clinton and the First Lady, along with Secretary of State Christopher and his wife, attended a dinner in the State Department's eighth floor Diplomatic Dining Hall to celebrate the 250th Commemoration of Thomas Jefferson's birth. Following the dinner, President Clinton "asked [Secretary Christopher] if it would be possible for him to stop by the Operations Center and visit the [State Department's] Rwanda Task Force, which had been doing some extraordinary work in recent days, helping secure the safety of Americans." Both the Secretary of State and his wife agreed to the President's request. According to an April 12 U.S. Department of State Daily Press Briefing, Deputy Assistant Secretary of State Prudence Bushnell happened to be present that night in the Operations Center and welcomed the President, introducing him to the various members of the Task Force. The President was impressed with the work that was done and was even permitted by the Director of the Operations Center to take photographs.[32]

Deputy Assistant Secretary Bushnell recalls that the completion of the evacuation procedure marked the point at which "we went from getting the Americans out, to doing nothing," and she explains that "the evacuation was the [easy] part because it was a focused issue, she had access to the Secretary, there were resources available, and decisions makers were available, and there was support, and although it was a real made-for-TV scenario, we were successful in getting our people out."[33]

THE WITHDRAWAL OF UNAMIR

It did not surprise many Rwandans and RPF officials that the United States was unwilling to intervene in Rwanda. However, both General Dallaire and the Rwandan population were caught by surprise when the United States and Belgium moved from inaction to total abandonment.[34] On April 7, while the United States was deciding whether or not to evacuate its expatriates, the Rwandan Presidential Guard kidnapped, tortured, and decapitated ten Belgian

UN troops at the military camp in Kigali. The deaths of ten UN troops brought back memories of Somalia and many in Washington believed that the UN should not make the same mistake that it had made in October 1993 when 18 Army Rangers were killed and one dragged through the streets in Mogadishu. As one senior U.S. official explained:

> When the reports of the deaths of the ten Belgians came in, it was clear that it was Somalia redux, and the sense was that there would be an expectation everywhere that the U.S. would get involved. We thought leaving the peacekeepers in Rwanda and having them confront the violence would take us where we'd been before. It was a foregone conclusion that the United States wouldn't intervene and that the concept of UN peacekeeping could not be sacrificed again.[35]

According to then Deputy Under Secretary of Defense for Policy and later Under Secretary of Defense Walt Slocombe, the Pentagon identified the plane crash rather quickly as an assassination, but it was the deaths of the Belgian peacekeepers that meant there would be a major crisis and real trouble.[36]

The day after the ambush of the Belgian peacekeepers, General Dallaire sought to reassure New York that UNAMIR was still a worthwhile mission by explaining that Rwanda was engulfed in "a very well planned, organized, deliberate and conducted campaign of terror. Aggressive actions have been taken . . . against particular ethnic groups . . . We face critical shortages that will reduce the abilities of and endanger the force within a matter of days . . . there is no doubt that Kigali would have been in a worse situation without UNAMIR."[37] This was not what the United States wanted to hear. With the reminders of Somalia, the Americans out of the country, and Congressional pressure to cut peacekeeping missions, policymakers failed to appreciate the gravity of General Dallaire's pleas. Ultimately, this would be illustrated by the partial withdrawal of UNAMIR.

As discussed in earlier chapters, UNAMIR was initially a favorable mission because it was deployed within the context of, what at the time, appeared to be an easily mediated peace process. We recall that the beginning of the genocide on April 6, 1994 and the ambush of ten Belgian peacekeepers the following day changed this perception. Many policymakers have characterized U.S. policy toward Rwanda during the genocide as an "absence of decision-making," yet in my discussions with members of both the RPF and the genocidal government, it became clear that the decision to support the partial withdrawal of UNAMIR was in fact a very crucial decision because of the confidence it gave the extremists to escalate their campaign of genocide and because of the sense of abandonment it bestowed upon the RPF and the Tutsis living in Rwanda. For these reasons, it is important to retrace the history of this decision in order to empirically illustrate the fact that while

Rwanda may have been neglected, U.S. policy in 1994 was by no means an absence of decision-making.

Following the April 7 ambush of the ten Belgian peacekeepers, U.S. Ambassador to Rwanda David Rawson recalls, "It was fairly evident that the mandate had to be changed because some of the troops that came in under a simple peacekeeping mandate were no longer committed. The Bangladeshis and the Belgians wanted out, so we had to change things, there had to be some recycling and there clearly had to be a changed mandate." Rawson remembers the general concern that "We had seen in our few days that the troops had without regard for the UN already begun massive murders and had in fact violated the presence of the embassy with no regard for diplomatic personalities. The perpetrators were going to carry out their plan irregardless of the international presence."[38]

With rumors that the Belgians and the Bangladeshis wanted to pull out of Rwanda, the interagency met at the lowest levels to make its recommendations on how to handle the UNAMIR question. With the evacuation of Americans occupying the U.S. government's attention from April 6 until April 10, the formal discussions about UNAMIR did not take place in Washington until April 13.

At 2:00pm on April 13, a Peacekeeping Core Group, led by Richard "Dick" Clarke from the National Security Council (NSC), and attended by officials from the Pentagon, the State Department, and various intelligence agencies, met to discuss various peacekeeping missions, one of which was UNAMIR. The meeting concluded that the "Department of State will direct the U.S. Mission to the UN to vote for pulling UNAMIR out of Rwanda."[39] It appears that either the recommendation to withdraw UNAMIR came out of the Peacekeeping Core Group teleconference and then was passed up the various bureaucracies for action, or senior officials tasked the Peacekeeping Core Group with providing the justification for a withdrawal. In an interview for this book, I asked then Assistant Secretary of State for International Organizations (IO) Douglas Bennet, who headed the bureau at the State Department that is responsible for peacekeeping, about the Peacekeeping Core Group's role in influencing his decision-making on UNAMIR. While Bennet did not recall the specifics, he remembered that both his Chief of Staff George Ward and he "sometimes attended these meetings." According to Bennet, "what was certain was that the U.S. was not going to commit, that was the general context of the [Peacekeeping] Core Group meetings." He explains that in these meetings "it was obvious that nobody there thought the U.S. could or should intervene." Given that this was a usual Peacekeeping Core Group meeting "many of which [he] attended, some of which Ward attended, [he] may have gone to the meeting, learned that we should pull out, and then gone out."[40]

Based on Bennet's recollection, it seems likely that following the April 13 meeting, Bennet either learned first-hand or from his Chief of Staff that the interagency favored a withdrawal of UNAMIR.

Following the Peacekeeping Core Group meeting on April 13, Assistant Secretary of State Bennet sent a memorandum through the Under Secretary of State for Political Affairs Peter Tarnoff to Secretary Christopher explaining that "Given the chaotic conditions in Rwanda, it is impossible for UNAMIR to fulfill its mandate. It is our view, therefore, that the force should withdraw from the country now. At an appropriate time, the force's mandate should be terminated."[41] Of particular concern to the Assistant Secretary and the Under Secretary was the fact that Belgian Foreign Minister Willie Claes "complained that Boutrros-Ghali is putting the onus on the Belgians for seeking the withdrawal and termination of the UN peacekeeping operation (UNAMIR) in Rwanda." Anxious to appease the Belgian concerns, Bennet and Tarnoff informed the Secretary that "the onus for withdrawal should not be placed on the Belgians."[42]

While this description offers insight into how the decision to withdraw UNAMIR was examined at the lower levels of the interagency bureaucracy, it does not indicate whether the interagency recommendations were responsible for Secretary Christopher's decision on the matter. In fact, there is no indication that the recommendations of the interagency made it to senior levels on April 13. In interviewing senior officials at both the White House and the State Department, it appears that the Peacekeeping Core Group is where the interagency discussion over UNAMIR ended. While Assistant Secretary of State Douglas Bennet explains that "theoretically, the working group would have compared notes on the issue and the respective parts of it would have addressed their principals," this did not occur.[43]

While it seems unlikely that the Secretary of State would have had the authority to instruct the U.S. Ambassador to the UN to call for a withdrawal of UNAMIR without consulting the President, the National Security Advisor, or the Secretary of Defense, this was the reality. Even if Secretary Christopher made the decision on his own, it seems that he would have at least had to brief the White House and the Pentagon on his decision, yet he did not. How could Secretary Christopher have cabled Ambassador Albright to call for a full withdrawal of UNAMIR without consulting the National Security Advisor or the Secretary of Defense? Why did he ignore an interagency process that had already begun examining the question of UNAMIR?

The events on April 14, one day after the Peacekeeping Core Group Meeting and the memorandum to Secretary Christopher, sheds some light on why Christopher appeared to make this decision without consulting his fellow Principals or the recommendations of the Peacekeeping Core Group. One week after the deaths of the ten Belgian peacekeepers, on April 14, Belgian Foreign Minister Willie Claes phoned Secretary of State Christopher and explained, "We are pulling out, but we do not want to be seen to be doing it alone." The Belgians wanted support for a full withdrawal of UNAMIR and Secretary Christopher was easily persuaded because of the Somalia legacy and because as State Department Political Military Advisor Tony Marley argues, "with the recommencement of the war in Rwanda in April of 1994, there no longer was peace for the UN peacekeepers to keep. The terms of the peace accord had broken down."[44] This fact made the decision more urgent, given the potential danger Christopher saw in leaving an ill-equipped force that was clearly not immune from attacks by the armed parties and the unwillingness to delay the wishes of their NATO ally. Given that the issue seemed cut and dried, Christopher made the decision to support the Belgian withdrawal of UNAMIR. Given the fact that interagency discussions addressed this issue the previous day, it would seem appropriate to ask what weight this dialogue had on the Secretary's decision. However, despite the interagency discussions on this issue, Secretary Christopher was neither aware of these discussions, nor was his decision influenced by them.

Recognizing that the Belgians and the Bangladeshis constituted the most significant components of UNAMIR, Secretary Christopher likely felt that he did not have to make a decision. He reasoned that UNAMIR could not continue without the support from the Belgians and Bangladeshis. Given the fact that the decision had already been made, Under Secretary of State Peter Tarnoff and Assistant Secretary of State Douglas Bennet merely reinforced the position of the Secretary and thus made it easier to phone the UN without consulting his counterparts at the White House or the Pentagon. Assistant Secretary of State for African Affairs George Moose also reassured the Secretary that this was the right decision. When asked what he was counseling Secretary Christopher to do in regards to UNAMIR, Moose explains, "We were counseling the Secretary not to oppose the Belgian request to get the hell out of there. We knew what the implications of that would be. I was not the only voice in here, but I certainly didn't feel that we were in a position to demand the Belgians keep their forces there after what happened."[45]

Given the fact that Dick Clarke was present at the Peacekeeping Core Group meeting, it is likely that Christopher would have assumed that Clarke would brief the National Security Advisor, who if he had any questions or concerns, would have made contact with the State Department. However, given the fact that the decision was already made by the State Department, Dick Clarke could just sign off on the decision. It is not unlikely; however, that if the Belgians and the Bangladeshis remained in Rwanda, there would have been a senior level interagency discussion over what to do about UNAMIR.

However, the withdrawal, in particular, of the Belgian contingent had serious and urgent implications for the United States According to U.S. Ambassador to the UN Madeleine Albright:

> Authorities in Brussels had appealed to the United States, as a NATO ally, to support the termination of the entire UN mission, but I cabled Washington that most Security Council members wanted to retain at least some elements. Nevertheless, on April 15, I was instructed to inform the UN that the United States favored 'full and orderly withdrawal of all UNAMIR personnel as soon as possible.'[46]

Sensing the urgency of the Belgian request and assuming that the Peacekeeping Core Group constituted enough of an interagency process to avoid criticism from colleagues for taking State Department unilateral action, Secretary Christopher, on April 15, sent a cable to U.S. Ambassador Albright that said:

> The [State] Department believes that there is insufficient justification to retain a UN peacekeeping presence in Rwanda that the international community must give highest priority to full, orderly withdrawal of all UNAMIR personnel as soon as possible . . . Mission is also instructed to make clear to other UNSC members that . . . we will oppose any effort at this time to preserve a UNAMIR presence in Rwanda . . . The Rwandan armed parties must bear full responsibility for the tragic situation, and continued violence and instability, in their country . . . In the current environment in Rwanda, there is no role for a UN peacekeeping force . . . Our opposition to retaining a UNAMIR presence in Rwanda is firm.[47]

U.S. Ambassador to the UN Madeleine Albright recalls the difficulty they would have had in going against the Belgians and maintaining UNAMIR. She explains that the Belgians "were our NATO ally, and . . . we didn't know about the massive aspect of [the killings at that point]. What was being focused on by the international community and the U.S. was the fact that the peacekeepers were under attack, and the Belgians wanted to leave." Albright's explanation omits an important fact; the most significant number of people were killed in those first few weeks of the genocide. The International Committee for the Red Cross was in Rwanda witnessing the death toll, the diplomats evacuating Rwanda in the first week saw the massive killings, and the UN troops, many of whom wanted to stay in Rwanda, bore witness to the deaths in Rwanda. If Ambassador Albright claims that "we didn't know about the massive aspect of [the killings]" at the time they decided to evacuate UNAMIR, it is because she deliberately ignored cables and information sent by these informants.

Echoing Secretary Christopher's concern, Albright reasoned that "the question was whether there was a U.N. force that was even capable of taking care of things, because the UNAMIR mandate had been for one thing, and all of a sudden it was caught in something else."[48] According to Nigerian Ambassador to the UN Ibrahim Gambari, the Belgian declaration that it would withdraw its troops had two fatal consequences for the mission: "One is that their operations, the logistics support was the backbone of the [force], which is not a big force—3,000 [or] so plus. But they were the backbone, so they left, not only with the personnel, but with the logistic backbone;" and second, "in order to convince their own public that the withdrawal was the right response, they went all out to persuade everybody else to leave, so as to ensure that the mission collapsed."[49] With these two devastating blows coupled with the publicity of yet another instance in which UN peacekeepers had been brutally ambushed, policymakers like Christopher and Albright felt that this situation was all too similar to what had happened in Somalia and therefore, did not feel comfortable taking a position different from Belgium.

The first withdrawal of troops occurred on April 19 when Belgian Colonel Luc Marchal left Rwanda with the Belgian troops, reducing UNAMIR to 2,100 troops.[50] The official withdrawal of UNAMIR, however, occurred on April 21, when the Security Council voted to withdraw all but 270 troops from 22 different countries.[51] Despite earlier U.S. efforts to push for a full withdrawal of UNAMIR, a memorandum from Assistant Secretary of State for African Affairs George Moose and Acting Assistant Secretary of State for International Organizations George Ward informed Deputy Secretary of State Strobe Talbot of the reviewed position on UNAMIR:

> UNAMIR cannot fulfill its mandate under the current circumstances and is unlikely to attract personnel or obtain equipment for an expanded operation. UNAMIR is currently affording some degree of protection to 12,000 refugees in Kigali. We should not advocate (and we could not get agreement in the Security Council for) abandoning these people, nor does it seem feasible for UNAMIR forces to take the refugees with them. UNAMIR is, thus, as a practical matter, stuck in Kigali until the situation there calms sufficiently for these people to disperse. Once this happens, however, we should urge an orderly withdrawal of all UNAMIR forces.[52]

Based on this position, it is clear that the United States decided to maintain a small symbolic presence of UNAMIR only because the United States did not want to be responsible for the immediate deaths of the 12,000 people under UNAMIR protection. While the United States appears to have reasoned that this was a moral compromise, it seems unlikely that 270 troops could be expected to protect 12,000 Tutsis. However, an April 20 U.S. Mission to the UN memo from Robert Grey through Ambassador Walker to U.S. Ambassador to the UN Madeleine Albright reveals that the United States recognized that the Nigerians "would never approve of the Council directing UNAMIR to withdraw."[53]

Ambassador Albright offers a slightly different explanation for retaining some elements of UNAMIR. At the time of Secretary Christopher's instructions, Ambassador Albright claims to have felt uneasy about a full withdrawal when within the Security Council there were states that adamantly supported maintaining UNAMIR. She recalls that after hearing the debate on the Security Council, in particular the "moving" pleas of Nigerian Ambassador to the UN Ibrahim Gambari, she "could see that [the U.S.] position was wrong." In an interview with PBS Frontline, Ambassador Albright explains how she sought to remedy the situation:

> [So] I had these instructions which made no sense at all. These were in informal meetings of the Security Council, where the real discussion goes on. I asked my deputy to take my seat while I left, and went out into the hall into these phone booths and called Washington. I decided not to call the State Department from whence my instructions really came, but the National Security Council, because they were dealing with it on a very imminent basis. Tony Lake, the National Security Adviser, was somebody that certainly knew a lot about Africa. He was the great expert. [Albright ended up talking to Dick Clarke instead of Tony Lake]
>
> I felt that I would get a better hearing if I called the National Security Council, which I did, and they said, "Well, no, we're worrying about this, and these are your instructions." I actually screamed into the phone. I said, "They're unacceptable. I want them changed." So they told me to chill out and calm down. But ultimately, they did send me instructions that allowed us to do a reinforcement of UNAMIR; not a massive changing of the mandate and enlarging it or withdrawing it, but the middle option allowed me to support that.[54]

While Ambassador Albright claims to have recognized the problems with the U.S. position on UNAMIR, it remains difficult to understand how a mere symbolic force of 270 troops from 22 different countries could possibly achieve anything significant. What was left behind to protect the Rwandan people was an ill-equipped force with a confused mandate and low morale. The withdrawal of troops was completed on April 25 and although the resolution called for a symbolic force of 270 to remain, Dallaire was able to maintain 503 troops.[55] When the withdrawal was discussed at the U.S. Rwanda Interagency Working Group (IWG) that same day, "the Group was strongly united in opposition to a withdrawal of any forces if such a move would put the 12–30,000 civilians being protected by UNAMIR at risk . . . and that the U.S. would like the Secretary General to come up with a plan for the continued protection of the civilian population before removing any of the remaining forces."[56] Secretary Christopher, however, continued to push for the withdrawal.

The motives behind this decision were heavily rooted in the Somalia debacle that had occurred just six months earlier and the resulting blame game that occurred between the United States and the UN. In an interview for this book, Under Secretary of Defense Walt Slocombe offers an explanation from a defense perspective:

> The murder of the Belgian peacekeepers was an example of what happens when you send in a token force that does not have much real capability and things go wrong, and as far as the peacekeepers are concerned that was our analysis, this was another situation in which the UN had gotten in with a force, that could not handle the situation. In our eyes, the UN was in another situation where a small force had gotten into a lot of trouble so it was hard to do anything useful.[57]

Slocombe's personal view "was and remains that too many of these UN peacekeeping forces are too big if they are not under threat and too small if they are under threat." He recalls that the concern in Washington was that, "the murder of the peacekeepers made it clear that the UN force could neither take care of itself, nor could it take care of others."[58]

Following the withdrawal of UN troops, the U.S. mission to the UN took no major actions regarding Rwanda. Ambassador Albright met with the RPF representative to the UN on several occasions throughout the genocide, but in one instance, she was told by the Deputy Permanent Representative to the UN Edward Walker and Deputy Political Councilor to the UN John Boardman that "[she] should be mostly in a listening mode during this meeting. You can voice general sympathy for the horrific situation in Rwanda, but should not commit the USG to anything."[59]

At the time of the withdrawal order, UNAMIR troops were protecting tens of thousands of people who sought refuge in stadiums and meeting grounds.[60] More than 3,500 people sought refuge at the UNAMIR headquarters in Kigali and according to RPF officials and Foreign Service Nationals, the UNAMIR troops gave ample warning to those who were being protected, but did not offer transport to other safe havens before they began to withdraw. As it became evident that they were abandoned by the very troops that promised them protection, Rwandan Foreign Minister and then RPF Liaison to the United States Dr. Charles Murigande recalls that many of those seeking protection asked to be escorted to the Amahoro Stadium where tens of thousands of people sought refuge. Despite a distance of only 1.5 km from UNAMIR headquarters, he recalls the UNAMIR troops refused to escort any of the Rwandans under their protection. Despite Murigande's claims, Dick Clarke sent a memorandum to Anthony Lake indicating "that the United States was leading efforts to ensure that the Rwandans under UN protection were not abandoned."[61] However, it is unlikely that many efforts were taken as the United States had just called upon the Security Council to withdraw all UNAMIR troops from Rwanda.

As a final plea, Murigande remembers that people lay in the streets and attempted to block the UNAMIR withdrawal, some even throwing their children onto the trucks.[62] One RPF commander, choosing to identify himself as "Joseph" remembers others screamed, "not to abandon us," and that "they are going to kill us if you leave."[63] In an effort to ward off the potential victims, Murigande claims that UNAMIR troops fired several shots into the air. This was one of the rare instances in which UNAMIR troops fired their guns, which led the RPF to question "why they would not shoot in the air to make the Interahamwe run away, but they would shoot in the air to make the victims run away."[64] As consultant for Human Rights Watch Alison Des Forges explains, UNAMIR actually did kill some of the genocidaires in order to protect people, however, these actions were not well publicized.[65]

Immediately after the withdrawal, Tito Rutaremara claims to have asked General Dallaire "Now please why don't you try and take people to safe havens or they are going to be massacred?" According to Rutaremara, Dallaire responded, "We don't want to do this, we want to be neutral." Rutaremara recalls that he attempted to reason with Dallaire by pointing to the fact that "when you are neutral in this situation you are actually going to be contributing to the massacres." On another occasion, Rutaremara recalls asking Dallaire:

> Fine, you want to be neutral and you don't want to fight the army or the people that are doing the killing, but there are all of these people hiding in churches doing nothing more than trying to survive and escape, why don't you take your people, go around those churches, call the international media and tell them to come and see and show the international community?[66]

What Rutaremara did not know is that General Dallaire, at great risk to his career disobeyed a number of orders from New York by trying to seize weapons caches and save lives with the minimal troop strength remaining in Rwanda.

NOTES

1. According to Deputy Under Secretary of Defense for Policy and later Under Secretary Walt Slocombe, the Pentagon identified the crash pretty quickly as an assassination not an accident.

2. Memorandum from Prudence Bushnell, Principal Deputy Assistant Secretary, Bureau of African Affairs, through Peter Tarnoff, Under Secretary for Political Affairs, to Secretary of State Warren Christopher, "Death of Rwandan and Burundian Presidents in Plane Crash Outside Kigali", April 6, 1994. Limited Official Use, in William Ferroggiaro, *A National Security Archive Briefing Book,* August 20, 2001, found in www.gwu.edu/~nsarchiv/NSAEBB/NSAEBB53/press.html.

3. Ibid.

4. Briefing from the Rwanda Washington Liaison Group Meeting. From Lieutenant Colonel Harvin to Under Secretary of Defense Wisner through Director for Africa in the bureau of International Security Affairs. April 7, 1994. Confidential. Declassified by authority of Office of the Secretary of Defense, 18 November 1998, case # 95-F-0894 in William Ferroggiaro, *A National Security Archive Briefing Book,* August 20, 2001, found in www.gwu.edu/~nsarchiv/NSAEBB/NSAEBB53/index.html.

5. Organization of African Unity, "International Panel of Eminent Personalities to Investigate the 1994 Genocide in Rwanda and the Surrounding Events," Chapter 13, p. 7, 2000, in "United Nations Independent Inquiry," December 1999, p. 1; see also, *Face the Nation*, CBS, April 10, 1994 in Samantha Power, *"A Problem From Hell:" America and the Age of Genocide,* p. 352.

6. Personal Interview, General George Joulwan, Washington, DC, September 7, 2004.

7. Ibid.

8. Personal Interview, Former Director of African Affairs and head of the Rwanda Task Force at the Pentagon, Vince Kern, Alexandria, VA, August 15, 2003.

9. Personal Interview, General George Joulwan, Washington, DC, September 7, 2004.

10. Personal Interview, Former U.S. Ambassador to Rwanda David Rawson, Via telephone to Michigan, September 26, 2003.

11. U.S. Department of State Daily Press Briefing, Friday, April 8, 1994. Michael McCurry and Prudence Bushnell, can be found at dosfan.lib.uic.edu/ERC/briefing/daily_briefings/1994.html

12. PBS *Frontline*, "Triumph of Evil."

13. Memorandum for the Secretary of Defense and Deputy Secretary of Defense from Assistant Secretary of Defense for SO/LIC, through Under Secretary of Defense for Policy. Subject: "Rwanda: Current Situation; Next Steps." Executive Summary/Cover Brief, I-94/16531, April 8, 1994. Confidential. Declassified by authority of OSD 18 November 1998, Case # 95-F-0894 in William Ferroggiaro, *A National Security Archive Briefing Book,* August 20, 2001, found in www.gwu.edu/~nsarchiv/NSAEBB/NSAEBB53/index.html.

14. Personal Interview, Former Deputy Assistant Secretary of State for African Affairs Prudence Bushnell, Washington, DC, December 9, 2002.

15. Personal Interview, Former National Security Advisor Anthony Lake, Washington, DC, November 20, 2002.

16. Personal Interview, Former Secretary of Defense Dr. William Perry, Stanford, CA, February 10, 2003.

17. Personal Interview, Former Deputy Assistant Secretary of State for African Affairs Prudence Bushnell, Washington, DC, December 9, 2002.

18. U.S. Department of State Daily Press Briefing, April 11, 1994, Michael McCurry. Can be found at dosfan.lib.uic.edu/ERC/briefing/daily_briefings/1994.html.

19. Personal Interview, General George Joulwan, Washington, DC, September 7, 2004.

20. PBS *Frontline* Interview, "Ghosts of Rwanda," Interview with Ambassador David Rawson, October 5, 2003.

21. In an October 3 & 4, 2003 interview with PBS Frontline for the documentary "Ghosts of Rwanda," Laura Lane described her role as the following, "I was kind of the everything officer. I was the junior officer. It was a very, very small embassy. There are no Marine security guards. There is an ambassador and a DCM and then I was just kind of everything else. There was an admin officer and GSO, but I did the visa work. I did the American citizens services work. I did the economic reporting, which was really, really interesting. I did the military security assistance work, so believe it or not, they actually had me go through [military] training. . . ."

22. PBS *Frontline* Interview, "Ghosts of Rwanda," Interview with Consular Officer Laura Lane, October 3–4, 2003.

23. Ibid.

24. PBS *Frontline* Interview, "Ghosts of Rwanda," Interview with Consular Officer Laura Lane, October 3–4, 2003.

25. Ibid.

26. Personal Interview, Former U.S. Ambassador to Rwanda David Rawson, Via telephone to Michigan, September 26, 2003.

27. Samantha Power, *"A Problem From Hell:" America and the Age of Genocide,* p. 352.

28. *Face the Nation,* CBS, April 10, 1994, in Ibid.

29. Memorandum for Under Secretary of Defense for Policy from Deputy Assistant Secretary of Defense for Middle East/Africa through Assistant Secretary of Defense for International Security Affairs, Subject: "Talking Points on Rwanda/Burundi", April 11, 1994. Confidential. Declassified by authority of: OSD, 18 November 1998, Case # 96-F-0894 in William Ferroggiaro, *A National Security Archive Briefing Book,* August 20, 2001, found in www.gwu.edu/~nsarchiv/NSAEBB/NSAEBB53/index.html.

30. Ibid.

31. Linda Melvern, *A People Betrayed: The Role of the West in Rwanda's Genocide,* p. 148; see also, U.S. Department of State Daily Press Briefing, April 11, 1994, Michael McCurry. Can be found at dosfan.lib.uic.edu/ERC/briefing/daily_briefings/1994.html.

32. U.S. Department of State Daily Press Briefing, April 12, 1994, Michael McCurry. Can be found at dosfan.lib.uic.edu/ERC/briefing/daily_briefings/1994.html.

33. Personal Interview, Former Deputy Assistant Secretary of State for African Affairs Prudence Bushnell, Washington, DČ, December, 12, 2002.

34. Samantha Power, *"A Problem From Hell:" American and the Age of Genocide,* p. 366.

35. Ibid.

36. Personal Interview, Former Under Secretary of Defense for Policy Walt Slocombe, Via phone to Washington, DC, February 7, 2004.

37. Michael Barnett, *Eyewitness to a Genocide*, pp. 114–115.

38. Personal Interview, Former U.S. Ambassador to Rwanda David Rawson, Via telephone to Michigan, September 26, 2003.

39. Memorandum to Middle East/Africa Division from Joint Staff LTC Bruce Bartolain, Remarks: "Sir, results of PKO Core Group Meeting (teleconferences) 1600 hrs today," Info to Director, Dep Dir, PMA, Chief, MEAF Div, April 13, 1994, Confidential. Declassified by authority of: OSD/JS, 18 November 1998, Case # 95-F-0894 in William Ferroggiaro, *A National Security Archive Briefing Book*, August 20, 2001, found in www.gwu.edu/~nsarchiv/NSAEBB/NSAEBB53/index.html.

40. Personal Interview, Former Assistant Secretary of State for International Organizations Douglas Bennet, Via Telephone to Connecticut, April 14, 2004.

41. In a personal interview with former Assistant Secretary of State for International Organizations, he explained that it was standard procedure to send memos to the Secretary through the Under Secretary of State, but that the Under Secretary of State was not involved in crafting the memorandum.

42. U.S. Department of State, Briefing Memorandum from Assistant Secretary of State for International Organizations through Under Secretary of State for Political Affairs Peter Tarnoff to Secretary of State Warren Christopher, "Phone Call to UN Secretary General Boutros-Ghali on Bosnia and Rwanda," April 13, 1994, Confidential in William Ferroggiaro, *A National Security Archive Briefing Book*, August 20, 2001, found in www.gwu.edu/~nsarchiv/NSAEBB/NSAEBB53/index.html.

43. Personal Interview, Former Assistant Secretary of State for International Organizations Douglas Bennet, Via Telephone to Connecticut, April 14, 2004.

44. Tony Marley, interview, "The Triumph of Evil," *Frontline*, PBS, January 26, 1999; available at PBS Online: www.pbs.org/wgbh/pages/frontline/shows/evil/interviews/marley.html.

45. PBS *Frontline* Interview, "The Ghosts of Rwanda," Former Assistant Secretary of State for African Affairs George Moose, November 21, 2003.

46. Madeleine Albright, *Madam Secretary: A Memoir*, New York: Easton Press, 2003, p. 150.

47. U.S. Department of State, cable number 099440, to U.S. Mission to the United Nations, New York, "Talking Points for UNAMIR Withdrawal", April 15, 1994. Confidential, in William Ferroggiaro, *A National Security Archive Briefing Book*, August 20, 2001, found in www.gwu.edu/~nsarchiv/NSAEBB/NSAEBB53/press.html.

48. PBS *Frontline* Interview, "The Ghosts of Rwanda," U.S. Ambassador to the UN Madeleine Albright, February 25, 2004.

49. PBS *Frontline* Interview, "The Ghosts of Rwanda," Nigerian Ambassador to the UN Ibrahim Gambari, January 15, 2004.

50. Samantha Power, *"A Problem From Hell:" America and the Age of Genocide*, p. 368.

51. UN Security Council Resolution 912, April 21, 1994, Ibid., p. 369.

52. U.S. Department of State Briefing Memorandum from Assistant Secretary of State for International Organizations Douglas J. Bennet through Under Secretary of State for Political Affairs Peter Tarnoff to Secretary of State Warren Christopher, "Phone Call to UN Secretary General Boutros-Ghali on Bosnia and Rwanda," April 13, 1994, Confidential in William Ferroggiaro, *A National Security Archive Briefing Book,* August 20, 2001, found in www.gwu.edu/~nsarchiv/NSAEBB/NSAEBB53/index.html.

53. United States Mission to the United Nations Memo from Robert T. Grey through Ambassador Walker to Ambassador Madeleine Albright, "Security Council Informals on Rwanda," Wednesday, April 20, 3:30pm, April 20, 1994 in William Ferroggiaro, *A National Security Archive Briefing Book,* August 20, 2001, found in www.gwu.edu/~nsarchiv/NSAEBB/NSAEBB53/index.html.

54. PBS *Frontline* Interview, "The Ghosts of Rwanda," U.S. Ambassador to the UN Madeleine Albright, February 25, 2004.

55. Samantha Power, *"A Problem From Hell:" America and the Age of Genocide,* p. 369.

56. April 21 Department of Defense Briefing by LtCol Harvin for the Deputy Assistant Secretary of Defense for Middle East/Africa. Secret. Declassified by authority of: OSD, 18 November 1998, Case #: 95-F-0894.

57. Personal Interview, Former Under Secretary of Defense for Policy Walt Slocombe, Via phone to Washington, DC, February 7, 2004.

58. Ibid.

59. Confidential memorandum to Ambassador Albright from John S. Boardman, through Ambassador Walker, "Subject: Your Meeting with Rwanda Patriotic Front (RPF) Representative Claude Dusaidi, Thursday, April 28, 3:00 P.M.," April 28, 1994, in Samantha Power, *"A Problem From Hell:" America and the Age of Genocide,* p. 357.

60. Howard Adelman & Astri Suhrke, *The International Response to Conflict and Genocide: Lessons from the Rwanda Experience,* Steering Committee of the Joint Evaluation of Emergency Assistance to Rwanda, Chapter 4, p. 4, March 1996; see also, Michael Barnett, *Eyewitness to a Genocide,* p. 127.

61. Samantha Power, *"A Problem From Hell:" America and the Age of Genocide,* p. 369.

62. Personal Interview, Foreign Minister of Rwanda Dr. Charles Murigande, Kigali, Rwanda, December 20, 2002; see also, personal interview, "Joseph" RPF Commander, Pretoria, South Africa, July 22, 2002.

63. Personal Interview, Foreign Minister of Rwanda Dr. Charles Murigande, Kigali, Rwanda, December 20, 2002; see also, personal interview, "Joseph" Former RPF Commander, Pretoria, South Africa, July 22, 2002.

64. Ibid.

65. Personal Interview, Human Rights Watch Consultant Alison Des Forges, Via telephone to Buffalo, NY, October 22, 2003.

66. Personal Interview, President of the Judicial and Constitutional Commission Tito Rutaremara, Kigali, Rwanda, December 20, 2002.

5

A Bureaucratic Nightmare

Rwanda never stood a chance in the American bureaucracy. Once the evacuations of the Americans and the UN officials were complete, the principals (cabinet members) at the White House, the State Department, and the Pentagon cast aside Rwanda and focused on other pressing issues like North Korea, Bosnia, and Haiti. Without the attention of the most senior officials, Rwanda sank deeper and deeper into the lower ranks of the bureaucracy. Those senior officials who knew Rwanda better than others chose to take the safe route instead of advocating the unpopular position that the United States ought to do something to save the Rwandans from the genocide. As a result, the prospect for an intervention in Rwanda was left in the hands of a small group of dedicated low-level officials who, despite their creativity and ambition in trying to devise some kind of an intervention, were unable to move any of their proposals without senior level support. The relevant Undersecretaries and Assistant Secretaries could have provided the link that would connect the work of the lower-level officials to the principals, but on most occasions, these senior officials were unwilling to play such a role.

Policymakers often argue that U.S. policy toward Rwanda during the genocide was characterized by an absence of decision-making. However, a more accurate assessment is that senior officials in the U.S. government adopted a policy of calculated non-interventionism. The principals and senior-level officials created an atmosphere that clearly ruled out intervention, but still permitted low-level officials to work the Rwanda issue within this context of doing nothing. Unfortunately, given an implicit and collective decision by the three bureaucracies not to intervene in Rwanda, there was little, if anything, that low-level officials could achieve without the interest of the principals, without the support of senior officials, and without the leverage and access that enables senior officials to implement policy.

Apathy at the White House

In the midst of a domestic focus on health care, the economy, and eradication of unemployment and a series of foreign policy crises confronting the administration, Rwanda could only emerge as a high foreign policy priority of national interest if President Clinton or National Security Advisor Anthony Lake made it a priority. As the President of the United States, Bill Clinton could have made the calculation that the crisis was so catastrophic that the moral obligation was in American national interest. He made no such calculation.

President Clinton was neither an Africanist, nor an expert on Rwanda. That being said, he had some familiarity with the crisis in Rwanda. Most notably, the President's interaction with Rwandan human rights activist Monique Mujawamariya just four months before the genocide offered some insight into Rwanda's dire situation and had a profound effect on him. In December 1993, Mujawamariya attended a White House breakfast to celebrate the proclamation of Human Rights Day. While Clinton was not in attendance at the breakfast, he met Mujawamariya in a receiving line and she was able to engage him in conversation for ten minutes. At the time of the meeting, Mujawamariya's face was still scarred from an attempt on her life that she had barely survived a few weeks earlier. Human Rights Watch consultant Alison Des Forge served as her interpreter and was therefore witness to the conversation as she made it possible for the two to communicate. According to Des Forges the talk was short, but Mujawamariya explained that the situation was critical and the human rights interests were being attacked. Mujawamariya expressed the need for some kind of U.S. pressure to move forward in the peace process and ensure that violence against civilians was halted. Des Forges recalls that Clinton was very warm and he was very much taken by her story, so much so that when the *Washington Post* falsely reported that she had been murdered, Clinton inquired two to three times a day about her well-being. Unfortunately for the Rwandan people, the President's personal concern for Monique Mujawamariya was never extended into an active policy.[1]

President Clinton saw no reason why the United States should undertake an intervention in Rwanda. There were other priorities, recent history showed that American troops on the ground in Africa could cause a domestic backlash, and the President did not know enough about the Rwanda situation to ask the right questions or to examine what actions, if any, the United States could undertake. Having endured a calamity over Somalia six months prior, President Clinton would have been unable to disassociate Rwanda from Somalia. The only association he made was that he did not want to repeat Somalia. In his eyes, intervention meant commitment of troops, American body bags, and domestic uproar. Ironically, the concept of "never again" seemed to have more resonance with regard to humanitarian intervention than it did with genocide.

Had the President determined that the United States needed to act, there are several actions or avenues he could have explored without committing military troops. If the President had felt it was both urgent and serious, it is not inconceivable that he would have called a meeting of the National Security Council to inform the cabinet that it was an issue he wanted discussed in the various bureaucracies. These meetings, led by the President, are reserved for the most serious matters and are attended by the cabinet and their deputies. Even if the President did not want to go as far as to call a meeting of the National Security Council, he could have ordered the Pentagon to develop contingency plans for Rwanda, or asked Anthony Lake to call a principals meeting to discuss possible responses to the genocide. The principals meeting, led by the National Security Advisor, is attended by relevant cabinet members to the particular issue on the table. Even if the President had not yet been convinced that the United States should take action in Rwanda, there was no evident harm in exploring options. If President Clinton did not want to call a meeting of the National Security Council, did not want to direct the Pentagon or the State Department to look into various types of interventions, and did not want to ask his National Security Advisor to call a principals meeting, he could have taken it upon himself to phone the Rwandan leadership and inform them that they were in violation of international law, pressure them to stop the massacres of innocent civilians, and warn that there would be consequences for their actions.

While the effectiveness of a phone call that did not take place is difficult to measure, the force of a call directly from President Clinton would have had significantly more impact than phone calls from Deputy Assistant Secretaries and directors. Despite these potential avenues for action, President Clinton, throughout the one hundred days of the genocide, never inquired about possible U.S. responses, never asked Anthony Lake to call a principals meeting to discuss the issue, and never picked up the phone to call the Rwandan leadership.

Even if President had no desire to take action in Rwanda, he gave no indication to the Rwandan leadership that he was serious about standing firm against the atrocities. There was no attempt at coercion. At this same time, Republicans in Congress were eager to criticize the Clinton administration, and as a result, it would have opened him up to potential criticism if he were to call for a response to Rwanda just six months after Congress had criticized the operation in Somalia.

Even though President Clinton did not take the initiative on Rwanda, Anthony Lake was in a position as the President's National Security Advisor to ensure that Clinton understood the severity of the situation in Rwanda. Lake met with NGOs, had a background as an Africanist, and saw some, although it is not clear how many, of the intelligence reports related to Rwanda.[2] Had he viewed the violence in Rwanda as a serious enough matter, he could have spoken directly with the President about it, called a principals meeting, sent memorandums, or made personal phone calls to the Secretary of State and Secretary of Defense to inform them that the White House wanted to know what the United States could do to respond to Rwanda. However, the plethora of high-interest issues distracted the National Security Advisor until it was too late and the genocide had already been completed. Lake describes his failure to call a principals meeting as his greatest mistake, regretting that "we never even sat down to assess the situation."[3]

In defense of Lake, former Director for African Affairs at the Pentagon Vince Kern argues that the reason Anthony Lake never called a principals meeting was because there were no decisions to make. He explains that there was nobody who was telling the State Department to stop their diplomatic efforts or to stop talking to the French, who were overtly supporting the genocidal government. Everybody in the interagency, according to Kern, agreed on most issues and there was therefore never anything that needed to be brought to the principals level. The notion that the United States should somehow surge into the lead and do something proactive such as a military intervention was non-existent.

Anthony Lake argues that his failure to address the issue of Rwanda was a result of his prioritization of issues such as North Korea, Bosnia, and Haiti. In the first week in May, Anthony Lake explained to the White House press that he and the Clinton administration had to make decisions about where it was strategic for the United States to involve itself:

> When I wake up every morning and look at the headlines and the stories and the images on television of these conflicts, I want to work to end every conflict. I want to work to save every child out there. And I know the president does, and I know the American people do . . . but neither we, nor the international community, have either the mandate, nor the resources, nor the possibility of resolving every conflict of this kind.[4]

With this approach to foreign policy issues, it is not surprising that the White House advocated a withdrawal of UNAMIR. In retrospect, it is easy to argue that Lake could have used the evacuation procedure as the first step toward determining what to do about the Rwanda crisis, but at the same time, it would have taken proponents for intervention in Rwanda that far outweighed those of North Korea, Bosnia, and Haiti, for Anthony Lake to place Rwanda above these other pressing issues. These proponents for a response to Rwanda did not materialize into a strong enough lobby to influence the National Security Advisor's thinking.

It would have been difficult for the National Security Advisor to rationalize a response to Rwanda when many of the NGOs were not calling for a military intervention, Congress was not calling for it, and there was only minimal pressure or exposure from the media. Even if one or more of these groups offered more intense pressure, it was already determined that the only existing force that could be used to stop the genocide was going to begin withdrawing on April 19.[5] Therefore, it would have taken overwhelming pressure for Anthony Lake to take a position different from that of the Secretary of State and the U.S. Ambassador to the UN. A decision to intervene in Rwanda might also have risked establishing a trend that could also drag the United States into the ethnic conflict in Bosnia, which compared to Rwanda, did not claim as many lives, but was nonetheless a theater for crimes against humanity.

Holly Burkhalter and Alison Des Forges of Human Rights Watch occasionally obtained a meeting with Anthony Lake, but as he recalls, they were not pushing for intervention until three weeks into the crisis. It is important to note that while most NGOs did not initially call for American troops to stop the genocide, many called for a strengthening of UNAMIR, greater pressure on the genocidal government, and jamming of the hate radio. Anthony Lake attributes the delay in calling for U.S. military intervention to the NGOs general reluctance to plead for a military response to a human rights issue. Other officials have speculated that what was occurring in Rwanda was so unfamiliar to even the NGO community, that it took at least three weeks for them to understand and accept the nature of the violence. These officials speculate that the genocide was something different from the Holocaust, Cambodia, and what was occurring in Bosnia and therefore, conclude that any NGO workers had difficulty grasping how a government could seduce one society, the Hutus, into exterminating another society, the Tutsis. However, this does not appear to be the case. Human Rights Watch consultant Alison Des Forges explains, "In terms of U.S. intervention, we never advocated that because we knew that was not going to go anywhere in Washington, except for very limited undertakings such as the radio which we did eventually call for."[6] This created a delayed response and as one official at the White House remembers that in the early stages, there was not a single letter, speech, op-ed piece, saying U.S. troops need to go into Rwanda to end the genocide.[7] Because Rwanda was not of economic, political, or strategic interest to the United States, and even more so because the UN force was going to be withdrawn,

Lake recalls that an "intervention [in Rwanda] was something so unimaginable that nobody thought it was possible, and there was therefore, no reason to bother trying for it."[8] True, Lake made briefings for the President in which he sometimes covered the most basic details about Rwanda (number of deaths, who is fighting, etc.), but as he explains, it was always within the parameters of the United States not doing anything and speculation as to "what was the most that we could do on the basis that we were going to do nothing."[9] For these reasons, Lake argues that the failure to respond to the violence in Rwanda was not a matter of ignoring information, but rather what he describes as "an error of omission not commission, in the sense that we never really made decisions. We did not make the wrong decisions, we just didn't make any, and that is where we failed."[10] Lake's recollection notwithstanding, the administration, whether it understood what it was doing or not, made a very crucial decision on April 15 to support a withdrawal of UNAMIR troops. Consequentially, this removed the one force that had potential to prevent the genocide from persisting. The resulting political environment was one that demonstrated senior level reluctance to either continue supporting efforts to stop the violence in Rwanda, or undertake any new initiatives.

With the evacuation of American expatriates, the fate of UNAMIR already determined, and no indication that either Clinton or Lake would make a recommendation for an American response, Rwanda issues at the White House fell into the hands of Richard "Dick" Clarke, who was head of International and Global Issues at the National Security Council,[11] Donald Steinberg who was the Senior Director for Africa, and to some extent, Susan Rice who was the Director for International Organizations. Clarke had been instrumental in the production of PDD-25 and as a result, interpreted the lack of initiative by Clinton and Lake as an indication that Rwanda was not vital to American interests and therefore, should not warrant a peacekeeping mission or a U.S. response. Rather than examining what the United States could do with the existing peacekeeping mission and how it could facilitate an end to the conflict, Dick Clarke continued to argue in favor of the withdrawal of UNAMIR.[12]

During the first half of the genocide, Clarke seized a leading role, his domineering style intimidating to some colleagues. According to the Pentagon's Director for African Affairs at the time Vince Kern, this was somewhat surprising because Clarke had come over to the NSC after having served as Assistant Secretary of State for Political Military Affairs.[13] Kern explains that Clarke went to the NSC and "resurrected his political career, becoming one of the most effective bureaucrats working in the interagency."[14] He argues that "Clarke could maybe not manage a couple hundred people, but he could really crack the whip in a small group interagency process." He recalled a Deputy Assistant Secretary once commenting that Clinton said "Dick Clarke was the only person who worked for him who could get things done."[15] According to Kern, Clarke's approach was to "win people over by the force of his arguments or to make them cower so that they would be silenced out of a fear that Dick Clarke would yell at them."[16] For these reasons, Clarke "acquired a reputation for bright ideas and bullying tactics." According to former director and senior director for counterterrorism, Daniel Benjamin and Steven Simon, Clarke worked under his own rules and "he infuriated other NSC senior directors by refusing to attend the twice-weekly staff meetings and by sending, in bold, red type, email messages that range from the merely snide to the blatantly insulting." One assistant secretary of defense put it cogently when he said, "Dick drove the Chiefs batshit."[17] Benjamin and Simon argue that Clarke's behavior stirred great controversy at senior levels and "It is no exaggeration to say that one person or another at the cabinet or sub-cabinet level or in the top NSC staff urged the National Security Advisor to fire Clarke almost every month."[18]

While Clarke took the lead role in distancing the U.S. government from Rwanda, he was not the only official overseeing the crisis at the White House. Donald Steinberg, who arrived on the Africa desk from the Public Affairs sector of the NSC, took part in a number of discussions about the violence in Rwanda, but found his ideas overturned by Clarke.[19] According to one White House official, the Africa desk was marginalized by the peacekeeping desk and the question was not one of what the Africa desk was doing, but what they were allowed to do.[20]

The President and the National Security Advisor's lack of initiative on Rwanda, their support for UNAMIR's withdrawal, in combination with the terms of PDD-25, led the peacekeeping desk at the NSC to believe that Rwanda was to be an early test case for the United States to prove to the United Nations and the Republicans in Congress that it was both willing and able to say "no" to peacekeeping if it was not in American strategic interest.[21] As the voice of the White House, Clarke made sure that all discussions about Rwanda took place with the understanding that an intervention was impossible without the necessary support from senior levels of the government.[22] Many NSC officials found the firm stance of the peacekeeping desk frustrating, and one official in the administration actually described Dick Clarke as "a man who has no heart." In an example of this frustration, one official from the White House explained that Donald Steinberg and other NSC policy advisors ran into constant opposition from the peacekeeping desk, which was constantly arguing that there were no forces to intervene, that the Pentagon was against it, that an intervention could jeopardize peacekeeping in more strategic areas, and finally, that the President did not see Rwanda as a national interest.[23] Most officials at the NSC understood Clarke's position and as one

White House official explains, even if officials did not agree with him, it was generally understood that "you could have been crucified if you stood up six months after Somalia and wanted to intervene in Rwanda."[24]

Clarke moved onto other issues half-way through the genocide and left the peacekeeping process to Susan Rice, who was viewed by many as extremely bright and highly effective.[25] According to some officials, Rice had seen Clarke's forceful technique and essentially adopted his style. However, as Director for African Affairs at the Pentagon Vince Kern explains, despite being "tough and hard charging, Susan Rice did not appear to have the malice in her that Dick Clarke appeared to have in him."[26] Furthermore, Rice was not in charge of Africa. As Director for Peacekeeping at the National Security Council, there were limited options she could have taken given the fact that the Secretary of State supported the withdrawal of UNAMIR from Rwanda. Without the presence of a robust peacekeeping mission in Rwanda, the pull needed to come from the Africa office at the National Security Council.

While most officials at the National Security Council did not publicly advocate for a greater response to Rwanda, there were some who tried to raise the issue within the White House. However, Dick Clarke, who had a firm position on peacekeeping repeatedly conveyed the message that "there is no support from the UN, the media, the African countries, Congress, and the NGOs. Are you saying that the US should do this unilaterally? Where is the support?"[27] Such a response was difficult to argue against, and according to one official at the NSC, this position in the first three weeks was reinforced by the fact that "there were very few NGOs that were doing much advocating at the time, [they all began advocating at the end of April.]"[28] Even when these claims of human rights violations transformed to pleas for intervention and use of the term genocide to describe the crisis, officials at the NSC remember that they were skeptical of the human rights NGOs. Policymakers had grown accustomed to the NGOs' frequent use of the term genocide and as a result, it was difficult for policymakers to distinguish between typical human rights reporting and a crisis that was truly unique.

THE STATE DEPARTMENT: "EXPECT LITTLE MORE THAN DIPLOMATIC STATEMENTS"

At the State Department, Secretary of State Warren Christopher developed his own list of crises that he deemed top priorities.[29] These were North Korea, Bosnia, and Haiti, where there was a clear political, economic, and strategic interest for the United States. It would have been unrealistic to expect Secretary Christopher to prioritize Rwanda over these other pressing issues without any indication from senior officials at the White House that the President or National Security Advisor wanted him to take the lead on an intervention in Rwanda.

Secretary Christopher was neither an Africanist, nor had he ever expressed significant interest in the politics of Africa outside of Egypt and Libya. Therefore, it seems unlikely that Christopher would have embraced a plea from any of the senior officials junior to him for an intervention in Rwanda. The unlikelihood of this was furthered by an absence of senior level will to propose, or even conceive of, a possible intervention in Rwanda.

As discussed in the previous chapter, Secretary Christopher appears to have taken the lead in ordering Ambassador Albright to call upon the Security Council to withdraw the UN Assistance Mission for Rwanda (UNAMIR). This action, along with Prudence Bushnell's claims that "Christopher never sent a single message or memorandum to his Assistant Secretaries asking for information, contingency plans, or analysis concerning a possible response to the Rwanda genocide," reinforced the sense in the Department that an intervention in Rwanda would be opposed at the most senior levels.[30]

Without pressure from the White House through a direct phone call, a memorandum, or a principals meeting, the only other way that Secretary Christopher might have been convinced to rethink his list of priorities would have been if the U.S. Ambassador to Rwanda David Rawson voiced a more forceful urgency for a U.S. response to the violence in Rwanda and opposed the withdrawal of UNAMIR. However, throughout the entire crisis, Ambassador Rawson never met with the Secretary of State.[31] Secretary Christopher had never prioritized issues in Africa, and while it is unlikely that pressure from the Ambassador would have led the Secretary of State to push for an intervention, it is possible that it would have at least compelled him to inform senior officials at the State Department, particularly Assistant Secretary of State for African Affairs George Moose, that he would support some kind of intervention in Rwanda. However, neither the Ambassador, nor the Assistant Secretary of State, tried to meet with Secretary Christopher about Rwanda and as a result, such pressure was never applied.

In the absence of such senior level pressure on the principal, the remote possibility that the Secretary would support some kind of intervention in Rwanda was never explored. Given the stance of the White House, it was inconceivable for the State Department to push for intervention in Rwanda without the support of the Secretary. Instead of providing this link, the Ambassador and Assistant Secretary Moose, by not trying to force Rwanda on the desk of the Secretary, failed to provide the link between the Principal and the junior officials who knew Rwanda best.

If Ambassador David Rawson was unable to personally convince Secretary Christopher that Rwanda should be discussed at senior levels in the State Department or that the UNAMIR force should be maintained, he could have also tried to meet with Anthony Lake in an effort to stress the need for the United States to intervene in Rwanda. As a returning U.S. Ambassador, David Rawson would not have had a difficult time obtaining a meeting with Anthony Lake and as a result, he could have taken advantage of Lake's experience working in African issues by explaining the urgency of a U.S. response to the genocide. One can only speculate as to what the effect of such a plea would have had on the National Security Advisor, but had Rawson urged Lake to take action in a way that did not commit troops, funds, or resources, such as forceful diplomatic statements condemning the massacres, it is likely that Lake would have at least phoned the Secretary of State, Secretary of Defense, or called a principals meeting.

By mid-April, Ambassador David Rawson, as was customary for a recently evacuated Ambassador, returned to work in the Africa Bureau alongside former Ambassador to Rwanda Robert Flaten. Rawson approached his new position with the understanding that Prudence Bushnell and Arlene Render took the lead on Rwanda in Washington and he would serve as an advisor when called upon. According to Rawson, his role was to attend the meetings, answer question when asked, and play a supportive role.[32]

Ambassador Rawson's passivity reflected his support for the administration's stance on Rwanda. By appearing to share this stance with his silence, Rawson gave Secretary Christopher no reason to question the withdrawal of UNAMIR or to address Rwanda alongside the high priorities of Bosnia, Haiti, and North Korea. After all, if the returning Ambassador to Rwanda was not making noise over Rwanda, many believed there was little cause for alarm. Once the evacuations of the Americans and the UN were complete, Secretary Christopher did not want to hear details of Rwanda, he did not want to consider an intervention in Rwanda, and he did not want to meet with people about Rwanda. This was not his focus, and it would take the force of the White House to convince him otherwise. According to Belgian Foreign Minister Willie Claes, Secretary of State Christopher's attitude was all too clear when he responded to the Foreign Minister's attempt to discuss Rwanda by informing him that, "I have other responsibilities."[33]

Ambassador Rawson's silence in Washington was eerily consistent with those senior officials who did not have an understanding of Rwanda. In retrospect, there are a number of different actions that the Ambassador could have taken to provide senior officials with incentive to discuss Rwanda; however, Rawson did not take these actions and it is therefore necessary to examine why he took a stance that fell in line with the administration's policy.

David Rawson grew up in the region, could speak the language fluently, was posted in Rwanda in the 1970s and as such, understood the nature of Rwandan politics, history, and culture better than almost everyone in Washington.[34] As an expert on Rwanda, how was it possible for Ambassador Rawson to witness the first week of the genocide, speak with RPF officials throughout the end of the civil war, and follow the crisis in such detail, yet still refrain from bringing a proposal for a U.S. response to the Office of the Secretary of State, Office of the Secretary of Defense, or the National Security Council? Rawson recalled a fear that, "If you get into a stalemate, and trench warfare in which the country totally exhausts itself, and there is anarchy in the countryside, then we could have taken a step backward into Somalia."[35] He also asserts that he had dedicated his entire post in Kigali to the Arusha Peace Process and as a result argues that, "We were naïve policy optimists . . . We were looking for the hopeful signs, not the dark signs . . . Once the Washington side buys into a process, it gets pursued, almost blindly."[36] Officials at the State Department, however, argue that the American Ambassador was strangely unclear about what was occurring in Rwanda and this indecisiveness prevented him from grasping the true severity of the genocide and bringing it before senior officials.[37] Given his knowledge of Rwanda and his perspective from serving as Ambassador, the situation in Rwanda ought to have been clearer to him than any other official.

Illustrating the lack of clarity Rawson communicated, former RPF liaison Charles Murigande recalls seeing television broadcasts after the evacuation in which the Ambassador explained that, "the situation is not as clear as some people claim, and that people are killing each other, and it is not clear exactly what is happening."[38] While many policymakers agree that they did not necessarily know that the violence in Rwanda constituted genocide until three weeks into April (a topic discussed in greater detail in chapter 6), intelligence officials at the State Department and the Defense Department recall the evidence was all too clear. According to one State Department official, it was clear as early as the first week that a lot of people were being killed, the nature of the killing was systematic, civilians were being massacred because of their ethnicity, and the situation was growing worse by the day.[39] However, Rawson's initial waffling on terminology led to confusion about what type of conflict was occurring in Rwanda.

This should not have been the debate. The Ambassador knew that hundreds of thousands of people were being killed, and whether or not it was occurring within the context of a civil war, a genocide, or an ethnic clash should not have mattered. The label of the killing did not change the fact that the violence and the body count in Rwanda was growing worse by the day, and that the withdrawal of UNAMIR and the refusal of the United States to issue a response contributed to the worsening situation.

There are several theories about what led to Ambassador Rawson's uncertainty. Some senior officials at the State Department argue that Rawson's uncertainty came from his inability to reach a conclusion as to who shot down the President's plane and his distrust of the RPF, who he believed had unjustifiably invaded Rwanda in 1990.[40] One can also make the argument that Rawson wanted to choose his words carefully in order to maintain influence over the situation. Beginning in 1992, U.S. Ambassador to the former Yugoslavia Warren Zimmerman had attempted to create a stir over Bosnia that would lead to intervention. However, Zimmerman's efforts were fruitless until the mid-90s. Given the interviews I conducted with those who knew Ambassador Rawson, it seems unlikely that he constrained himself out of a fear that too much demand for an intervention would reduce his influence. If this was the case, it is difficult to explain why Ambassador Rawson never proposed any intervention.

A more widely accepted explanation is that Rawson viewed the Habyarimana regime as the power that ended the violence in Rwanda and first attracted development aid to the country, making it difficult for him to believe the RPF claims that the Habyarimana government was extremist and promoted violence against Tutsis. Proponents of this theory argue that Rawson saw the government and the extremists as separate actors that differed in their treatment of Tutsis. Furthermore, the defining aspect of Ambassador Rawson's post in Rwanda had been to help facilitate an on-the-ground end to the four-year civil war that preceded the genocide by supporting the Arusha Peace Process and working to bring the RPF and the Rwanda Government together in a Broad-Based Transitional Government on terms that were agreeable to both sides. Distracted by his narrow focus on a return to the Arusha Peace Process and a distrust of the RPF, Ambassador Rawson portrayed the crisis in Rwanda as violent, but not necessarily systematic. In a recollection of the Ambassador's stance, RPF officials remember hearing a speech by Ambassador Rawson on April 10, in which he announced over Radio MPR that, "everybody is killing everybody."[41]

RPF officials argue a different explanation for Ambassador Rawson's decisively non-interventionist position regarding Rwanda. While their view is likely to be biased, it presents a different perspective than those of Ambassador Rawson's colleagues. All senior RPF officials interviewed argued that Rawson was distracted by his preoccupation with including the extremist CDR in the peace process. As a result, they assert that he tended to view the crisis from a different angle and seemed unaffected by the killings in Rwanda. In an example of this, on the morning of April 15 Ambassador Rawson and his wife invited current Foreign Minister and former RPF liaison to the

United States Charles Murigande to their home in Washington DC. According to Murigande, he explained over breakfast the details of the atrocities and the fact that there was a genocide in Rwanda. He recalls the Ambassador's skeptical response to this information and remembers being "shocked and disappointed by his attitude."[42] Murigande remembers that immediately after discussions about the crisis and in a period when more than 10,000 people were being killed daily, the Ambassador's wife explained, "[We] had a very beautiful home in Kigali and from our balcony we could contemplate Kigali had a very nice view, and I wonder when we will be able to go back." Murigande responded, "Madam very soon you will be able to go back." Mrs. Rawson asked "why are you so optimistic?" He paused for a moment and then said that "very soon there will be no Tutsi to kill anymore and you can go back. The job will be done and you can enjoy the view from your balcony."[43]

Lacking attention from the Secretary of State and confronted with alternate views from Ambassador Rawson, the responsibility for Rwanda remained in the Bureau of African Affairs under the leadership of Assistant Secretary of State for African Affairs George Moose. At the time the plane was shot down, Moose was in Cairo for the Organization of African Unity (OAU) meeting, and his backup, Principal Deputy Assistant Secretary of State (PDAS) for African Affairs Ed Brynn was on leave. As a result, responsibilities for Rwanda fell into the hands of Deputy Assistant Secretary of State for African Affairs Prudence Bushnell. Bushnell spoke with Moose over the phone several times while he was in Cairo. Because she had earlier served Moose as the Deputy Chief of Mission in Dakar, Senegal he trusted her ability to monitor the situation. According to Prudence Bushnell, most of her phone calls to Moose were informative and focused on "this is what I am doing, this is what I am going to do, and this is what I want to do."[44]

When Moose returned to Washington a few days after the genocide broke out, he left the oversight of Rwanda in Bushnell's hands. One State Department official observed that Moose seemed to be in the difficult position regarding Rwanda of "[looking] callous if [he said] it is not in our interest, and [going] against a lot of grain if [he wanted] to do the intervention."[45] However, as the Assistant Secretary of State for Africa, Moose had a duty to oversee the administration's most pressing concerns in Africa, which at the time were the Somalia pull out and the progress of South Africa's transition to democracy. Not only were these issues more pressing for U.S. national interest, but Moose also had an extremely capable Deputy Assistant Secretary who had devoted much of her attention to Rwanda. Moose was, however, engaged in some aspects of U.S. policy toward Rwanda, but because of the Somalia and South Africa priorities he did not take the lead.

Only one senior official at the State Department played an active role in promoting a U.S. response to the violence in Rwanda. Assistant Secretary of State for Democracy, Human Rights and Labor John Shattuck was in direct contact with the Deputy Assistant Secretaries, Directors, and desk officers who were focusing on Rwanda and met with several human rights activists. Despite advocating a response to Rwanda, Shattuck lacked the influence to even sway the policy direction, unlike the regional and geographic bureaus. The Bureau of Democracy, Human Rights and Labor (DRL), did not formulate policy, but relied on influence to advocate that human rights violations should prevent certain countries from receiving the benefits of U.S. policy. In addition to his affiliation to an inherently weak bureau, John Shattuck recalls that he "had been under siege during the month of April for the positions [he] was taking in the internal debates over China, Bosnia and Haiti." He spent "almost every day in meetings at the State Department or the White House in which [his] role in trying to implement the President's executive order linking human rights to trade benefits for China was undercut."[46]

Assistant Secretary of State Shattuck knew that his role in advocating for a forceful response to Rwanda would not be popular among his senior colleagues, but even so, he continued to make an effort. Shattuck's interest in Rwanda escalated on April 19 after hearing escaped victim of the genocide Monique Mujawamaija describe the details of the atrocities in Rwanda. According to Shattuck, Monique was "deeply discouraged by the reception she had received at the White House" and in response to her testimony, he "vowed after [their] meeting that [he] would travel to Rwanda to do what [he] could to influence [American] policy on the rapidly escalating human disaster."[47] Shattuck spent the majority of April preparing for his trip to the Great Lakes region. During his preparations for the diplomatic trip Shattuck recalls running into a wall of State Department lawyers who wanted to make sure that he understood that use of the term "genocide" was a "legal conclusion, not a statement of fact" and who informed him that he could only use the term "mass killings" to describe the genocide.[48]

In the final days of April, John Shattuck and Ambassador Rawson traveled to Ethiopia, Tanzania, Burundi, and Uganda. They were not permitted to enter Rwanda due to safety concerns, but the Air Force plane flew low enough for them to obtain a visual confirmation of the magnitude of the genocide and as Shattuck described, "Like logs slowly flowing in the current, hundreds of human bodies could be seen heading downstream toward Lake Victoria."[49] He stated that during this low flying tour of the Rwanda genocide, Ambassador Rawson even pointed out the bridge below [them] where he said reports indicated the bodies were being counted at a rate of ten per minute.[50] The trip to East Africa had a profound effect on the Assistant Secretary, and he returned to Washington on a mission to work with all those at the State Department who also wanted to campaign for a U.S. response to Rwanda.[51]

With George Moose focusing on other African issues, Prudence Bushnell, with Assistant Secretary Shattuck's support of the efforts, led desk officers and low-level officials to do something to stop the killing. Shattuck felt that Prudence Bushnell was acting heroically and explains that her efforts energized him to support her actions.[52] Bushnell regularly led inter-bureau meetings with representatives from the Bureau of African Affairs (AF), the Bureau of Population, Refugees, and Migration (PRM), the Bureau of Intelligence and Research (INR), and the Bureau of Democracy, Human Rights and Labor (DRL), whom she fondly called her "Rwanda groupies." She recalls the content of these meetings with those charged with tracking Rwanda focused on "what can we do?" This question had to be asked; however, within the context of policy limits that would severely limit whatever actions seemed feasible.[53]

Bushnell also attended and frequently chaired interagency meetings with representatives from the U.S. Agency for International Development (USAID), CIA, Office of the Secretary of Defense (OSD), Joint Chiefs of Staff (JCS), and the NSC. These meetings became known as the Rwanda Interagency Working Group (IWG). For convenience, these meetings were usually held via the closed circuit teleconference.[54] In Bushnell's opinion, the "impersonal environment created by the video screens trivialized the enormity of what was happening in Rwanda. Many officials made discussion and decision-making difficult and inefficient."[55] On April 26, in one of the most important sessions of the IWG, Bushnell gathered participants together to discuss the "next steps in Rwanda: 1) Stop the On-going Massacres Now; 2) Achieve a Ceasefire; 3) Resume Negotiations within Arusha Framework; 4) Prevent Violence from Spreading Outside Rwanda's Borders; 5) Launch Immediate Humanitarian Assistance; and 6) Create a Public Affairs Strategy on U.S. Policy on Rwanda."[56] These "next steps" became the guidelines for the May, June, and July discussions about possible small-scale interventions.

Director for African Affairs at the Pentagon, Vince Kern, remembers that in addition to the Interagency Working Group meetings led by Deputy Assistant Secretary of State Bushnell, all participating agencies also attended interagency teleconferences called the Peacekeeping Core Group. Kern explains that the NSC, which took the lead in these meetings, "certainly [permitted] the [junior level] diplomatic discourse that the State Department, Pru principally, were making to try and get people to stop the violence." However, this encouragement stopped short of supporting any measures that went beyond diplomatic statements. He recalls that the approach at these Closed Video Teleconference System (CVTS) meetings was to "find a way to get the violence to stop, but from a distance, we no longer had Americans at risk in the country, we no longer had an embassy in the country, Americans were now safe, but what could the U.S. do to play a role in trying to end the violence? It was difficult because we had very few cards to play."[57] Not surprisingly, according to Tony Marley, the Political Military Advisor for the State Department, the meetings "[often] became emotional as people's frustration would be reflected in comments or . . . they would manifest themselves in different ways."[58]

In both types of meetings, visible tensions emerged between those with little ties and interest in Rwanda—like the NSC and DoD—and those like Prudence Bushnell and the others within the State Department and USAID who saw the conflict as something other than a test case for the formula outlined by PDD-25.

> The vast majority, however, that participated [in the teleconferences] had never been to Rwanda, didn't know Rwandans and were approaching these conferences from institutional interest, bureaucratic interest that had nothing to do with Rwanda, itself, and so they approached it much more business-like, or much more cynically, perhaps, than those . . . [who] had personal relationships with Rwanda.[59]

Prudence Bushnell and the State Department representatives also met with a number of NGOs to obtain their perspectives on the Rwanda crisis. Human Rights Watch members Alison Des Forges and Janet Fleishman came to meet with Bushnell frequently and as she recalls, they used to "beat her up about Rwandan issues." Bushnell argues that they did not see her personally as the enemy, and eventually they seemed to understand that she was doing all she could. Bushnell represented a government that was doing nothing, and NGOs tried hard to pressure her and the Africa office to do something.[60] In retrospect, the NGOs came to the State Department to "beat up" the wrong officials. More often than not, when they met with senior policymakers outside of the Africa bureau, discussions focused on Haiti, Bosnia, and North Korea, rather than Rwanda. On some rare occasions Human Rights Watch found its way to the offices of Assistant Secretaries, but for the most part, the NGOs were prevented from meeting at high levels.

Within the narrow limits of the acceptable policy parameters, Bushnell and her team tried to be as forceful as possible. On April 29 Prudence Bushnell "telephoned Rwandan Ministry of Defense Cabinet Director Colonel Bagosora . . . to urge him to stop the killings." During this phone conversation, Bushnell listened to the government of Rwanda's story that "the RPF offensive is triggering the massacres" and she responded by telling Colonel Bagosora that "the world does not buy the [Government of Rwanda's] story on the killings and that credible eyewitness and respected organizations reported Rwandan military complicity in the killings . . . [and] criminal acts, aiding and abetting civilian massacres."[61] The unwillingness of the Rwandan government to accept responsibility or offer legitimate justification for their actions, led Bushnell to fully comprehend that she was dealing with irrational extremists.[62]

Bushnell also phoned RPF Commander General Paul Kagame and his adversary Rwandan Army Chief of Staff Augustin Bizimungu, whom she nicknamed "Bizi the Bad."[63] To both, Bushnell presented talking points agreed upon in interagency meetings: stop the killing, agree to a cease fire, and return to the Arusha process. According to Bushnell, their conversations were often surreal. Kagame could only be reached by satellite phone in the bush and often the antenna was down. To contact Bizimungu at the opening of his work day, Bushnell would set her alarm for 2:00AM and use her kitchen phone to engage in conversations that she described as "utterly bizarre." Bizimungu's secretary came to recognize Bushnell's voice and cheerfully answered, "bonjour Madame Bushnell, como cava?" Bizimungu was equally polite and often answered the phone with the same cordial greeting. However, when it came to convincing the Chief of Staff to stop the killing, Bushnell got nowhere. In one conversation, in total frustration and outrage at his stoic attitude, Bushnell surpassed the limits of her talking points by telling Bizimungu that "President Clinton would hold him personally responsible for any future deaths that occurred." Bizimungu responded sarcastically, "How nice of the President to think of me." President Clinton never gave Bushnell the order or permission to do this, but she was "desperate, so [she] lied."[64]

Conversations with RPF Commander General Kagame were equally difficult for very different reasons—it was the Tutsis who were being slaughtered. During one initial phone call Kagame departed from his usual rational, businesslike manner, asserting with uncharacteristic passion, "Madame, they are killing my people." He went on to describe how people were hiding in the woods in desperation to save the lives of their family and children. Not surprisingly, Kagame had no more enthusiasm for injunctions to declare a ceasefire than his enemy Bizimungu. According to the General, a ceasefire would only facilitate the killing of innocents. Limited by policy instructions to stick to her talking points, Bushnell could only show her compassion by ending each conversation with the words "General I wish you peace."[65] Bushnell's efforts to alter U.S. policy went unrewarded and by the time the United States agreed to support the deployment of UNAMIR II in mid-May, the worst phase of the genocide was already over.

At the same time that Bushnell placed phone calls to the Rwandan and RPF leaderships, she also went on the radio stations that she knew broadcasted in

Africa. She went on BBC, VOA, and "[she] was saying stop the killings."
When she returned to the closed circuit teleconferences and informed people
about what she was doing, they "remained indifferent."[66] Bushnell defends
her actions by explaining that in a time when most senior policymakers were
driven by national interest, she was driven by moral imperative and felt compelled to take a stand for what was the right thing to do:

> If you have massive killings going on before your very eyes and you know that
> beyond a certain level of the bureaucracy, nobody cared, you had a few NGOs
> that cared, but the people, the media, the government, the Europeans, none of
> them cared, and yet there was killing going on, so I tried to be as creative as
> possible. And if that meant setting my alarm for 2:00am and lying to Biz-
> imungu or taking the President's name in vain then that is what I was going to
> do. How could Clinton get mad at me anyway, I was just trying to save peo-
> ple's lives.[67]

While Bushnell's actions fell within the confines of her job, her actions
took on a different form than most of her colleagues, in particular, those at the
senior-level. Why was she willing to take this career risk and challenge an entire administration that disagreed with her? To begin with, Bushnell was
heavily influenced by her trip to Rwanda and Burundi just two weeks before
the genocide. At the time of this trip, a failed coup attempt in Burundi resulted
in widespread violence that nearly prevented Bushnell from traveling to Bujumbura.[68] After arriving at the Acting Ambassador's residence she heard
gunshots and explosions. Bushnell, her small delegation, and the Ambassador
decided to stage a TV press conference in Burundi where Bushnell appealed
for people to stop the killing. She gave the speech calling for all sides to stop
the fighting, and remarkably, that night, there were no gunshots in the city of
Bujumbura. The next day, Bushnell went to go buy souvenirs at the local mar-
ket and two women came up to her and asked, "Madame, are you the one
from TV yesterday?" When she answered them, the two women responded,
"Thank you for doing this." Bushnell recalls how "it was amazing, I was
American and I said 'stop the fighting' on television and they stopped fighting. I thought to myself how it is really easy and we can stop the killings in
Rwanda if we just make an appeal. I was trying to translate this experience to
Rwanda."[69] Inspired by her experience in Burundi, Bushnell explored a number of strategies to try and stop the killings, but her colleagues were "more
bureaucratically astute than [she] was" and as a result, did not share excite-
ment for her plan of action.[70]

According to Bushnell, the character of the Central African Office of the
Bureau of African Affairs had a tremendous influence on her. The desk officers were "younger and less experienced and they were horrified and even

traumatized by what was going on in Rwanda." Bushnell recalls having to face these young policymakers who wanted to know "what was the point of being the world's most powerful nation if you are not going to use it." She felt vulnerable to their passion and "if somebody had an idea, even if it was not a great idea, [she] at least acknowledged it. The Bureau of African Affairs was generating its own energy."[71]

Costs, Logistics, and Practicalities: Reluctance at the Pentagon

The Pentagon's role in the failure of the U.S. government to intervene in the genocide differed from the State Department and the White House in that it was their job to respond to requests for a U.S. response and intervention plans, not suggest them. That said, in rare moments when solutions were proposed, Pentagon officials erected logistical, financial, and bureaucratic obstacles that crushed proposals for action of any kind. Because these proposals for action came from the lower ranks of the bureaucracy, Pentagon officials who participated in meetings about Rwanda had no pressure from senior officials that would cause them to embrace proposals for action.

Operating in the shadow of Somalia, most senior officials at the Pentagon did not even want to discuss intervention in Rwanda. The Pentagon remained paralyzed at the level of the Secretary because there were no orders coming from either the State Department or the White House. Because there was no proposed response to Rwanda, and because the UNAMIR force was being withdrawn in early April, Secretary of Defense William Perry was not part of discussions pertaining to Rwanda.

Had the Secretary of State or the President decided not to withdraw UNAMIR and suggested that the United States should intervene in Rwanda, Secretary of Defense William Perry asserts that both he and Chairman of the Joint Chiefs of Staff General John "Shali" Shalikashvili "could have easily put an equipped force together."[72] However, both the President and the Secretary of State remained opposed to either an American or a UN presence in Rwanda and as a result, Secretary Perry explains that "[officials at the Pentagon] didn't even have to argue against [intervention], it just wasn't an issue."[73] However, given the political context and the logistical challenges, it is understandable why no proposal for military intervention ever reached the desk of the Secretary of Defense. In an interview for this book, Perry explained that the "administration faced great difficulty in that the United States did not have the logistics in the Great Lakes region to deploy a Bosnia size force,"[74] and he acknowledges that this kind of a deployment would have resulted in a proposal to the President addressing the question of "if we sent a lightly armed brigade, which was a very small force compared to the size of the rebel force, would that have been enough, just by the presence of American troops to halt the fighting?"[75] Given that this was not an option that the U.S. government looked into, Secretary Perry did not know the answer to this question. Secretary of Defense Perry argues that this would have required a judgment call as to whether or not "the symbolic significance of American troops would have been very high and probably would have resulted in the rallying of troops from elsewhere to serve as the primary force."[76] While it is easy to argue that the deployment of American troops to Rwanda would have encouraged other countries to follow their lead, it would have been unrealistic to expect President Clinton to make an undoubtedly risky judgment call just six months after Somalia.

Without any proposals or talking points on Rwanda in the early stages after the evacuation, Secretary of Defense Perry had no incentive to follow-up on the situation, request information, or even discus the matter with the President. Although Perry would have been unlikely to support a military intervention, he argues that a proposal would at least have compelled him to sit down and talk about it.[77] In reflecting back on his time as the Secretary of Defense William Perry theorizes that "had Rwanda exploded before the October 3 firefight in Somalia, there is a good probability that the United States would have sent a small symbolic force to Rwanda to stop the genocide or at least sat down to talk about it."[78]

Without an order from the White House or the Secretary of State, the Pentagon had no incentive to devise its own contingency plans for Rwanda, particularly at a time when they were feuding over budget constraints with Congress. The officials at the Pentagon were weary of military engagement where there was no strategic interest and as Secretary Perry recalls, the United States was coming off the "heels of Somalia and the thought that we could have gotten authority for sending another military operation over [to Africa] was not very attainable and there would have been absolutely no political support."[79] General Colin Powell, as the former Chairman of the Joint Chiefs of Staff, firmly explained this position, asserting that "as long as I am chairman of the Joint Chiefs of Staff, I will not agree to commit American men and women to an unknown war, in an unknown land, for an unknown cause, under an unknown commander, for an unknown duration."[80] No senior official felt Rwanda was worth risking their career over and with so many other pressing issues, they felt comfortable delegating matters related to the genocide to their deputies, principal deputies, and directors.

In an interview for this book, Under Secretary of Defense Walt Slocombe addressed these very issues. He recalled that "One of the lessons which we had drawn from Somalia, which was also a big issue in the debate of Rwanda, the military does not decide where to go, the policy, the mission, but given the mission, they have a big role in saying what it takes to execute it."[81] In the case of Rwanda, there was no mission.

As Director for African Affairs, and later Deputy Assistant Secretary of Defense Vince Kern explains, "It would have been unimaginable for Secretary Perry, having gotten his job because his predecessor Les Aspin had gotten fired for the events that occurred just six months earlier in Somalia, to approach President Clinton and say 'Once again Mr. President I think we ought to put American troops on the ground in Africa.'" Kern argues that "even if a Secretary of Defense had thought it was a good idea he was not going to recommend it because he knew that there was no way the president was going to do it and that congress was going to cut off funds if they tried."[82]

In addition to watching his former boss, Les Aspin, get fired and widely criticized for the deaths of 18 American Rangers in Somalia, Secretary Perry was also constrained by the fact that he was the unexpected successor to Aspin. Bobby Inman, a retired Navy Admiral and private businessman, was the Clinton administration's first choice, but after a series of statements described by Kern as "strange," he was withdrawn as the nominee for Secretary of Defense. William Perry, who had been serving as the Deputy Secretary of Defense, waited out the drama over Inman and by the time he actually became the new Secretary of Defense it was just a month or two before Rwanda. This further constrained the Secretary, who as an insider in the Pentagon did not necessarily have the clout of his predecessor who had served as Chairman of the Armed Services Committee.[83]

Prior to the beginning of genocide, Deputy Assistant Secretary of Defense for African Affairs James Woods, who was the most senior official in the Pentagon working exclusively on Africa, had been discouraged early on from pushing for increased involvement in Central Africa.[84] In the spring of 1993, Woods recalls a senior official asking all Assistant Secretaries and Deputy Assistant Secretaries of Defense to prepare a list of potential trouble spots that may cause the Clinton administration problems in foreign policy. However, when he suggested adding Rwanda and Burundi to the list, he was told by then Under Secretary of Defense for Policy Frank Wisner:

> Look, if something happens in Rwanda-Burundi, we don't care. Take it off the list. U.S. national interest is not involved and we can't put all these silly humanitarian issues on lists, like important problems like the Middle East and North Korea and so on. Just make it go away.[85]

As a result of this response from the Under Secretary of Defense, Woods believed that Rwanda was a political non-starter even before the genocide began and as such, was unlikely to push for an intervention when he knew there would be no support.[86] Walt Slocombe explains, however, that for strategic reasons Rwanda and Burundi were not at the top of that list. He recalls that on Secretary Christopher's order, he began to work the Bosnia issue for which he met with his French counterparts. Slocombe remembers these French counterparts inquiring as to the U.S. position on Rwanda and their question about whether or not it was an election issue. In regards to the French inquiry, Slocombe recalls that "I knew where they were and I knew there had been terrible ethnic violence over a period of years, but I have to tell you they were not big issues in the election campaign, but thereafter we were aware of one of a low level potential hot spot."[87]

With the Secretary of Defense out of the equation and the Undersecretary of Defense seemingly uninterested in Rwanda, responsibility for overseeing U.S. defense policy toward Rwanda, as occurred at the White House and the State Department, filtered down to the lower ranks of the bureaucracy. However, responsibility for overseeing Rwanda at the Pentagon did not fall into the hands of Deputy Assistant Secretary of Defense for Africa James Woods. Instead the genocide occurred during a transition in the leadership for African issues that saw Rwanda fall into the hands of lower-level officials. Woods' involvement in policymaking toward Rwanda ended just before the genocide. According to Vince Kern, "Woods had wanted to retire and a decision was made at the time within the Office of the Secretary of Defense (OSD) that when he retired we would no longer have a separate Deputy Assistant Secretary of Defense (DASD) for Africa (AF)." Kern continued by explaining that "Africa would be taken and subsumed by Molly Williamson, who was the DASD for Middle East and Southeast Asia."[88] This was problematic because it meant that Africa was not going to get as much attention at senior levels because as Kern explains, "there is no way that anyone could be reasonably expected to be at the top of their game doing Africa, Middle East, and South East Asia, and since Molly Williamson, who had served in Israel, was more of an expert in the Middle East, Africa became less of a priority."[89]

Woods had actually wanted to retire earlier, but as Director for African Affairs Vince Kern recalls, "he delayed his retirement because Molly Williamson indicated that when she took over Africa, she wanted to have what she thought would be a clean slate a clear deck, and the end of March was when we were withdrawing our forces from Somalia. So, what she wanted was to take over when that had completed."[90] As a result, Woods did not retire until March 31, 1994. Little did Molly Williamson know that less than a few days later she would take over Africa at the start of a genocide and a time of crisis in Africa, particularly in Rwanda. Upon Woods' retirement he joined former Assistant Secretary of State Herman Cohen in a consulting firm, but without a clearance and no longer part of the government, James Woods was not a part of the decision-making process toward Rwanda at any point during the genocide. While Woods no longer had the clearance to take part in policymaking on Rwanda, he remained somewhat engaged by briefing senior officials in the early stages of the genocide. On April 7 Woods and Assistant Secretary of Defense Ted Warner briefed Under Secretary of Defense Frank Wisner and his Deputy Walt Slocombe.[91]

When the genocide broke out just six days after Molly Williamson took over Africa at the Pentagon, she quickly figured out that Rwanda was going to be if not all consuming, very consuming in the days after April 6. As Kern points out, "it became clear that this was going to be a major bureaucratic endeavor to try and see what we could do to respond to the events there." This led Williamson, who was preoccupied with the Somalia pullout and the Middle East, to look for a way to reduce the bureaucratic load that she inherited as the Deputy Assistant Secretary of Defense for Middle East and Africa. Kern recalls Williamson approaching him in the first week of the genocide and saying "Vince I want you to do that, meaning assume the responsibility for Rwanda."[92] Why would the Deputy Assistant Secretary of Defense who was responsible for Africa delegate responsibility over the genocide to her Director? As Kern explains, "There is a phrase we have in the military where you either lead, you follow, or you get out of the way, and Molly was clever enough to get out of the way. She knew that she couldn't do the rest of her job, the middle east, southeast Asia, and the rest of Africa if she was going to be overwhelmed with African issues."[93]

Because there was still a small UN deployment on the ground in Rwanda and because there were requests for the United States to supply resources to the mission, Deputy Assistant Secretary of Defense for Peacekeeping Sarah Sewall also played a role in overseeing Rwanda at the Pentagon. However, like Woods, Sewall claims that she was discouraged early on. The United States had pressured the Security Council to withdraw UNAMIR, leading Sewall to believe that the United States was not interested in increasing the involvement of either the United States or the UN in Rwanda. In retrospect, this was an accurate assessment. She recalls not pushing to fight this stance because she had been told by her superiors that "Congress hates peacekeeping, Congress wants to cut off funds, Congress does not want us to be supportive of peacekeeping with U.S. military personnel, and there is no way that we could convince them of anything."[94] Sewall explains that the paralysis of the Pentagon was not a matter of the Pentagon's lack of will to intervene in Rwanda, but rather the fact that "Rwanda ran up against what had become a very beleaguered peacekeeping apparatus and the amount of time that they spent defending peacekeeping policy, the UN, and any role for blue helmet forces and financial support, already placed [senior Pentagon officials] on the defensive and discouraged [them] from pushing the issue any further."[95]

According to Vince Kern, the interagency was beginning to meet more and more frequently and eventually it became daily. During both the IWG Closed Video Teleconference System (CVTS)[96] meetings and the peacekeeping CVTSs, Vince Kern and Sarah Sewall shared the screen from the Office of the Secretary of Defense. Kern represented International Security Affairs Africa Region and Sewall represented peacekeeping.[97] Kern explains that there was a "split between functionalists and regionalists with the functionalists being more interested in looking at the impact of Rwanda on peacekeeping and regionalists looking more at the impact of peacekeeping on Rwanda, but because the functionalists were essentially in control of this, the regionalists did not get as much attention for our point of view as we would have liked."[98]

Most of the activity at the Pentagon related to Rwanda occurred at the Deputy Assistant Secretary level and below. The Under Secretary of Defense for Policy (USDP) Frank Wisner was interested in receiving information about Rwanda, but never offered any indication from senior levels that something should be done in response to the genocide. Vince Kern recalls passing reports to Under Secretary Wisner, but because he was getting ready to leave office and become the U.S. Ambassador to India, he began withdrawing from involvement in issues that he did not consider to be a top priority. As relayed in an April 7 Under Secretary of Defense for Policy briefing, Lieutenant Colonel Harvin, the Rwanda desk officer in the bureau of International Security Affairs (ISA/AF), explained that "USDP expressed his belief that any U.S. planning for action in Rwanda should be closely coordinated with the Belgians and French . . . [USDP] said that he didn't feel an OSD Rwanda Task Force was needed . . ."[99]

As Wisner was withdrawing from his position as Under Secretary, Deputy Under Secretary of Defense for Policy Walter Slocombe was preparing to take over for him. According to Vince Kern, Walter Slocombe took an interest in Rwanda and contrary to his predecessor decided that there needed to be a Rwanda Task Force.[100] In a confidential May 17 memorandum to the Assistant Secretary of Defense for Democracy and Peacekeeping, Assistant Secretary of Defense for Special Operations and Low-intensity Conflict, the Assistant Secretary of Defense for Legislative Affairs, and a number of other Deputy Assistant Secretaries and offices, Africa Region Director Vince Kern declared that "We are being called on to prepare numerous reports to the Secretary of Defense (SecDef) and complex analyses of various aspects of the Rwanda problem. Per SecDef direction and in order to improve the flow of both information and coordination, I am establishing a Rwanda Task Force. I have been assigned as the Task Force Director by Mr. Slocombe."[101] According to Walt Slocombe, "The decision was made at Secretary Perry's direction that we were going to have task forces for all major crisis areas so that as a crisis developed there would be a DoD-wide team. There had already been one for Somalia, Haiti, and Bosnia. As the crisis developed in Rwanda, we decided to create it so that we would be bureaucratically prepared and informed enough to respond to whatever requests came from the White House and the State Department."[102]

As Vince Kern explains, the Rwanda Task Force changed the level of efficiency through which the Rwanda crisis could be addressed at the Pentagon.[103] First, it allowed him to go out and recruit some more people to assist in intelligence gathering and generation of analysis. Prior to the creation of the Rwanda Task Force, the make up of Kern's office was such that it was not equipped to handle the Rwanda crisis amidst a portfolio of Africa, Middle East, and Asia. Kern did not have the luxury of a Rwanda desk officer and while he had a central Africa desk officer, he had about twelve countries to oversee. Kern explains that occasionally the desk officers for Southern and West Africa would assist with Rwanda, but in the days before the Rwanda Task Force, "Rwanda was a two man job, [Vince Kern] and [his] desk officer."[104] The Rwanda Task Force enabled Kern to bring on officials from the Defense Intelligence Agency (DIA), a major to work with a lieutenant colonel, and also two second lieutenants from the Air Force. Kern instructed the two lieutenants to arrive at the Pentagon at 5:00am every day and find all the sources of information both classified and unclassified. Kern explains that he asked them to compile daily situation reports on the battlefield situation, the humanitarian situation, and various other categories so that by the time he arrived around 6:00am, he could take a look at them and make the necessary changes before sending it up to the Under Secretary of Defense for Policy.[105] Kern claims that in addition to sending the info up to Under Secretary Slocombe, he also distributed the daily situation reports throughout the Pentagon "so that there would be a common collection of data about what was going on in Rwanda."[106]

According to Vince Kern, Under Secretary Slocombe took notice of these reports and while he never acted specifically on them, he brought them up with Kern directly. Kern recalls one occasion in which his office hosted a party for a colleague who was getting a promotion. Walt Slocombe came down to congratulate the recipient and Kern remembers that when he introduced the Under Secretary to the two lieutenants and explained that they were the officers who wrote the Rwanda situation reports, Slocombe, who normally would not take so much time to speak with two lieutenants, came over to talk with them and was asking questions about where they got their sources. According to Kern, the Under Secretary was "very much interested."[107]

The second advantage to the Rwanda Task Force was that it allowed Vince Kern to tap people in other offices like peacekeeping, humanitarian assistance, the various Special Operations Low-Intensity Conflict (SOLIC) offices, and several others. Kern explained that these offices were experts in dealing with crises like Rwanda and they were experts on radio and cyops. With the creation of the Rwanda Task Force, Kern had the authority to ask them to prepare a paper, a thought piece, or talking points for his meetings.[108]

The third and arguably most important advantage to the establishment of a Rwanda Task Force was the authority it granted Vince Kern to go directly to Under Secretary of Defense Slocombe. Prior to the creation of the Rwanda Task Force, Kern had to get three Assistant Secretaries of Defense to sign off on any document going up to the Under Secretary of Defense. Kern remembers this being problematic because one would often be out of the building or take too long to sign off on the document. He also recalls that if one Assistant Secretary of Defense had changes he had to go through the process all over again. It was the bureaucratic mess and papers moved very slowly. The Rwanda Task Force changed this and papers that Slocombe wanted to keep for his own interest or pass along to Secretary Perry began to move far quicker.

Despite the generation of information coming out of the Rwanda Task Force and the CVTSs that Kern and Sewall attended, there was little beyond information sharing that occurred at the Pentagon. Slocombe may have shown interest in Rwanda, but it never caused him to take major action or urge the Secretary to make a response. As for the Joint Chiefs of Staff (JCS), they participated in the CVTS conferences, but like Sewall and the peacekeeping office, the JCS approached Rwanda from a functional side rather than a regional side. According to Kern, once there was a successful evacuation and no Americans were killed or sent into harms way, the JCS "sat on the side line and waited. If somebody came up with a certain mission that the U.S. should undertake and they were ordered to do it, the JCS would have; however, once the evacuation ended, the JCS faded into the background."[109]

It is understandable why senior officials at the Pentagon chose not to advocate greater attention for Rwanda. The Pentagon was inundated with issues related to Bosnia, North Korea, and Haiti, in large part because the White House informed Pentagon officials that these were high-risk trouble spots and as a result, most officials did not think to push for an intervention in Rwanda. Furthermore, as of April 25, there was no longer a sizable UN force to work with. According to State Department and NSC officials, there were some instances in which officials at the State Department and the NSC sought to increase the Pentagon's involvement in discussions over Rwanda; however, according to one White House official, senior Defense officials always responded with the same question, "Is the President saying this is a national security matter? If yes, we will sacrifice our interests in Europe and make ourselves vulnerable so that we can stop the conflict in Rwanda."[110]

At the intelligence level of the Defense Department, Rwanda was discussed more frequently and the Defense Intelligence Agency (DIA) had the government's most detailed intelligence on Rwanda.[111] As a result, desk officers and regional officers saw a number of the reports being distributed by DIA officials.[112] Despite the fact that the DIA was one of the Pentagon's most useful resources, most of their reports on Rwanda concerned the progress of the war, information about the mobilization and movements of the RPF and the Rwandan Armed Forces, and to some extent satellite photos that illustrated massacre sites.[113] However, in the context of the Pentagon, this information was only passed up the ranks if it pertained to the safety of Americans. As one DoD official recalls, "during the evacuation we used this information to provide daily update briefings to the Chairman of the Joint Chiefs of Staff, senior DoD officials, and for interagency meetings."[114] Upon the completion of the evacuation, requests for daily briefings ceased and while the number of reports being produced by the DIA did not change, they mostly occupied the file cabinets of desk officers.

However, on one occasion, National Security Advisor Anthony Lake attempted to obtain a brief overview on the calamitous situation in Rwanda from the Pentagon:

> I remember going over to the Pentagon for a meeting over what a US presence in Kigali for evacuation in Rwanda would entail and, I am embarrassed to say, I remember asking what this was all about in Rwanda. They responded that they did not know. They did not have any information on what was happening in Rwanda and what kind of conflict we were dealing with. This was reflective of the fact that they hadn't done much of anything.[115]

But, Anthony Lake did not come to the Pentagon to meet with the Rwanda desk officers and the regional officers. He came to meet with senior officials who could offer minimal insight into the crisis from brief talking points. In other instances, Dick Clarke claims that he phoned the Pentagon from the NSC peacekeeping office to gain insight into the nature of the conflict in Rwanda. He recalls that their apparent knowledge was shockingly minimal as "they had to start asking whether it was Hutu and Tutsi or Tutu and Hutsi."[116]

NOTES

1. Personal Interview, Consultant for Human Rights Watch Alison Des Forges, Via telephone to Buffalo, NY, October 6, 2003.
2. Personal Interview, Former National Security Advisor Anthony Lake, Washington, DC, November 20, 2002.

3. Personal Interview, Former National Security Advisor Anthony Lake, Washington, DC, November 20, 2002.

4. White House, press briefing. Policy on Multilateral Peacekeeping Operations, Washington, DC, 5 May 1994. Transcript by Federal News Service, Washington, DC, document number WL-05-01, 5 May 1994, in Linda Melvern, *A People Betrayed: The Role of the West in Rwanda's Genocide*, pp. 190–191; the accuracy of this quote was verified in personal interview, Former National Security Advisor Anthony Lake, Washington, DC, November 20, 2002.

5. Ibid.

6. Personal Interview, Human Rights Watch Consultant Alison Des Forges, Via telephone to Buffalo, NY, October 6, 2003.

7. Personal Interview, Former White House Official [A], Washington, DC, November 21, 2002.

8. Ibid.

9. Ibid.

10. Personal Interview, Former National Security Advisor Anthony Lake, Washington, DC, November 20, 2002.

11. This was a position that included "counterterrorism, counternarcotics programs, peacekeeping operations, humanitarian interventions, and U.S. relations with the UN." (Daniel Benjamin and Steven Simon in *The Age of Sacred Terror,* p. 232)

12. Samantha Power, *"A Problem from Hell:" America and the Age of Genocide,* p. 368. According to Dick Clarke, "Once we knew the Belgians were leaving, we were left with a rump mission incapable of doing anything to help people . . . They were doing nothing to stop the killings." However, as Power argues, "Clarke underestimated the deterrent effect that Dallaire's very few peacekeepers were having."

13. Clarke was fired in 1992 by Secretary of State James Baker for "appearing to condone Israel's illicit transfer of U.S. technology to China." (Daniel Benjamin and Steven Simon in *The Age of Sacred Terror,* p. 232)

14. Personal Interview, Former Director for African Affairs and Head of the Rwanda Task Force at the Pentagon, Vince Kern, Alexandria, VA, August 15, 2003.

15. Ibid.

16. Ibid.

17. Daniel Benjamin and Steven Simon, *The Age of Sacred Terror: Radical Islam's War Against America,* New York: Random House, 2003, p. 232.

18. Ibid.

19. Samantha Power, "Bystanders to Genocide," *The Atlantic Monthly*, September 2001.

20. Personal Interview, Former White House Official [A], Washington, DC, November 21, 2002; see also, Samantha Power, "Bystanders to Genocide," *The Atlantic Monthly*, September 2001.

21. Hearing of the International Security, International Organizations, and Human Rights Subcommittee of the House Foreign Affairs Committee, May 17, 1994, in Michael Barnett, *Eyewitness to a Genocide,* p. 139; see also Michael MacKinnon, pp. 107–108; see also Boutros Boutros-Ghali, *Unvanquished: A US-UN Saga*, New York: Random House, 1999, in Organization of African Unity, "International Panel of Em-

inent Personalities to Investigate the 1994 Genocide in Rwanda and the Surrounding Events," 2000, Chapter 12, p. 5.

22. Personal Interview, Former Deputy Assistant Secretary of State for African Affairs Prudence Bushnell, Washington, DC, December 9, 2002.

23. Ibid; see also Samantha Power, "Bystanders to Genocide," *The Atlantic Monthly*, September 2001.

24. Personal Interview, Former White House Official [A], November 21, 2002; see also, Samantha Power, *"A Problem from Hell:" America and the Age of Genocide*, p. 340. Samantha Power quotes one U.S. official as saying, "Anytime you mentioned peacekeeping in Africa, the crucifixes and garlic would come up on every door." This meant that there was a general reluctance to undertake peacekeeping missions in Africa or to even talk about it.

25. Samantha Power, *"A Problem from Hell:" America and the Age of Genocide*, p. 359.

26. Personal Interview, Former Director for African Affairs and Head of the Rwanda Task Force at the Pentagon, Vince Kern, Alexandria, VA, August 15, 2003.

27. Personal Interview, Former White House Official [A], Washington, DC, November 21, 2002.

28. Personal Interview, Former White House Official [A], Washington, DC, November 21, 2002.

29. In Secretary Christopher's memoirs, *In the Stream of History: Shaping Foreign Policy,* Christopher argues that, "The administration had judged that our European partners with long involvement in the region should take the lead in the Rwandan peacekeeping effort." (p. 468) While Christopher argues that Rwanda was one of the decades greatest tragedies, he assumes no responsibility for the U.S. role and in his only two explanations for why Rwanda deteriorated to genocide, he explains that "Rwanda and Burundi stood out as tragic cases in which environmental degradation exacerbated political unrest, causing massive human suffering" (p. 414) Christopher only mentions Rwanda five times in the text of his memoirs and his analysis never extends beyond two sentences per instance. The only decisions regarding Rwanda that Christopher points to are those related to stopping the cholera outbreak in Zaire, but this occurred after the genocide.

30. Personal Interview, Former Deputy Assistant Secretary of State for African Affairs Prudence Bushnell, Washington, DC, December 9, 2002.

31. Personal Interview, Former U.S. Ambassador to Rwanda David Rawson, Via telephone to Michigan, September 26, 2003.

32. Personal Interview, Former U.S. Ambassador to Rwanda David Rawson, Via telephone to Michigan, September 26, 2003.

33. Belgian Foreign Minister Willie Claes quoted in Samantha Power, *"A Problem From Hell:" America and the Age of Genocide,* p. 352.

34. Ibid, p. 346.

35. Linda Melvern, *A People Betrayed: The Role of the West in Rwanda's Genocide,* p. 169.

36. Samantha Power, *"A Problem from Hell:" America and the Age of Genocide,* p. 347.

37. Personal Interview, State Department Official [A], Via telephone to Washington, DC, February 28, 2003; see also personal interview, Former Assistant Secretary of State for Democracy, Human Rights and Labor John Shattuck, Via telephone to Boston, MA, February 24, 2003.

38. Personal Interview, Foreign Minister of the Republic of Rwanda Dr. Charles Murigande, Kigali, Rwanda, December 20, 2002.

39. Personal Interview, State Department Official [A], Via telephone to Washington, DC, February 28, 2003.

40. Personal Interview, Former Assistant Secretary of State for Democracy, Human Rights and Labor John Shattuck, Via telephone to Boston, MA, February 24, 2003.

41. Personal Interview, Foreign Minister of Rwanda Dr. Charles Murigande, Kigali, Rwanda, December 20, 2002.

42. Ibid.

43. Personal Interview, Foreign Minister of Rwanda Dr. Charles Murigande, Kigali, Rwanda, December 20, 2002; In a personal interview with Ambassador Rawson it was confirmed that the brunch did in fact take place; however, during out discussion there was no confirmation of this story.

44. Personal Interview, Former Deputy Assistant Secretary of State for African Affairs Prudence Bushnell, Washington, DC, December 9, 2002.

45. Personal Interview, State Department Official [A], Via telephone to Washington, DC, February 28, 2003.

46. John Shattuck, *Freedom on Fire: Human Rights Wars and America's Response,* Cambridge: Harvard University Press, 2003.

47. Ibid.

48. Ibid.

49. John Shattuck, *Freedom on Fire: Human Rights Wars and America's Response,* Cambridge: Harvard University Press, 2003.

50. Ibid.

51. Personal Interview, Former Assistant Secretary of State for Democracy, Human Rights and Labor, Via telephone to Boston, MA, February 24, 2003.

52. Personal Interview, Former Assistant Secretary of State for Democracy, Human Rights and Labor, Via telephone to Boston, MA, February 24, 2003.

53. Personal Interview, Former Deputy Assistant Secretary of State for African Affairs Prudence Bushnell, Washington, DC, December 9, 2002.

54. Ibid.

55. Personal Interview, Former Deputy Assistant Secretary of State for African Affairs Prudence Bushnell, Washington, DC, December 9, 2002.

56. Agenda for Interagency Strategy Meeting, April 26, 1994. Confidential. Declassified by authority of:OSD/JCS, 18 November 1998, Case #: 95-F-0894; see also, Confidential Briefing on IWG Meeting on Rwanda, drafted by LtCol Harvin, April 26, 1994. Confidential. Declassified by authority of: OSD/JS, 18 November 1998, Case # 95-F-0894.

57. Personal Interview, Former Director for African Affairs and Head of the Rwanda Joint Task Force at the Pentagon, Vince Kern, Alexandria, VA, August 15, 2003.

58. Tony Marley, interview, "The Triumph of Evil," *Frontline,* PBS, January 26, 1999; available at PBS Online: http://www.pbs.org/wgbh/pages/frontline/shows/evil/interviews/marley.html.

59. Tony Marley, interview, "The Triumph of Evil," *Frontline,* PBS, January 26, 1999; available at PBS Online: http://www.pbs.org/wgbh/pages/frontline/shows/evil/interviews/marley.html.

60. Personal Interview, Former Deputy Assistant Secretary of State for African Affairs Prudence Bushnell, December 9, 2002.

61. U.S. Department of State, cable number 113672, to U.S. Embassy Bujumbura and U.S. Embassy Dar es Salaam, "DAS Bushnell Tells Col. Bagosora to Stop the Killings", April 29, 1994. Limited Official use, in William Ferroggiaro, *A National Security Archive Briefing Book,* August 20, 2001, found in http://www.gwu.edu/~nsarchiv/NSAEBB/NSAEBB53/press.html.

62. Personal Interview, Former Deputy Assistant Secretary of State for African Affairs Prudence Bushnell, Washington, DC, December 9, 2002.

63. Ibid.

64. Personal Interview, Former Deputy Assistant Secretary of State for African Affairs Prudence Bushnell, Washington, DC, December 9, 2002.

65. Personal Interview, Former Deputy Assistant Secretary of State for African Affairs Prudence Bushnell, Washington, DC, December 9, 2002.

66. Ibid.

67. Personal Interview, Former Deputy Assistant Secretary of State for African Affairs Prudence Bushnell, Washington, DC, December 9, 2002.

68. Bujumbura is the capital city of Burundi and was the site of much violence at this time, even more so than Rwanda.

69. Personal Interview, Former Deputy Assistant Secretary of State for African Affairs Prudence Bushnell, Washington, DC, December 9, 2002.

70. Ibid.

71. Personal Interview, Former Deputy Assistant Secretary of State for African Affairs Prudence Bushnell, Washington, DC, December 9, 2002.

72. Personal Interview, Former Secretary of Defense Dr. William Perry, Stanford, CA, February 10, 2003.

73. Personal Interview, Former National Security Advisor Anthony Lake, Washington, DC, November 20, 2002.

74. Personal Interview, Former Secretary of Defense Dr. William Perry, Stanford, CA, February 10, 2003.

75. Ibid.

76. Personal Interview, Former Secretary of Defense Dr. William Perry, Stanford, CA, February 10, 2003.

77. Ibid.

78. Ibid.

79. Personal Interview, Former Secretary of Defense Dr. William Perry, Stanford, CA, February 10, 2003.

80. Ivo H. Daalder, "US Policy for Peacekeeping," in William J. Durch (ed.), *UN Peacekeeping: American Politics and Uncivil wars of the 1990's*, Henry L. Stimson

Center, New York: St. Martin's Press, 1996, p. 42, in Linda Melvern, *A People Betrayed: The Role of the West in Rwanda's Genocide,* p. 191.

81. Personal Interview, Former Under Secretary of Defense for Policy Walt Slocombe, Via phone to Washington, DC, February 7, 2004.

82. Personal Interview, Former Director for African Affairs and Head of the Rwanda Task Force at the Pentagon, Vince Kern, Alexandria, VA, August 15, 2003.

83. Personal Interview, Former Director for African Affairs and Head of the Rwanda Task Force at the Pentagon, Vince Kern, Alexandria, VA, August 15, 2003.

84. Ibid.

85. James Woods, interview, "Triumph of Evil," *Frontline,* PBS, January 26, 1999; available at PBS Online: http://www.pbs.org/wgbh/pages/frontline/shows/evil/interviews/woods.html; see also Organization of African Unity, "International Panel of Eminent Personalities to Investigate the 1994 Genocide in Rwanda and the Surrounding Events," Chapter 12, p. 8, 2000; see also Samantha Power, *"A Problem From Hell:" America and the Age of Genocide,* p. 342.

86. See Organization of African Unity, "International Panel of Eminent Personalities to Investigate the 1994 Genocide in Rwanda and the Surrounding Events," Chapter 12, p. 5, 2000.

87. Personal Interview, Former Under Secretary of Defense for Policy Walt Slocombe, Via phone to Washington, DC, February 7, 2004. It is important to note that Slocombe said this in response to the French question. He is careful to note that he said this because the French asked about it, not because he meant that only issues in the election were worth paying attention to.

88. Ibid.

89. Ibid.

90. Personal Interview, Former Director for African Affairs and Head of the Rwanda Task Force at the Pentagon, Vince Kern, Alexandria, VA, August 15, 2003.

91. Briefing for Under Secretary of Defense for Policy. From Lieutenant Colonel Harvin to Under Secretary of Defense Wisner through Director for Africa in the Bureau of International Security Affairs, April 7, 1994. Secret. Declassified by authority of Office of the Secretary of Defense, 18 November 1998, case # 95-F-0894.

92. Personal Interview, Former Director for African Affairs and Head of the Rwanda Task Force at the Pentagon, Vince Kern, Alexandria, VA, August 15, 2003.

93. Ibid

94. Personal Interview, Former Assistant Secretary of Defense for Peacekeeping and Humanitarian Affairs Sarah Sewall, Via telephone to Boston, MA, February 13, 2003.

95. Ibid.

96. Each government agency has a secure room that is sound proof for the purpose of a CVTS. In each room there is a main table with microphones that can be seen through video screens by other agencies and there are also chairs on the perimeter of the room that cannot be seen on the video screens. Due to the difficulty of physically gathering all parties together for meetings, interagency discussions that are frequent and consistent, such as the IWG or the Core Peacekeeping Group, meet through these video teleconferences.

97. Personal Interview, Former Director for African Affairs and Head of the Rwanda Task Force at the Pentagon, Vince Kern, Alexandria, VA, August 15, 2003. The only place where the regionalists were in charge was at the State Department which was led by DAS Pru Bushnell, and even there it wasn't an A/S, it was not a PDAS, it was a DAS largely because Rwanda, Burundi, and some of those issues had been issues that Prudence Bushnell was working on.

98. Ibid.

99. Briefing for Under Secretary of Defense for Policy. From Lieutenant Colonel Harvin to Under Secretary of Defense Wisner through Director for Africa in the Bureau of International Security Affairs, April 7, 1994. Secret. Declassified by authority of Office of the Secretary of Defense, 18 November 1998, case # 95-F-0894.

100. Personal Interview, Former Director for African Affairs and Head of the Rwanda Task Force at the Pentagon, Vince Kern, Alexandria, VA, August 15, 2003.

101. Memorandum from Director, African Affairs Vince Kern for ASD/Democracy and Peacekeeping (DASD Sewall), ASD/Special Operations and Low Intensity Conflict (Brigadier General Taylor/DASD Irvin), ASD Legislative Affairs (Ms. Mathias/Col Landrum), DSAA (Col Raphael), Comptroller (Mr. Hall), General Counsel (Mr. McNeil), Public Affairs (Col Powers), DIA (Mr. Thom), J-5 (Col Baltimore), Subject: "Rwanda Task Force," 17 May 1994, Declassified by authority of: OSD, 18 November 1998, Case #: 95-F-0894.

102. Personal Interview, Former Under Secretary of Defense for Policy Walt Slocombe, Via phone to Washington, DC, February 7, 2004.

103. Vince Kern met with the Rwanda Task Force every two or three days and they either prepared him for a SVTS conference or worked with him afterwards to determine what to do with the information obtained from the SVTS.

104. Personal Interview, Former Director for African Affairs and Head of the Rwanda Task Force at the Pentagon, Vince Kern, Alexandria, VA, August 15, 2003.

105. Personal Interview, Former Director for African Affairs and Head of the Rwanda Task Force at the Pentagon, Vince Kern, Alexandria, VA, August 15, 2003.

106. Ibid.

107. Ibid.

108. Ibid.

109. Personal Interview, Former Director for African Affairs and Head of the Rwanda Task Force at the Pentagon, Vince Kern, Alexandria, VA, August 15, 2003.

110. Personal Interview, Former White House Official [A], Washington, DC, November 21, 2002.

111. Alan Kuperman, *The Limits of Humanitarian Intervention*, pp. 32–37.

112. Personal Interview, DoD Official [A], Via e-mail, March 1, 2003.

113. Alan Kuperman, *The Limits of Humanitarian Intervention*, p. 32.

114. Personal Interview, Department of Defense Official [A], Via e-mail, March 1, 2003.

115. Personal Interview, Former National Security Advisor Anthony Lake, Washington, DC, November 20, 2003.

116. Samantha Power, *"A Problem From Hell:" America and the Age of Genocide*, p. 330.

On April 7, 1994, ten UN Belgian peacekeepers were ambushed at a military camp in Kigali. The ambush sparked the partial withdrawal of the UN from Rwanda.

All Rwandans were forced to carry ethnic identity cards, noting their ethnicity, address, and other personal information that would be used to round-up Tutsi during the genocide.

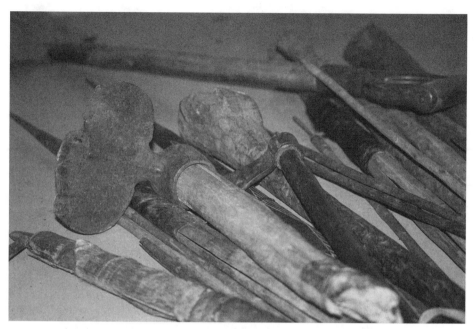

Weapons of mass destruction; it was ordinary farm tools that were used to carry out the majority of the massacres.

A survivor displays a cross at the genocide memorial in Kigali.

Skulls and bones litter the church at Ntarama, where 5,000 innocent Tutsis were brutally slaughtered in the spring of 1994

A young survivor embraces one of the thousands of unknown victims at Nyamata.

It was not uncommon for Tutsis to be speared to death.

The neatly organized remains of those who perished do not even begin to illustrate the brutality of the massacres.

Remains of unknown victims from Rwanda's genocide.

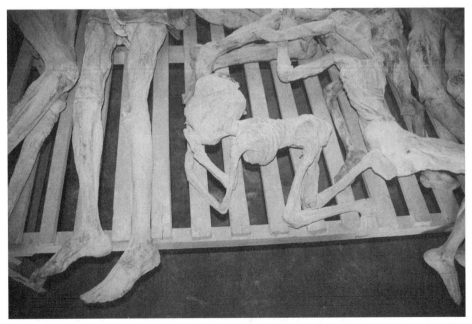

The exhumed bodies at Murambi in the south of Rwanda are a reminder that the majority of the victims were women and children.

The frozen gestures are a reminder of the pain and suffering that Tutsi children must have experienced in these final moments of their lives.

Hutu extremists often decapitated their victims.

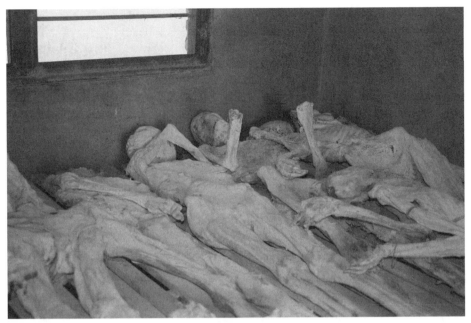

Some victims had their limbs cut off before the fatal attack was executed. Hutu extremists wanted the death to be as slow and painful as possible.

The small shoes at the Kigali Genocide memorial are a tragic reminder that many of the victims in Rwanda's genocide were children.

Tutsi survivors reveal a mass grave in Kigali.

The perpetrators of the genocide, or the "men in pink" as they are known, are forced to perform services around the country as part of their jail sentence.

6

Calling It Genocide

"My deepest regret from my years in public service is the failure of the United States and the international community to act sooner to halt those crimes [in Rwanda]."[1]

—Former U.S. Ambassador to the UN Madeleine Albright

More than 20,000 corpses littered the streets of Kigali in the first week of the genocide. On April 13, at the beginning of the second week of the atrocities, the Rwanda Patriotic Front (RPF) declared that "genocide" was taking place in Rwanda. Referencing the rising body count of innocent Tutsis, RPF Chairman Colonel Alexis Kanyarengwe announced that the extremists sought the extermination of Tutsis in Rwanda.[2] Four days later on April 17, the RPF issued a plea to the international community over Radio Muhabura, "the world cannot and should not forget the genocide which is being perpetrated in Rwanda today."[3] By the time the RPF issued this appeal, the number of massacred bodies had grown from 20,000 to hundreds of thousands. African Rights testimonies conducted after the genocide reveal that by April 21, more than 250,000 people, mostly Tutsi, were killed in Rwanda.[4]

Believing that hundreds of thousands of Tutsi bodies laying in the streets, the hills, and the churches of Rwanda was more than enough evidence to convince the United Nations to recognize the genocide, the RPF representative to the UN Claude Dusaidi sent a letter on April 23 to New Zealand Ambassador to the UN Colin Keating expressing frustrations over the international community's refusal to call the conflict a genocide. In the letter Dusaidi wrote: "When the institutions of the UN was created after the Second World War, one of its fundamental objectives was to see to it that what happened to the

Jews in Nazi Germany would never happen again." Dusaid's letter was not followed with any action. By late April the RPF's frustration with the international community transformed to hopelessness. As the numbers continued to rise at 10,000 deaths a day, the RPF announced on April 29, "the genocide is almost completed."[5]

Only a handful of foreigners stayed in Rwanda during the genocide. They were associated with the Seventh Day Adventist Church, several journalist organizations, and most notably, the International Committee for the Red Cross (ICRC). Of them, Phillip Gallaird of the ICRC offered the most reliable estimates of the number of deaths in Rwanda.[6] Because his ICRC mission in Rwanda extended throughout the country and had the best access to massacre sights and the most frequent interaction with the wounded, he became the source that policymakers and journalists would look to when trying to determine the death toll. He recalls that "About numbers, I remember a couple of funny phone calls from BBC London who made the first call around the 20th of April asking me the same question, 'What's your estimation of the number of people killed?' and I told them at least 250,000." According to Gallaird, "One week later they called again and asked me, 'What's your estimation today?' So I told them, 'You can double it. Five hundred thousand people have been killed.'" Gallaird became frustrated by these questions and just "one week later they made a last call about this very specific question . . . and I answered, 'Listen, after half a million, sir, I stopped counting.' . . . Everybody knew every day, live, what was happening in this country. You could follow that every day on TV, on radio."[7]

During this time Phillip Gallaird "went almost twice, three times a week to the Ministry of Defense" and on one occasion actually met face to face with Colonel Bagosora, the architect of the genocide. During their meeting, he told him "Colonel, do something to stop the killing. This is absurd. This is suicide." Gallaird recalls that Bagosora answered in "words [that] you never forget—his answer was, 'Listen, sir, if I want tomorrow I can recruit 50,000 more *Interahamwe*.'" Gallaird explains that his response was forceful: "I took him by the shirt—I'm 58 kilograms and he must be 115—I took him by the throat, looked in his eyes and told him, 'You will lose the war.' He didn't answer anything."[8]

THE GENOCIDE CONVENTION
AND THE IMPLICATIONS OF TERMINOLOGY

Looking back on the genocide, critics of the U.S. government and the UN argue that a moral and legal obligation went unfulfilled. The legal obligation is in reference to the 1948 Convention on Punishment for the Crime of Genocide, more commonly known as the "Genocide Convention." After the conclusion of World War II, the United Nations drafted this convention as a way of defining genocide and formally declaring it a crime under international law. Ironically, the fact that the Genocide Convention provided a definition for genocide gave policymakers and lawyers a specific definition that they could circumvent when describing the situation in discussion.

In Article II, the Genocide Convention calls on five acts to be punishable: genocide, conspiracy to commit genocide, direct and public incitement to commit genocide, attempt to commit genocide, and complicity in genocide. More specifically, Article II outlines the specific actions that constitute genocide:

> Article II: In the present Convention, genocide means any of the following acts committed with intent to destroy, in whole or in part, a national, ethnical, racial or religious group, as such:
>
> (a) Killing members of the group;
> (b) Causing serious bodily or mental harm to members of the group;
> (c) Deliberately inflicting on the group conditions of life calculated to bring about its physical destruction in whole or in part;
> (d) Imposing measures intended to prevent births within the group;
> (e) Forcibly transferring children of the group to another group.[9]

The lack of a specific methodology for determining what constitutes (a) through (e) under Article II makes it possibly to loosely interpret the language of the definition. Even if the language of the Genocide Convention cited more specific criteria for determining the punishable crimes related to genocide, there were no provisions to the treaty that compelled signatory nations to intervene.

In Article IV, the treaty states, "Persons committing genocide or any of the other acts enumerated in article III shall be punished, whether they are constitutionally responsible rulers, public officials or private individuals."[10] While Article VI explains that individuals should be punished in "a competent tribunal," neither Article IV, nor other sections of the treaty indicated how this should be done. There is no mention of the use of force and the language for responding to genocide was so vague that the United States could have labeled Rwanda a genocide, issued a statement condemning the violation of international law, and legally justified honoring the terms of the Genocide Convention. If this was the case, one has to ask why the United States continued to use other terminology to describe the violence in Rwanda.

The answer to this question is rooted not in a fear that the United States was legally bound to the Genocide Convention, but rather in recognition that third parties might have their own definition of what warrants action. Specifically, there was a concern that by calling the conflict by its rightful name, NGOs, the media, and the UN might use an acknowledgement of genocide by the United States as an opportunity to interpret the language of the Genocide Convention in such a way that it called specifically for U.S. intervention. These third parties, through the media, might redefine the language of the Genocide Convention in the public's eyes.

The issue of whether or not the violence in Rwanda constituted genocide was the main issue of discussion regarding a U.S. response to Rwanda. Skilled lawyers in both the State Department and the Defense Department spent countless hours ensuring that the United States did not call the conflict genocide in either an official or unofficial setting. State Department lawyers argued that the use of the term "genocide" would provide the non-government world and the international community with a link between the United States and the Genocide Convention.

REASSESSING THE NATURE OF THE CONFLICT

On April 8, two days after the assassination of President Habyarimana, senior ranking representative of the Ministry of Defense Colonel Theoneste Bagosora took control and "assembled party leaders to fashion a civilian government . . . from the Hutu Power end of the political spectrum."[11] The interim government was inaugurated under the leadership of Dr. Théodore Sindikubwabo on April 9 and orchestrated a number of political assassinations in order to eliminate moderates from the political scene. The interim government's stay in Kigali was brief and by April 12, due to the RPF advance on Kigali, the government fled south toward Gitarama. That same day Radio Rwanda "broadcast a press release from the Ministry of Defense." The press release called upon citizens to "act together [to] carry out patrols and fight the enemy [Tutsi]."[12]

The combination of civilian massacres and political assassinations during this first week of the genocide confused policymakers who still believed that the killing was confined to Kigali. Reflecting back on the initial week of the genocide, policymakers often claim that they thought both Hutus and Tutsis were being killed and that the violence was confined to Kigali. While the majority of the initial killing occurred in Kigali and in the early days moderate Hutus were killed along with Tutsis, "assailants were killing and pillaging Tutsi [by mid-day April 7] in the northwest, in the town of Gisenyi, and at Byangabo, Busogo, Busasamana, Mudende, Muramba, Kivumu, and Rambura; south of Kigali, at Ruhuha and Sake; northeast of Kigali at Murambi; in Gikongoro at Muko and in the far southwestern town of Cyangugu."[13] Policymakers claim that they were unaware of this killing outside of the capital during the first week of the genocide. This false perception led many in Washington to downplay the killing. Many officials incorrectly assumed that killing could only constitute a campaign of extermination if it extended beyond the capital. As a result, no policymaker in Washington even entertained the possibility that extremists were implementing a final solution during the first week of the genocide.

It seems possible to entertain the notion that policymakers failed to understand the violence as genocide during the first week, but what is more difficult to comprehend is the common recollection among policymakers that they did not know it was genocide until after the second week. During the period from "April 11 to the first of May, killers carried out the most devastating massacres of the genocide."[14] Given the fact that the most horrific and numerous killings began at the end of the first week of the genocide, how is it possible that policymakers and government officials in Washington failed to recognize the violence as genocide?

In an attempt to answer this question, one State Department official drew on the argument that they believed the massacres were confined to Kigali. He explained that on April 10 the RPF troops began moving south from the northern prefectures of Byumba and Ruhengeri and came within a few kilometers of Kigali by April 12. Encroachment by the rebels on the capital forced the Rwandan government to flee to Gitarama and it initially appeared as though the RPF were going to capture the capital. However, when the Rwandan Armed Forces (FAR) fled the city, the *Interahamwe* militias filled the power vacuum and began the most severe stage of the genocide, using roadblocks to prevent the Tutsis from fleeing the capital and declaring that they intended to liquidate the *Inyenzi* [Tutsis].[15]

Given the lack of intelligence resources the United States had in the region it is possible that intelligence officials did not have all of the facts during the first week of the genocide. However, according to State Department officials, the Bureau of Intelligence and Research (INR) at the State Department received a number of reports by April 15 indicating that the killing had spread and the countryside [the areas outside of Kigali] was exploding.[16]

A few days after the interim government fled Kigali on April 12, it became increasingly clear that the massacres were part of a campaign of genocide and not solely a military strategy to protect Kigali and hold on to power. One State Department official close to the intelligence recalls that on April 15 they began to seriously question the intent of the extremist FAR, *Interahamwe*, and Presidential Guard. This same official remembers that by April 21 they became more certain of their intentions and fully understood their plans:

After two weeks [following the April 6 assassination of President Habyarimana] we knew that this was a systematic effort to exterminate Tutsi, this was a genocide. I was reluctant to draw such a conclusion before because we didn't know enough yet, and we didn't know enough of the details. We just knew that a hell-of-a lot of people were being killed. By April 21, 22, 23, we were certain that this was genocide.[17]

Not everybody in the State Department saw it this way. The desk officers, action officers, directors, and intelligence officials were close to the information coming in from the field and were more interested in the details than their superiors.

Given the fact that much of the intelligence either never made it up the bureaucratic ranks or was ignored by senior officials, not everybody in the State Department was prepared to call it genocide. There were, however, some exceptions to this. As the *Interahamwe* intensified their attacks in the second week of the genocide, Assistant Secretary of State for Democracy, Human Rights and Labor (DRL) John Shattuck claims that his bureau prepared "plenty of press guidances condemning the massacres" in an effort to stir-up interest in the deteriorating situation.[18] Unfortunately, in the early stages of the genocide, the reporters present at the State Department press conferences were more concerned with the crises in North Korea, Bosnia, and Haiti.

On April 19, in the same period that intelligence officials were reassessing the nature of the conflict in Rwanda, Kenneth Roth, the Executive Director of Human Rights Watch, represented the organization in an appeal to the Security Council for action:

> We urge your attention to the fact that the Rwanda military authorities are engaged in a systematic campaign to eliminate the Tutsi . . . the organized campaign has become so concerted that we believe it constitutes genocide as defined by Article II of the Convention on the Prevention and Punishment to the Crime of Genocide.[19]

The following day, Human Rights Watch estimated that "as many as 100,000 people may have died to date, and the RPF warned that hundreds of thousands of defenseless victims were being slaughtered."[20] That same day, UNHCR announced that "16,870 people had been killed in nine villages around Cyangugu," a prefecture distant from Kigali.[21] On April 21, the International Committee for the Red Cross (ICRC) issued an even more serious claim that "hundreds of thousands were dead."[22] On April 27, the Pope issued a statement indicating that the crisis in Rwanda constituted genocide. Oxfam eventually joined the ranks of NGOs labeling the conflict genocide in its April 28 press release declaring, "Oxfam fears genocide is happening in Rwanda."[23] Following the lead of Human Rights Watch and Oxfam, the U.S. Committee for Refugees, on May 2, called upon President Clinton to call the crisis in Rwanda a genocide, believing that under the terms of the Genocide Convention such a label would result in U.S. action. In addition to the body count estimates, NGOs began to provide eyewitness accounts of the human rights violations, which ultimately led Assistant Secretary Shattuck to conclude by late April that there was a genocide in Rwanda.[24] This marked the beginning of the relatively small-scale campaign for an American response to the genocide.

A PREOCCUPATION WITH TERMINOLOGY

The interagency discussions over the appropriate label for the violence in Rwanda began on April 26 when Deputy Assistant Secretary of State Prudence Bushnell pulled together policymakers from every relevant government agency to hold the largest meeting on Rwanda to that date. That same day, the Bureau of Intelligence and Research (INR) wrote and distributed an intelligence report entitled "Genocide in Partition," describing the conflict in Rwanda as genocide and explaining the systematic nature of the killings.[25] According to one State Department official, INR officials presented the report during the meeting and found themselves confronted by the State Department's lawyers who "stood up and said you can't call this genocide; this is acts of genocide."[26] Tony Marley, Political Military Advisor for the State Department, explains that, "those that wanted nothing done didn't want to even acknowledge the fact that it could be genocide because that would weaken their argument that nothing should be done."[27] As the organizer of the meeting, Bushnell recalls that she did not want to get caught up in the g-word discussions because she "knew [the U.S. government] was not going to do anything, [it] didn't have the resources, so whether we called it a genocide or a suicide didn't matter. The fact is that people were killing each other."[28] Despite this unpopular stance, discussions about the label of the conflict were a necessary prelude to discussions over intervention; however, there was still a tremendous amount of resistance from the legal elements of the Public Affairs Office and officials who were traveling to the region were ordered not to call the crisis a genocide in their meetings.[29]

As mentioned earlier, the number of press guidances related to Rwanda increased by the end of April.[30] On April 28, one reporter asked State Department spokesperson Christine Shelley if the violence in Rwanda could be considered genocide. Shelley, clearly given an order from a higher authority to avoid using the term genocide, answered the reporter by strategically circumventing the question:

> Well, as I think you know, the use of the term "genocide" has a very precise legal meaning. . . Before we begin to use the term, we have to know as much as possible about the facts of the situation, particularly about the intentions of those

who are committing the crimes. . . . I'm not an expert on this area, but generally speaking there—my understanding is that there are three types of elements that we look at in order to make that kind of determination. . . . Types of actions[,] . . . .kind of brutality[, and]. . .assess the intent of the perpetrators. The intent of the perpetrators is something which we have to undertake a very careful study of before we can make a final kind of determination. The intentions, the precise intentions, and whether or not these are just directed episodically or with the intention of actually eliminating groups in whole or in part, this is a more complicated issue to address. . . . I'm not able to look at all of those criteria at this moment and say yes, no. It's something that requires very careful study before we can make a final determination.[31]

The State Department, through Christine Shelley, informed the press that it was still trying to determine whether or not the violence in Rwanda constituted genocide; however, as they put on this façade for the media, a deliberate decision to ignore the fact that this was genocide took place behind closed doors.

There was a fear, in particular among Pentagon officials that use of the term genocide may escalate to commitment. A secret May 1 discussion paper for the Deputy Assistant Secretary of Defense for Middle East/Africa Region, Molly Williamson, advised her to "be careful" on the issue of discussing "language that calls for an international investigation of human rights abuses and possible violations of the Genocide Convention." The underlining rationale behind this was that "genocide finding could commit the USG (U.S. Government) to actually 'do something.'"[32] However, the Director for African Affairs and head of the Rwanda Task Force, Vince Kern, explains that the discussion paper's reference to "do something" was in fact an expression of negative sarcasm over the State Department's circumvention of the term genocide, as seen in Figure 6.1.[33]

.Issues For Discussion:

1. Genocide Investigation: Language that calls for an
international investigation of human rights abuses and possible
violations of the genocide convention.
    Be Careful. Legal at State was worried about this yesterday--
Genocide finding could commit USG to actually "do something"

CLASSIFIED BY: DIR, AFR REGION   **DECLASSIFIED BY AUTHORITY OF:**
DECLASSIFY ON: OADR   **OSD**
                          SECRET   **DATE: 18 Nov 1998**
   **CASE #: 95-F-0894**

Figure 6.1.   Discussion Paper, Office of the Deputy Assistant Secretary of Defense for Middle East/Africa Region, Department of Defense, May 1, 1994. Secret[34]

The U.S. government also influenced the UN Security Council to muffle its language about the nature of the conflict in Rwanda. The Security Council had originally received a draft proposal stating:

> The horrors of Rwanda's killing fields have few precedents in the recent history of the world. The Security Council reaffirms that the systematic killing of any ethnic group, with intent to destroy it in whole or in part constitutes an act of genocide as defined by relevant provisions of international law . . . the council further points out that an important body of international law exists that deals with perpetrators of genocide.[35]

According to consultant for Human Rights Watch Alison Des Forges, a decision had not yet been reached about what to call the violence in Rwanda. The President of the UN Security Council, who was at the time Colin Keating from New Zealand, was anxious to maintain the language of the draft resolution. This led Keating to threaten to declare the meeting of the Security Council an open meeting, thus revealing the true position of the United States and Great Britain.[36] As a result, Keating achieved a compromise on April 29 with the United States and Great Britain where the word "genocide" would not be used, but the definition would remain. Keating removed a clause stating that, "the systematic killing of any ethnic group, with intent to destroy it in whole or in part constitutes an act of genocide as defined by relevant provisions of international law."[37] The new resolution read as follows:

> The Security Council condemns all the breaches of international humanitarian law in Rwanda, particularly those perpetrated against the civilian population, and recalls that persons who instigate or participate in such acts are individually responsible. The Security Council recalls that the killing of members of an ethnic group with the intention of destroying such a group in whole

As discussed in chapter 4, Assistant Secretary of State John Shattuck traveled to the Great Lakes Region at the end of April. In response to his meetings with East African leaders and his own visual confirmation of what was occurring in Rwanda, Shattuck broke the common approach of avoiding the g-word when on May 8, after returning from what he described as "an eye-opening trip to Rwanda, [he] decided that even though [he] made no progress toward the formation of a new peacekeeping mission, [he] would do [his] best to tell the truth about what [he] had heard was happening in Rwanda." Shattuck wanted to explain that a genocide was occurring in Rwanda, but after pressure from the State Department lawyers, he told the international press that "crimes against humanity and acts of genocide" were being committed and that "those responsible should be investigated and brought to justice."[38]

On May 9, the Defense Intelligence Agency (DIA) used the term "genocide" to describe the killings in Rwanda. In a report entitled "Rwanda: The
Rwanda Patriotic Front," the DIA noted that the "Presidential Guard began
the systematic execution of prominent Tutsi . . . [and] it appears, that, in addition to the random massacres of Tutsis by Hutu militias and individuals,
there is an organized, parallel effort of genocide being implemented by the
army to destroy the leadership of the Tutsi community."[39] The DIA classifi-
cation of the violence in Rwanda as genocide went largely ignored and the administration continued to avoid use of the term.

Exactly one week later, the State Department's Bureau of African Affairs
issued a similar claim to that of the DIA. In a draft legal analysis, Assistant
Legal Adviser for African Affairs Joan Donoghue explained how the killings
in Rwanda fit the Genocide Convention's definition of what constitutes a
punishable violation of the treaty:

> There can be little question that the specific listed acts have taken place in
> Rwanda . . . most of those killed in Rwanda have been Tutsi civilians, including
> women and children . . . some of the prohibited acts have apparently been com-
> mitted with the requisite intent to destroy, on whole or in part, the Tutsi group
> as such, as required by the Convention . . . INR further concludes that '[t]here
> is substantial circumstantial evidence implicating senior Rwandan government
> and military officials in the widespread, systematic killing of ethnic Tutsis, and
> to a lesser extent, ethnic Hutus who supported power-sharing between the two
> groups. . . . it seems evident that the killings and other listed acts have been un-
> dertaken with the intent of destroying the Tutsi group in whole or in part.'[40]

On May 18, just two days later, in a memorandum from the Bureau of Intelligence and Research (INR) to Assistant Secretary of State for African Affairs
George Moose, Tobi Gati outlined the specific aspects of the Geneva Convention being violated by extremists in Rwanda. She explained that "there is
substantial circumstantial evidence implicating senior Rwandan government
and military officials in the widespread, systematic killing of ethnic Tutsis,"
and that already, between "200,000 and 500,000 . . . between 8 and 40 percent of the Tutsi population," mostly "women and children" already lost their
lives. By INR's standards, the three criteria for genocide were met by the
atrocities in Rwanda: "killing members and causing serious bodily or mental
harm to members of the group, deliberately inflicting on the group conditions
of life calculated to bring about its physical destruction in whole or in part,
and imposing measures intended to prevent births and forcibly transferring
children of the group to another group."[41]

By May 21, the State Department faced increased pressure to label the crisis a genocide. The evidence was overwhelming and the body count was in

the hundreds of thousands. In a rare memorandum to the Secretary of State, the Assistant Secretaries of State for Democracy, Human Rights and Labor (DRL); African Affairs (AF); and International Organizations (IO) advised that, "Department officials should be authorized to state the Department's conclusion that 'acts of genocide have occurred' in Rwanda." The memorandum reviewed the Genocide Convention's definition of genocide and argued that, "there is a strong basis to conclude that some of the killings and other listed acts carried out against Tutsis have been committed with the intent of destroying the Tutsi ethnic group in whole or in part." The Secretary of State was assured that "a USG [U.S. Government] statement that acts of genocide have occurred would not have any particular legal consequences."[42] It was believed that "acts of genocide" is different than "genocide" in that the former implies that only some of the actions fit the Genocide Convention definition of "genocide," while the latter implies that a coordinated campaign is underway. Therefore, "acts of genocide" is considered less severe because it does not imply that the violence as a whole is genocide.

The language of the May 21 memorandum, despite clearly outlining why the events in Rwanda constituted genocide, also indicated that application of the compromised term "acts of genocide" was necessary to save face and prevent a necessity to act. The memorandum read, "if we do not seize the opportunity presented by fora such as the UNHCR to use the genocide label to condemn events in Rwanda, our credibility will be undermined with human rights groups and the general public, who may question how much evidence we can legitimately require before coming to a policy conclusion."[43] Behind closed doors, the U.S. government admitted that agreeing to a compromise term was no more than a symbolic action. It was a way for policymakers to appear as though they were concerned without having any obligation to take action.

Three days later, Secretary of State Christopher announced that, "the delegation is authorized to agree to a resolution that states that 'acts of genocide' have occurred in Rwanda or that 'genocide has occurred in Rwanda,'" as seen in Figure 6.2. However, the Secretary still restricted the use and application of the term by explaining that the "delegation is not authorized to agree to the characterization of any specific incident as genocide or to agree to any formulation that indicates that all killings in Rwanda are genocide."[44] At this stage, the State Department's deliberate attempt to circumvent use of the g-word even surprised officials at the White House, and according to National Security Advisor Anthony Lake, the State Department "was ridiculous in its blatant refusal to use the g-word."[45] The National Security Advisor became so frustrated with this charade that during the June 26–27 White House Conference on Africa, he recalls referring to the violence in Rwanda as "genocide" rather than "acts of genocide," a term which he did not have authorization to use.[46]

RECOMMENDATIONS

That you authorize Department officials to state publicly that "acts of genocide have occurred" in Rwanda (all bureaus support).

Approve ____✓ (WC) 5/21/94____ Disapprove ____

That you authorize U.S. delegations to the UN Human Rights Commission and other international fora to agree to resolutions and other instruments that refer to "acts of genocide" in Rwanda, state that "genocide has occurred" there or contain other comparable formulations (all bureaus support).

Approve ____✓ (WC) 5/21/94____ Disapprove ____

WC.

Attachments:

    Tab 1 - INR Memorandum
    Tab 2 - Legal Analysis

UNCLASSIFIED

~~CONFIDENTIAL~~
(with ~~SECRET~~ attachments)

Figure 6.2. May 21, 1994 Action Memorandum to Secretary of State Warren Christopher in which he authorizes the use of the term "acts of genocide" to describe the violence in Rwanda.

NOTES

1. Madeleine Albright, *Madam Secretary: A Memoir*, New York: Easton Press, 2003, p. 147.
2. Personal Interview, Former RPF Chairman Colonel Alexis Kanyarengwe, Kigali, Rwanda, December 18, 2002.
3. (Clandestine) Radio Muhabura, 1900 GMT, April 17, 1994, in FBIS-AFR-94-075, April 19, 1994, the report was translated and published by the CIA on April 19, 1994, in Alan Kuperman, *The Limits of Humanitarian Intervention,* p. 31.
4. Alan Kuperman, *The Limits of Humanitarian Intervention,* p. 16.
5. Linda Melvern, *A People Betrayed: The Role of the West in Rwanda's Genocide*, p. 177.
6. In a September 12, 2003 PBS *Frontline* interview for the documentary "Ghosts of Rwanda," Phillip Gallaird offered a detailed account of how he unexpectedly found himself involved in aiding victims of genocide. Gallaird had come to Rwanda in July 1993 because after "working for more than ten years in Latin America [and] a couple of years in the Middle East [he] was a bit fed up." He recalls asking a friend of his "if he knew about any place in Africa, just to work in another context, in another conti-

nent," and his friend informed him that "there is a very interesting process in Rwanda where civil war and guerilla fights started three to four years ago in the beginning of the '90s." Because the politics sounded interesting to him and because he enjoyed fishing—Rwanda was known to have some of the best fishing in Africa—he ended up working in Rwanda. Little did he know the project that he would have to undertake.

7. Ibid.

8. Ibid.

9. U.N.T.S. (United Nations Treaty Series), No. 1021, vol. 78 (1951), p. 277.

10. Ibid.

11. Alison Des Forges, *Leave None to Tell the Story,* p. 197.

12. Radio Rwanda, "Defence Ministry communique urges Rwandans to ignore 'the lies' of RPF radio," April 12, 1994, SWB, AL/1970 A/5, April 13, 1994 in Ibid.

13. Alison Des Forges, *Leave None to Tell the Story,* p. 209.

14. Ibid, p. 211.

15. Personal Interview, State Department Official [A], Via telephone to Washington, DC, February 28, 2003.

16. Personal Interview, State Department Official [A], Via telephone to Washington, DC, February 28, 2003.

17. Ibid.

18. Personal Interview, Former Assistant Secretary of State for Democracy, Human Rights and Labor John Shattuck, Via telephone to Boston, MA, February 24, 2003.

19. Linda Melvern, *A People Betrayed: The Role of the West in Rwanda's Genocide,* p. 169; *see also,* Letter from Human Rights Watch to UN Security Council, April 19, 1994, in Alan Kuperman, *The Limits of Humanitarian Intervention,* p. 31.

20. Johnathan Moore (ed.), *Hard Choices, Moral Dilemmas in Humanitarian Intervention,* Oxford: Rowman and Littlefield, 1998, p. 81, in Ibid, p. 176.

21. Ibid.

22. Press Release, Human Rights Watch/Africa, April 20, 1994, in Alan Kuperman, *The Limits of Humanitarian Intervention,* pp. 27–28.

23. Linda Melvern, *A People Betrayed: The Role of the West in Rwanda's Genocide,* p. 178.

24. Personal Interview, Former Assistant Secretary of State for Democracy, Human Rights and Labor John Shattuck, February 24, 2003.

25. Personal Interview, State Department Official [A], Via telephone to Washington, DC, February 28, 2003.

26. Ibid.

27. Tony Marley, interview, "The Triumph of Evil," *Frontline,* PBS, January 26, 1999; available at PBS Online: http://www.pbs.org/wgbh/pages/frontline/shows/evil/interviews/marley.html.

28. Personal Interview, Deputy Assistant Secretary of State for African Affairs Prudence Bushnell, Washington, DC, December 9, 2002.

29. Personal Interview, Assistant Secretary of State for Democracy, Human Rights and Labor John Shattuck, Via telephone to Boston, MA, February 24, 2003.

30. According to A/S for DRL John Shattuck, by late April there were daily press guidances about the crisis in Rwanda that were being provided by DRL.

31. Samantha Power, *"A Problem From Hell:" America and the Age of Genocide*, pp. 359–360.

32. Discussion Paper, Office of the Deputy Assistant Secretary of Defense for Middle East/Africa Region, Department of Defense, May 1, 1994. Secret, in William Ferroggiaro, *A National Security Archive Briefing Book*, August 20, 2001, found in http://www.gwu.edu/~nsarchiv/NSAEBB/NSAEBB53/press.html.

33. Personal Interview, Former Director for African Affairs and Head of the Rwanda Task Force at the Pentagon, Vince Kern, Alexandria, VA, August 15, 2003.

34. Discussion Paper, Office of the Deputy Assistant Secretary of Defense for Middle East/Africa Region, Department of Defense, May 1, 1994. Secret, in William Ferroggiaro, *A National Security Archive Briefing Book*, August 20, 2001, found in http://www.gwu.edu/~nsarchiv/NSAEBB/NSAEBB53/press.html.

35. Linda Melvern, *A People Betrayed: The Role of the West in Rwanda's Genocide*, p. 180.

36. Personal Interview, Consultant for Human Rights Watch Alison Des Forges, Via telephone to Buffalo, NY, October 6, 2003.

37. Ibid.

38. John Shattuck, Chapter 2 unpublished book, expected publication date September 1, 2003; cited with permission of the author.

39. Defense Intelligence Report, Defense Intelligence Agency, "Rwanda: The Rwandan Patriotic Front's Offensive", May 9, 1994. Secret/NOFORN, in William Ferroggiaro, *A National Security Archive Briefing Book*, August 20, 2001, found in http://www.gwu.edu/~nsarchiv/NSAEBB/NSAEBB53/press.html.

40. Draft Legal Analysis, Office of the Legal Adviser, Department of State, drafted by Assistant Legal Adviser for African Affairs Joan Donoghue, May 16, 1994. Secret, in William Ferroggiaro, *A National Security Archive Briefing Book*, August 20, 2001, found in: http://www.gwu.edu/~nsarchiv/NSAEBB/NSAEBB53/press.html.

41. Memorandum from Assistant Secretary for Intelligence and Research Tobi T. Gati to Assistant Secretary of State for African Affairs George Moose and Department of State Legal Adviser Conrad Harper, "Rwanda—Geneva Convention Violations", circa May 18, 1994. Secret/ORCON, in William Ferroggiaro, *A National Security Archive Briefing Book*, August 20, 2001, found in http://www.gwu.edu/~nsarchiv/NSAEBB/NSAEBB53/press.html.

42. Action memorandum from Assistant Secretary of State for African Affairs George E. Moose, Assistant Secretary of State for Democracy, Human Rights and Labor John Shattuck, Assistant Secretary of State for International Organization Affairs Douglas J. Bennet, and Department of State Legal Adviser Conrad K. Harper, through Under Secretary of State for Political Affairs Peter Tarnoff and Under Secretary of State for Global Affairs Tim Wirth, to Secretary of State Warren Christopher, "Has Genocide Occurred in Rwanda?", May 21, 1994. Secret, in William Ferroggiaro, *A National Security Archive Briefing Book*, August 20, 2001, found in http://www.gwu.edu/~nsarchiv/NSAEBB/NSAEBB53/press.html.

43. Ibid.

44. Confidential cable from Secretary of State Warren Christopher to the U.S. Mission to the UN in Geneva and embassies, "Subject: UN Human Rights Commission: 'Genocide' at Special Session on Rwanda," May 24, 1994, in Samantha Power, *"A Problem From Hell:" America and the Age of Genocide*, p. 362.

45. Personal Interview, Former National Security Advisor Anthony Lake, Georgetown, MD, November 20, 2002.

46. Ibid.

7

Too Little, Too Late

Developments in the debate over terminology greatly affected the government's willingness to intervene in Rwanda. The use of the watered down term of "acts of genocide" on May 21 created the mechanism that some bureaucrats, particularly senior officials, needed to encourage discussions over a way forward for Rwanda. Between early May and the genocide's conclusion in July, officials discussed a number of possible courses of action, but in almost every instance policymakers delayed action or expressed concern over launching an intervention while violence persisted in Rwanda. These officials used Congress, legal terminology, and other government agencies as the reason for not supporting intervention. Despite acknowledgement that at least "acts of genocide" had occurred in Rwanda, the United States continued to avoid either discussing or launching effective interventions until the RPF seized control of Kigali and a ceasefire was established. Why were officials so adamantly opposed to even a small-scale and perhaps non-military intervention in Rwanda?

In an interview for this book Under Secretary of Defense for Policy Walt Slocombe outlined the fundamental problem with an intervention in Rwanda. He explains that "nobody had any doubt as to what was going on in Rwanda, how awful crisis was, the degree of horror, and there certainly was not anybody saying that this is not happening, but there was the very legitimate issue of we cannot intervene and no matter how nice the idea may have sounded, we believed that we could not run around the world knocking off lousy governments."[1] Slocombe recalls that "Every morning, you get a detailed report on events that are going on in the world, I don't know that the Rwanda massacres were reported every day, but even so it took a little while to realize the scale." Under Secretary Slocombe raised another important variable which was that "an intervention to stop the massacres raised the issue choosing sides in a civil war. We had learned from Bosnia that you cannot intervene in one of these crises without taking sides and that complicates things."[2]

The issue of why the United States could not intervene, from a defense perspective, lent itself to the notion that there was not going to be another Somalia debacle and if an intervention in Rwanda was to take place it would have been a very serious and robust force, which neither the White House, nor the State Department was willing to consider. According to Slocombe, Chairman of the Joint Chiefs of Staff General Shalikashvili ran his shop on the premise that "we are not interested in a fair fight, we want to win." Under Secretary Slocombe explains that "even before the actual firefight in Mogadishu six months earlier, the U.S. was not keen to get into another conflict and the DoD position on Rwanda was such that, if we were going to go in, we were going to go in with an overwhelming force."[3] However, as Slocombe points out, there were two additional issues complicating the matter; "Rwanda was not an easy place to get into and it would take time and preparation to get there."

Complicating matters further was the issue of what to do once troops arrived. The killing was decentralized and carried out by ordinary civilians in the countryside. These ordinary men killed because of a hatred of Tutsis, not because of the Rwandan government. Therefore, the expected coercive effect of a U.S. military presence might not have had the desired impact. From a defense perspective, how could an overwhelming military presence, convince civilians from killing their civilian neighbors with machetes?

Slocombe argues that further complicating matters was the fact that the United States viewed the conflict as a civil war that RPF General Kagame was winning. The common, yet incorrect assessment that the genocide was a civil war stemmed from the fact that the genocide was preceded by four-years of civil war between the Rwandan Armed Forces and the RPF. However, once Habyarimana's plane was shot down on April 6, 1994, the context changed from civil war to genocide and while the same actors that were fighting the civil war remained engaged in the conflict, their reasons for fighting changed with the context. The Rwandan Armed Forces now sought extermination of the Tutsis and the RPF sought an end to the genocide and assurances that extremists would never again control Rwanda. True, the early days were characterized by political assassinations, but after the first week of the genocide, the RPF sought to end the killing by expelling the government. To policymakers, the RPF attempt to take control was reflective of its aspirations to win the civil war and govern the country.

In retrospect, given the consequences and the outcome of the Rwanda genocide, Slocombe states that "he wishes we had done it," but he also recognizes that the Pentagon's position was such that an "intervention would have had to be a very substantial military operation and they would have devoted a lot of time, money, and people, which was not something that could be done overnight given the difficulty in reaching Rwanda." Given the fact that the Pentagon would have had to factor in speed, the potential for serious resistance from locals, and the prerequisites necessary to secure the required safe zones, it might have taken 20,000 troops to accomplish this.[4] However, in reality the issue was not the number of troops or the logistics (20,000 is considered a relatively small force), but rather the fact that policymakers would not support sending American troops in any number to Africa just six months after the deaths of eighteen Army Rangers in Somalia.

In interviews for this book it is clear that senior policymakers at the State Department, the Pentagon, and the White House did not entertain the possibility of unilateral military intervention. This is not surprising. What is shocking, however, is the failure of the Clinton administration to appreciate the potential value and impact of small-scale interventions, a number of which did not even require commitment of troops. The U.S. government could have explored these options by looking at the possibility of naming the killers, supporting a coalition of the willing comprised of African states, and jamming the radio. None of these interventions fully materialized, but following some pressure from sympathetic members of Congress and the persistence of the genocide, a second UN deployment was eventually deployed. Unfortunately, this second deployment of the UN was accompanied with logistical complications that prevented the force from playing a role until after the genocide had ended.

NAMING THE KILLERS AND PUNISHING THE PERPETRATORS

Given the fact that the administration was unwilling to commit major resources to an intervention in Rwanda, it seems that they may have at least been willing to undertake initiatives that would not require such commitments. Forceful diplomacy was one such option. Yet, throughout the genocide, senior officials underestimated the power of firm diplomatic statements. The United States knew the names of the perpetrators, yet no senior official ever ordered them to stop the campaign of genocide. When Monique Mujawamariya, a Rwandan human rights activist affiliated with Human Rights Watch, came to the White House with Alison Des Forges, Anthony Lake explains that he asked her "what should we do for Rwanda?" Mujawamariya said, "'You, meaning the U.S. government, know who the people responsible for this are: announce their names over the radio and call on them to stop the violence.'"[5] She continued by explaining that they "'should broadcast methods of reconciliation throughout Rwanda' and said that 'Human Rights Watch could provide the text for this.'"[6] Within 48 hours, Clinton taped a one-minute message that the White House broadcasted over the radio on VOA.[7] However, this message served more as an appeal than a command. The White House "[called] on the leadership of the Rwandan armed forces, including Army commander-in-chief Colonel Augustin Bizimungu, Colonel Nkundiye, Captain Pascal Simbikangwa, and Colonel Bagosora, to do everything in their power to end the violence immediately."[8]

During the genocide, there were no efforts on the part of the United States or the UN to restrict the representation of the genocidal government in its agencies, organizations, and institutions. Despite the fact that General Dallaire sent information directly to the UN describing the Rwanda government's complicity in the genocide, Rwanda's UN Ambassador Jean-Damascene Bizimana continued to sit as a non-permanent member of the Security Council.[9] Furthermore, the United States did not encourage the UN to place travel restrictions on ministers in the Rwanda Interim Government and on May 16 the United States even permitted Rwanda Foreign Minister Jerome Bicamumpaka to travel to New York and declare before the UN Security Council that "the systematic killings were being carried out by the RPF."[10] Despite the fact that the Rwandan Ambassador and his staff represented a government carrying out genocide, the United States also allowed Rwanda to maintain its diplomatic mission in Washington DC.

On July 15, President Clinton finally gave an order to freeze Rwandan assets in the United States and close the Rwanda embassy in Washington DC. Clinton argued that the United States could not "allow representatives of a regime that supports genocidal massacres to remain on our soil,"[11] yet by this time the genocide had been over for eleven days. While one can only speculate as to what the effect would have been if Clinton closed the Rwandan embassy and prevented representation of its government at an earlier date, it can be assumed that such an action would have at least demonstrated a public U.S. condemnation of the Rwandan government's policies.

The U.S. unwillingness to sever relations with the Rwandan government during the genocide is difficult to grasp. However, even more astonishing is the apparent reasons for this delay. It seems that throughout the entire genocide, a number of policymakers still believed there was hope for the Arusha Peace Process. Despite the fact that this seems inconceivable, some policymakers believed that the United States needed to maintain ties with all actors involved with the hope of returning to the bargaining table. In a May 1 discussion paper for the Deputy Assistant Secretary of Defense for Middle East/Africa Molly Williamson, it was suggested that in regards to the question of should the United States support punishment of the organizers of the genocide, the United States should "[hold out] till ceasefire has been established [because they] don't want to scare off the participants."[12] If the goal had been to stop the atrocities, scaring off the perpetrators would seem a positive outcome. However, this fact was overridden by a belief as late as July 1994 that there was still hope for the Arusha Peace Process.

A "COALITION OF THE WILLING" UN DEPLOYMENT

Whereas naming the killers would have required a direct U.S. confrontation with the Rwandan government, there were options that could have been more effective and not required this direct action. Even though there was never any proposal for a unilateral or multilateral U.S.-led military intervention, prospects for a military intervention led by other nations were not immediately ruled out. By the first week in May, proponents of intervention suggested the deployment of troops, mostly from African countries, that would form a "coalition of the willing."[13] During John Shattuck's trip to East Africa during the last week of April, he concluded that East African leaders were open to being part of a regional initiative to end the genocide in Rwanda and address the humanitarian crisis.[14]

Despite this willingness on the part of African states to consider taking part in a regional initiative, permanent members of the Security Council feared that without the support of a leading power the mission could end in disaster and further embarrass both the UN and the United States. Deputy Assistant Secretary of Defense Sarah Sewall argues that, "nobody really wanted to come in and take on a new and very different mission without a lead nation coming in and equipping and leading them."[15]

During a trip to South Africa for Nelson Mandela's inauguration, one official from the White House recalls senior policymakers, led by Vice President Al Gore, discussed a proposal with OAU Secretary General Dr. Salim Ahmed Salim and UN Secretary General Boutrous Boutrous-Ghali that called for "a coalition of the willing with air support, logistical support, financial support, and equipment." Boutrous-Ghali responded to the proposal by explaining that, "there just were not the trained troops that were capable of operating together."[16] During this meeting in South Africa, one White House official argues, "It became clear that if anybody was going to do this [intervention] it would have to be a unilateral initiative by a western country,"[17] but with no support for this, policymakers were unenthusiastic about a permanent member of the Security Council launching a unilateral mission in Rwanda.[18]

For reasons already stated and reiterated throughout this book, this was not an option. Summarizing the position of the interagency, Lieutenant Colonel Harvin wrote: "While most seem to think that only the imposition of a large and heavily armed force can stop the killing (Chapter VII),[19] no one (except Susan Rice at the NSC and a few folks in refugee affairs at State/AID) appear ready to sign up to that (expensive, and potentially bloody) option." From the Pentagon's perspective, "lots of careful thinking needs to be done before we start supporting the concept of putting people in Rwanda."[20]

At the May 11 Interagency Working Group (IWG) teleconference there were significant developments for the possibility of a UN coalition of the willing. Offers from the Nigerians, Tanzanians, Ghanaians, Canadians, and Namibians made the prospect of a second UN mission real. At this same meeting, the interagency discussed the International Committee for the Red Cross (ICRC) request for a C-130 aircraft to provide airlift capabilities for an additional 240 metric tons of food, medical supplies, and tents from Nairobi to Bujumbura. The unanimous decision among interagency participants was that the "U.S. would help fund such an aircraft lease, but that there would be no U.S. military aircraft involved."

Despite the apparent willingness of some in the interagency to discuss this matter, other participants, particularly the Office of the Secretary of Defense (OSD) asked the questions of "who will pay?, and, isn't there a Congressional Notification required somewhere along the line?"[21] The C-130 debate pinning OSD and Joint Staff (JCS) against the Department of State, foreshadowed the following discussion on a reinforcement of UNAMIR. In his May 11 briefing of the IWG meeting, Lieutenant Colonel Harvin explained that following the discussion over the C-130, the "meeting degenerated into a NSC/State attempt to sign-up our Principals to support a Chapter VII operation wearing Chapter VI[22] sheep's clothing, with OSD and Joint Staff in stiff opposition." He also made clear that "NSC and State seem convinced that the Vice President's mention during his visit to South Africa of the U.S. not liking the UN's proposed plan to put a large number of forces in Kigali and our expressed interest in examining other solutions means that we have signed up to the alternative solution that he introduced (setting up camps for the refugees where they can be safe and cared for)."

The Pentagon, in particular the Joint Staff, did not share the stance of the State Department and the NSC, arguing that "the U.S. is not committed to supporting the [South Africa] option, but [the U.S.] is committed to examining it and other alternatives." The stance at the Pentagon was not a result of indifference, but rather a concern that establishing safe havens along the Burundi/Rwanda border would place the internally displaced persons (IDP) "right in the path of escape for any renegade Hutu forces that might be pursued by the RPF." Even though DoD adamantly opposed this commitment, the Joint Staff and OSD participants agreed that "If the Deputies determine that such an action is the way we want to go, then that is the way we want to go, however, we want the details fairly presented to the Deputies so they understand exactly what they are signing up for."[23]

The interagency discussions, in particular the Peacekeeping Core Group, changed dramatically on May 12. Dick Clarke, who had been adamantly opposed to an intervention of any kind in Rwanda, issued an overnight task to Joint Staff to "begin formal mission planning for 'something'." Representatives from the Office of the Secretary of Defense observed that "the results of this meeting are somewhat foggy in the mind of the attendees—it will either be a large fixed force in Kigali, or a large force that moves inward from the neighboring border areas 'securing' the territory along the corridors as it advances."[24]

The question one has to ask is why Dick Clarke, the man most obstinately opposed to an intervention in Rwanda, felt compelled to task the Joint Staff to do "something." Dick Clarke almost certainly received unexpected instructions from Anthony Lake or President Clinton to come up with a contingency plan for some kind of damage control. Was this because John Shattuck, without authorization had used the term "acts of genocide" to describe the killings in Rwanda? Was this because the DIA issued a report on May 9 labeling the conflict in Rwanda a genocide? Or was this because the President or National Security Advisor were moved by something they had seen on television, heard on the radio, or read in the paper?

While each of these suggestions could serve as a reason for Dick Clarke's shift, it is more likely a result of the dynamics of the UN Security Council. Following the UN estimate in early May that "200,000 people had been killed," the UN Security Council "reopened the debate on Rwanda and asked the UN Secretariat for contingency plans."[25] At this juncture, members of the Security Council looked increasingly at the possibility of deploying a second UN mission to Rwanda. Given this renewed debate and the likely pressure placed on the United States for support, it is not surprising that Dick Clarke was forced to discuss these matters in the interagency.

By May 16, this momentum for a reinforced UNAMIR deployment seemed to die down. In a secret memorandum to the Secretary of Defense and Deputy Secretary of Defense, then Principal Under Secretary of Defense for Policy (PDUSDP) Walter Slocombe explained the DoD working level opposition to the UN Secretary General's proposal for a UN peacekeeping force of 5,500 to be deployed and operate out of Kigali. Slocombe also indicated that due to unsafe conditions at the Kigali Airport, the Interagency Working Group and the Peacekeeping Core Group's opposition to the U.S. government providing a C-130 to fly missions into Kigali in direct support of the UN peacekeeping forces.[26]

A DILEMMA OF SOVEREIGNTY: JAMMING HATE RADIO

Broadcasts from Radio Rwanda and Radio Television Libre Mille Collines (RTLM) played a significant role in rousing anti-Tutsi sentiments and brainwashing the civilian population to commit atrocities against the Tutsi population. Broadcasting inflammatory messages of hate and announcing the names and addresses of those who had not yet been killed certainly contributed to the efficiency of the killing, in particular after most Tutsis had gone into hiding. The non-governmental organizations (NGO) played a major role in lobbying the U.S. government to consider initiatives to jam the hate radio. Human Rights Watch pushed for several radio interventions calling on the U.S. government to broadcast methods of reconciliation (supplied by Human Rights Watch if necessary) throughout Rwanda. Alison Des Forges, a senior consultant for Human Rights Watch and a widely recognized expert on Rwanda, appealed to the NSC, the State Department, and the Pentagon to do what they could to jam the hate radio.[27]

As a result of these discussions and meetings, several policymakers believed that jamming the hate radio could prevent extremist messages from being promoted and halt the announcement of Tutsi names, addresses, and hiding places. According to the State Department's Political Military Advisor Tony Marley, there were three methods for radio jamming in Rwanda:

1) Transmit counterpropaganda from a U.S. aircraft with Loudspeakers,
2) Block Radio Rwanda and RTLM from broadcasting their Messages, and
3) Destroy the radio antennas.[28]

According to Director for African Affairs at the Pentagon Vince Kern, the radio jamming solution emerged in the interagency teleconferences because "there was so little the U.S. could do other than the jawbone, such as talk to the two sides and work through the UN, that when somebody suggested radios people just latched on."[29] The Pentagon was more skeptical than most about the radio jamming. Kern argues that it "wasn't something new that Hutus were being told that Tutsis were cockroaches; it is not like suddenly they were getting a new source of information, these guys are bad you have to do something about it, this was going on for generations." Kern continued by explaining that "the moment we might have been able to actually do something about the radios had passed;[30] the sorts of things that people talked about doing with the radio did not make sense, we couldn't strike the station or the radio tower."[31] Perhaps a more provocative question is why the hate radio was there in the first place.[32]

There was a clear danger in permitting these broadcasts to persist. Policymakers, however, were concerned with what they perceived to be the far greater danger of an escalation in U.S. involvement. As such, policymakers used legal and strategic explanations for why the U.S. could not initiate radio jamming. On May 1, a discussion paper reached the desk of the Deputy Assistant Secretary of Defense for Middle East and Africa, recommending that the United States not "[engage] in additional propaganda activities to get a message into Rwanda to counter the radio stations that [were] urging the killings" because such actions presented the danger of a "significant increase in [the U.S.'] role."[33] As a result, the Pentagon denied the State Department's request "for the preliminary planning of utilizing DoD assets to jam radio broadcasts originating in Rwanda." The Pentagon did not oppose the operation of radio jamming, but opposed U.S. involvement in such an operation because it had potential to escalate to a greater commitment. Officials at the Pentagon offered a compromise proposal that suggested "[offering] equipment to neighbors and [urging] them to do it."[34]

In spite of the Pentagon's position outlined in the May 1 discussion paper, Secretary of State Warren Christopher approached Secretary of Defense William Perry in early May to ask if the Pentagon could provide an airplane to broadcast counter-propaganda. According to Secretary Perry, Christopher intended for the airplane to fly over the region with "huge loudspeakers to provide announcements with the hope of having a calming effect that would halt the malicious hate messages being spread over the radio."[35] Perry informed Christopher that "he didn't think it would be very useful," but the Pentagon could provide an airplane for that purpose.[36] However, due to bureaucratic delays this agreement between the Secretary of State and the Secretary of Defense never materialized.

The National Security Council also took part in discussions concerning the operation of radio jamming. Anthony Lake met with Secretary of Defense Perry for a luncheon discussion on May 4 in which "he raised with Secretary Perry the possibility of jamming Rwandan radio broadcasts."[37] After hearing the National Security Advisor's objectives, Secretary Perry "concluded [that] jamming [was] an ineffective and expensive mechanism that [would] not accomplish the object the NSC Advisor [sought]." In reality, the Secretary of Defense likely drew this conclusion based on the position that the Pentagon was not interested in committing resources to be used against a country with which the U.S. had diplomatic relations. Reinforcing this claim in a May 5 confidential memorandum for the Deputy Assistant to the President for National Security Affairs at the National Security Council, Undersecretary of Defense Walt Slocombe explained that, "International legal conventions complicate airborne or ground based jamming and the mountainous terrain reduces the effectiveness of either option."[38] He also expressed concern over the price of the initiative which would cost the U.S. government "approximately $8500 per flight hour and requires a semi-secure area of operations due to its vulnerability and limited self-protection." Under Secretary Slocombe rationalized that this money could be better spent "[assisting] Rwanda in the relief effort, particularly in neighboring countries, like Tanzania."[39] The Pentagon's belief that diplomatic ties needed to be severed in order to conduct radio jamming led to a rift between policymakers at the State Department and the Pentagon. The cost of the procedure proved to be a convenient way for the Pentagon to reinforce its position that it did not want to conduct such operations.

Policymakers and UN representatives engaged in a legal debate over whether or not the UN or the U.S. had the legal authority to interfere with the communications of another nation with which it still had diplomatic relations. Lawyers representing the United Nations and the United States opposed a U.S. initiative to jam the Rwandan radio broadcasts on the basis that it violated international law and Rwanda's sovereignty. Director for African Affairs at the Pentagon and head of the Rwanda Task Force, Vince Kern, argues that "we never got passed the legal barrier on the radio issue. I often and I still wish that State would have broken diplomatic relations, I understand why they didn't, the argument was that they could talk to these people even though we knew they were bad guys, and my argument back was we talked to Kagame without having diplomatic relations with the RPF."[40] While Kern admits that it still may not have had any effect to jam the radio, cutting off relations with the Rwandan government would have at least taken away the legal blockade. He argues that "without cutting off relations with the government of Rwanda, jamming RTLM would have technically been the same as jamming the BBC."[41] Deputy Assistant Secretary of State for African Affairs Prudence Bushnell, like Vince Kern, was also frustrated by the legal blockade against jamming the radio. According to Bushnell, they "talked about radio jamming a lot at the interagency conferences and the excuse about international law was [bogus]. We just didn't want to do anything."[42]

Even if someone in policy had been able to jump the legal hurdle, the Joint Chiefs of Staff at the Pentagon were not sure about where the assets would come from because as Vince Kern explains, the planes the United States would have had to use to do the operation were in Haiti. In order to use the planes from Haiti to jam the radio in Rwanda, the United States would have had to be less effective elsewhere in the world, principally Haiti, because the Pentagon would have had to remove some of the assets from the Haiti operation. Because Anthony Lake was admittedly preoccupied with Haiti, it is unlikely that this decision would have sat well with him. Therefore, even if somebody had gotten over the legal hurdle or had the State Department been willing to break relations with the government, there would have been pushback from the Joint Chiefs of Staff about whether or not the planes in Haiti were better off in Haiti or Rwanda. However, as Kern points out, "the U.S. never got to that practical phase. People felt very strongly about the radios only because it was the only thing on the table that was proactive."[43] While Kern's assessment characterizes the perspective of those at the Department of Defense, there were many at the State Department and in the NGO world who believed that radio jamming would save thousands of lives. Given the fact that the radio was used to declare where specific Tutsis were hiding, living, and trying to escape to, it seems that the radio served as an important mechanism for facilitating the genocide.

THE VOICES IN CONGRESS

Given the fact that none of these discussed interventions ever materialized into a formal proposal that would have required funding from Congress, it is not surprising that during the genocide Congress rarely had to speak out against an intervention in Rwanda. In interviews for this book, it became abundantly clear that policymakers knew that asking Congress for funds to intervene in Rwanda would be out of the realm of possibility. Despite this assumed Congressional opposition, there were some who sought to undermine the barrier against intervention. While these Congressmen and Senators were only marginally influential in their efforts to create awareness about Rwanda, their role is not insignificant.

This small congressional lobby for an intervention—it consisted of members of the Africa Sub-committee and the Foreign Relations Committee—began to develop in late April and came together by early May. Congressional records indicate that discussions of "genocide" in Rwanda began on the Congressional floor as early as April 26, 1994. Senator Simon spoke before the Senate and explained that, "[T]he eruption in Rwanda [is] of brutal, systematic, and indiscriminate violence, resulting in the deaths of more than 100,000 people to date. These actions constitute genocide, and clearly violate all international standards of human rights."[44] During this speech, Senator Simon urged the Senate to pass Senate Resolution 207. The resolution "[called] upon the United Nations, the United States, and the entire international community

to act swiftly and in a capacity that [would] ensure the safety of civilians
. . ."[45] Senate Resolution 207 resolved that the Senate do the following:

1) Deplore the brutal and systematic massacre of civilians and individuals sympathetic to the political opposition in Rwanda by the Rwandan military and
   associated groups;
2) Urges the United Nations and the Organization of African Unity to continue
   efforts to broker a cease-fire;
3) Calls on all parties . . . to exercise restraint, accede to an immediate and un-
   conditional ceasefire, ensure the safety of innocent civilians, and recommit
   to the Arusha Accords;
4) Calls on the United Nations to consider carefully both military and diplomatic options which are consistent with the Arusha Accords; and
5) Urges President Clinton to continue diplomatic efforts at the highest levels
   to achieve prompt resolution of the political and humanitarian crisis in
   Rwanda.[46]

While the April 26 Senate Resolution 207 sat, those in Congress who were
interested in stirring interest in Rwanda banded together. According to the
Chairman of the Sub-committee on African Affairs Paul Simon, the committee began receiving news and intelligence reports about "these people being
slaughtered in Rwanda and it seemed to me to be the fundamental solution to
try and stop it."[47] Alison Des Forges, who had been briefing Simon on
Rwanda asked General Dallaire if he would call Senator Simon. According to
Des Forges, Dallaire explained that as a UN official he could not call a U.S.
senator. Des Forges recalls asking Dallaire if he would receive a phone call
from the Senator, to which he responded that he would. Following their discussion, Des Forges contacted Senior Director for Africa at the White House
Donald Steinberg and asked him to get Senator Simon Dallaire's telephone
number.[48] After receiving the General's number from his staff, Simon remembers being concerned that it would not be possible to get through to him
amidst the chaos. On May 13, Simon solicited the partnership of Senator
James Jeffords and telephoned General Dallaire in order to find out how the
killings could be stopped. According to Simon, Dallaire described the situation and said, "It is going to get much worse and we are only in the beginning
stages and if I can get 5,000 to 8000 troops right away we can get a stop to
it." Dallaire informed Simon and Jeffords "he was under UN orders not to intervene and that this created a major strain on his operation." Simon told General Dallaire that he would "do [his] best to see that we got some action but
did not give him any specifics about what [he] could have done to help."[49]

In response to their conversation with General Dallaire, Senators Simon
and Jeffords decided to write a letter to President Clinton suggesting that the

U.S. take action in Rwanda. In the letter, they suggested that the U.S. "send a signal to the present government . . . that a government which does not strive to halt the civil war, eliminate the massacres . . . will not receive assistance from the United States." The letter continued by demanding a reinforcement of UNAMIR, an arms embargo, financial and logistical support, and assurance that there would be no delay in taking action.[50] However, the fact that Senators Simon and Jeffords were referring to the conflict in Rwanda as a civil war as late as mid-May, still indicated a lack of understanding. At this late stage, most government officials who followed Africa in any capacity knew that the violence in Rwanda was something other than a civil war.

After ten days without a response from the White House, Senator Simon attempted to phone National Security Advisor Anthony Lake, but due to Lake's unavailability he spoke with Deputy National Security Advisor Sandy Berger who explained that "there was no public support for U.S. participation in such an operation." On June 9, after 27 days without a response, President Clinton responded to Senator Simon and agreed that some action needed to be taken.[51]

Senator Simon worked with Senator Jeffords to try and pass a resolution through the congressional floor condemning the violence in Rwanda and establishing pressure on the administration to act. However, Senator Simon recalls, "The problem in Congress is not opposition in helping Africa, it is just plain indifference. Resolutions regarding Africa move very slowly through the process. We had to overcome indifference on the floor and at the White House." In addition to indifference at the government level, Senator Simon explains that the lack of media attention also prevented him from taking major action on Rwanda. True there were a few stories in *Time* and *Newsweek*, but these were not the graphic images that covered the pages of magazines during the Somalia famine of the early 1990s. He thought about the possibility of calling a press conference on Rwanda, but after seeing George Mitchell return from settling the Irish question to a press conference of one TV camera, Simon feared that the media would be a "no show."[52] Senator Simon "regrets not even trying," but also recognizes that, "At that point you are in the Senate and there are other issues and it is difficult to justify taking up time on the floor over the issue of Rwanda when there are pressing domestic issues."[53]

Throughout the period of the genocide various officials in the bureaucracy were called before Congress to testify on the issue of Rwanda. On one occasion, Prudence Bushnell recalls receiving a barrage of criticism from Congressman Donald Payne who, according to Bushnell, told her that she was not doing enough to push for action in Rwanda. Bushnell, shocked by his criticism, recalls looking at him and saying, "Congressman Payne, not doing enough? I am doing all that I can." Congressman Payne then clarified for

Bushnell that he did not intend to single her out, but viewed her as a representative of the State Department.[54] However, while there were sporadic Congressional questions regarding inaction in Rwanda, these instances of interest never involved more than a small contingent of Congressmen and were usually reserved for members of the Foreign Relations Committee or the Subcommittee on Africa.

Recalling that the first mention of Rwanda in a Congressional context took place on April 26 in reference to Senate Resolution 207, the next recorded discussion about Rwanda on the Congressional floor did not take place until June 8. At this late stage, when it had already been reported that hundreds of thousands of people were massacred, Senator David Durenberger stood before the Senate to discuss "the international community's failure in Rwanda."[55] He expressed great concern "that we have not acted more quickly" and concluded that, "Our present inaction is the direct result of the leadership vacuum that exists at the White House—a vacuum that is mirrored at the Department of State and at the National Security Council." Disturbed by the indifference of the Clinton administration, Senator Durenberger continued by asserting that, "Instead of being a moral voice rallying support for the thousands of refugees—or speaking up in righteous wrath against the genocide—the United States has been paralyzed by the same malaise that has caused the Europeans and other nations to refuse to provide direct support to stop the bloodshed."[56]

On June 10, Senator Daniel Moynihan, who had served as both the U.S. Ambassador to the UN and the President of the Security Council, spoke before the Senate about "[stopping] the genocide in Rwanda." Moynihan stated, "I am not aware of anyone who actually disputes the conclusion that this is, in fact, genocide." He continued by demanding that, "We must act so that those who would undertake genocide in Rwanda, to commit ethnic cleansing in Bosnia, to use systematic rape as a weapon of war anywhere do have a concern for the opinion of the world. How the world responds to genocide in Rwanda will perforce be a precedent." Senator Moynihan called upon Congress to "provide the funds that are required to participate effectively."[57] On June 13, Congressmen Hastings introduced House Resolution 453, which resolved that the House of Representatives do the following:

1) Strongly condemns the atrocities being carried out in Rwanda
2) The House of Representatives calls such atrocities [in Rwanda] genocide[58]

On June 16, Senator Pell stood before the Senate and explained why the killings in Rwanda could only be described as genocide, arguing that, "the attacks against Rwandan civilians easily fit the provisions of the Genocide

Convention."[59] On July 22, Senator Ted Kennedy supported the Congressional pressure placed on the Clinton administration to "move with urgency to get UNAMIR forces in the country to help stabilize the situation."[60] Five days later, Senator Moynihan reinforced his original position and issues a similar statement that, "Without further delay, the UN peacekeeping force in Rwanda known as UNAMIR needs to become fully operational."[61]

Throughout the Rwanda genocide, Congress convinced the bureaucracy and the White House that intervention in Rwanda was financially impossible. The Republicans in the Senate, led by Minority leader Bob Dole adamantly opposed peacekeeping after Somalia, and on one occasion in early August 1994, one month after the genocide had ended, the Republican Senator from South Dakota Larry Pressler asked the question, "Remember Somalia? Will Haiti or Rwanda be next? This cannot continue." Pressler continued by stating, "I am tired of policies that say one thing and actions which practice something else . . . Will the President stand firm and adhere to policies outlined both in the recently signed Foreign Relations Authorization Act and the recently endorsed administration decision directive on reforming multilateral peace operations? Already, President Clinton has failed the first test of resolve."[62] While policymakers were beginning to realize the consequences of watching 800,000 deaths take place in Rwanda between April and July, Senator Pressler was for the first time articulating the need to take an even stronger position of no intervention in Rwanda.

THE RETURN OF UNAMIR

Given the earlier rejection by policymakers of any of the discussed interventions, what led to the eventual U.S. decision to support a reinforcement of UNAMIR in the late stages of the genocide? UNAMIR suffered from a lack of equipment, funds, and supplies necessary to carry out its mission in Rwanda. The UN troops ran out of medical supplies, ammunition, and even batteries. The machinery was inadequate and out of the 300 vehicles donated to UNAMIR, only eight functioned.[63] There was a serious shortage of food, insufficient drinking water, a lack of fuel for the functioning vehicles, and UNAMIR did not have an ambulance to attend to its own forces.[64] By the second week of May, the UN began to consider the possibility of reinforcing the UN presence in Rwanda. Advocates of a reinforcement proposed a UN "non-paper on Rwanda"[65] asking for an "expanded UNAMIR force of at least 5,500 troops based in Kigali with a mandate to provide security for displaced persons in various parts of Rwanda and to assist in the provision of humanitarian services to them."[66] The United States expressed great concern over a

UN reinforcement in Rwanda "while a civil war and heavy fighting are raging in and around that city and its airport."[67] American policymakers feared that sending a second UNAMIR force into Kigali without a chapter VII mandate posed a grave threat to the troops "given the interim government's lack of command and control over renegade army units and extremist militias." The United States did not want to risk another massacre of UN troops like those of the Americans in Somalia and the Belgians in Rwanda. Furthermore, the United States feared that the difficulty the UN would confront in airlifting troops, supplies, and equipment into Kigali would require American assistance and thus, increase the role of the United States.[68]

On April 29, UNHCR reported that more than 250,000 refugees had fled from Rwanda into western Tanzania and this mass exodus resulted in a revitalization of discussions concerning a reinforced UN deployment in Rwanda. The United States and the United Kingdom were adamantly opposed to this plan of action. Consultant for Human Rights Watch Alison Des Forges explains that on April 30 Security Council President Colin Keating threatened the United States and the United Kingdom with the possibility of declaring the meeting "open," revealing the callous attitudes of both superpowers. Ultimately, Keating prevailed and Des Forges recalls receiving a phone call that night from the Czech delegate in which he explained "we have won, we are going to have a new force." The next morning, Des Forges received a phone call explaining that the force was no longer going to happen. After asking the Czech delegate why, he responded with information that the RPF opposed the force. Des Forges was surprised and recalls thinking that this was impossible, but after phoning her RPF contact in Brussels she learned that the RPF believed the genocide was over. The next day, the RPF came out with a press release relaying the same information and explaining that if an international force enters Rwanda it will be engaged as if it were the enemy.[69]

With the commitment of a force averted, Under Secretary of State for Political Affairs Peter Tarnoff and the Director of the Joint Staff, cabled the U.S. mission to the UN on May 13 with the suggestion that they should propose safe havens as an alternative to the reinforcement of UNAMIR. Rather than using additional forces to secure Kigali, the United States proposed "the possibility of using an expanded force to create one or more secure zones in Rwanda along the border for the protection of refugees and delivery of humanitarian relief to them."[70] U.S. officials argued that an expanded force could also "provide an environment conducive to refugee repatriation and could serve in a preventive capacity to deter the spread of violence to neighboring countries."[71] Ambassador Albright brought this suggestion before the Security Council, but in the end was convinced to approve the reinforcement of UNAMIR.

On May 17, after a heated debate in the Security Council and despite initial opposition from the United States, the UN passed Resolution 918, calling for an arms embargo on Rwanda, the deployment of 5,500 UNAMIR II troops, and a Secretary General's report on human rights abuses in Rwanda.[72] The United States supported the embargo because it did not require logistical or financial support, but the U.S. did "not envision [that] it [would] have a significant impact on the killings because machetes, knives and other hand implements [were] the most common weapons" used by the genocidaires.[73]

While the embargo was relatively easy to implement, soliciting member states to deploy troops under UNAMIR II proved more difficult than the Security Council had anticipated. The Nigerians suggested using African troops to reinforce the UN mission and asked western powers to contribute equipment for an African-led force. However, according to Bruce Jones, "interviews with U.S. officials about their reasons for not responding positively to Nigerian proposals to use U.S. equipment to protect African peacekeepers revealed attitudes of callousness and indifference."[74] The initial deployment of UNAMIR II troops was slower than either the United States or the UN would have liked. Director for African Affairs at the Pentagon Vince Kern explains that "We were trying to get the UN to move faster than it was on getting forces out there. We decided at an interagency meeting to divvy up the responsibility for troop contributing countries among western donor countries and call it 'adopt a battalion.'"[75] Kern recalls that he "always hated the term adopt a battalion because it sounded paternalistic, but he didn't fight it because he liked the idea, and if the feeling of adopting would make western powers act more than a word like 'assisting', he was not going to stand in the way of those forces getting to people in Rwanda."[76]

Despite the introduction of the "adopt a battalion" idea, bureaucratic infighting in the U.S. government and between the United States and the UN over issues related to equipment, specifically armored personnel carriers (APCs) delayed the deployment of UNAMIR II.[77] In particular, the State Department and the Pentagon clashed over this issue of the APCs. According to Deputy Assistant Secretary of Defense for Peacekeeping Sarah Sewall, "It is almost embarrassing to explain something that is so difficult and ought to be so simple. State couldn't believe how long this was taking." The Pentagon explained to the State Department that the delays resulted from Congressional pressure over the issue of reimbursement. "Congress did not like that the U.S. was supplying people or supplies to UN" and used recently passed legislation as a way of preventing excessive commitment of equipment. State kept proposing various ways for the Pentagon to speed up the process and send the APCs, and in each instance, the Pentagon "faced opposition from defense proprietors and Congress about funds and reimbursement." Sewall remembers that the State Department proposed "all kinds of ways to get support of the equipment, but their feuding with the Pentagon revealed its inability to understand the restrictions that Congress had placed on the Pentagon."[78]

After almost two weeks of debate, the United States informed the Security Council on May 28 that they would be willing to lease [50] APCs to the UN for $4 million and informed the Security Council that the transportation would take no more than two weeks.[79] The bureaucratic delay of the APC delivery to Rwanda embarrassed the United States, but in actuality it revealed more about the bureaucratic flaws of the United Nations. As the UN began to deploy UNAMIR II, Boutros Ghali kept making statements in the *New York Times* and elsewhere saying that the delays were a result of the United States being slow in providing APCs. In actuality, it was the UN's bureaucratic nature and actions that led to the slow pace in providing the APCs.

The APCs that the UN wanted were MI-113s (tracked APCs) because that was the equipment they were used to using. According to Director for African Affairs at the Pentagon, the UN's attitude was that "we have done it this way before, we want to do it again, so we want MI-113s." Kern explains that if MI-113s were the only possibility, the Pentagon would have said "it is not the best kind of equipment, but if it is the best we can do and if that is what the UN wants, the U.S. can provide it." However, this was not the case. The UN already had an offer from the South Africans for Mambas (wheeled APCs). The Mambas were a much better APC for the conditions in Rwanda because it was a wheeled APC, because it was mine-resistant, and because it had been prepared for the rough conditions in Africa.[80] Deputy Assistant Secretary of Defense for Peacekeeping Sarah Sewall favored the Mamba option because the MI-113s "would have eaten up the roads, which were the one good thing that they had." Having traveled to Rwanda, Sewall was uncomfortable with this request and she tried to explain that the mission and the country would benefit from APCs with wheels rather than tracks and as a result, the delays persisted. Kern explains that the roads were not the only issue because "if it was between saving a life or a road, the Pentagon would have chosen to save a life." Kern explains that it was a matter of the Mamba being a more appropriate vehicle and the fact that the United States was pleased to see South Africa get involved in peacekeeping because they had the best and largest army in Africa, they had never been involved in peacekeeping before, and the fact that the apartheid regime had fallen meant that the United States was now willing to work with the South Africans. Kern argues that the United States completely favored this idea and if anybody was reluctant about South African involvement in peacekeeping it was the South Africans. He suggested that they were reluctant to be seen as the "big kid on the block" by other Africans, or even worse be seen by other Africans as a "puppet state of the U.S." However, the South Africans embraced the donation of Mambas because it was a way for them to get involved in peacekeeping without committing troops. Because it was steadfast in only using the APCs it was accustomed to using, the UN rejected this offer and was persistent in its request for the MI-113s.[81]

After a great deal of debate in New York, the United States agreed to sell the UN MI-113s. However, the UN did not want to buy the APCs, they just wanted to lease them. This created an entirely new bureaucratic delay as the Pentagon then had to draw up a lease agreement through the Defense Security Assistance Agency (DSAA). Vince Kern recalls that he "moved heaven and earth to expedite a two week process in a matter of days because he wanted to get those APCs out there and get those UNAMIR II troops deployed." Kern remembers that they got the draft from the DSAA on either a Tuesday or a Wednesday [June 3] and the UN said that it would not be able to review the lease until that following Monday [June 7] when the lease committee usually meets. This frustrated officials at the Pentagon because while Boutros-Ghali was accusing the U.S. of being slow in providing APCs, the UN was unable to meet outside of their normal schedule. This delayed the APC delivery an additional week.[82]

Once the UN signed the lease, the United States located American-owned MI-113s in Germany that could be used in Rwanda. There were some UN-owned APCs nearby in Somalia, but they were needed for the mission in Mogadishu. Vince Kern recalls that the United States had the MI-113s loaded onto C-130 cargo planes in Germany and just as they were ready to begin the delivery, the UN explained that the MI-113s needed to be painted white instead of the green and olive U.S. army colors. Kern remembers that they then had to unload all of the APCs, paint them, wait for them to dry, and then reload them back onto the airplane. This contributed to several more days of delay. Once the APCs dried and were reloaded, the cargo plane delivered them to Entebbe, Uganda. However, when they arrived in Entebbe, Kern recalls that the UN representative on the ground refused to accept them. The UN representative stated that nobody in New York had authorized him to accept the APCs. Kern remembers the frustration that the United States was there with a UN cargo plane on the ground and the MI-113s were ready to offload, but because the UN representative would not accept them, they remained on the airplane.[83] Shortly after the cargo plane arrived, a U.S. defense attaché who had been posted in Malawi arrived in Kampala to receive the APCs and help facilitate their delivery to Rwanda. This defense attaché took his own initiative and got the authority from Kampala to offload the APCs, take the 50 caliber machine guns off of them and store them at the U.S. embassy, and then work out a deal with the Uganda military to store the gunless APCs behind a locked fence at Entebbe airport.[84]

After a great deal of negotiation, the U.S. representatives finally convinced the UN representative on the ground that he was authorized to sign for the

APCs. However, at this point, the UN representative said that he could not permit the delivery of the APCs because he was not authorized to sign for the amount that the APCs would cost. Vince Kern remembers relaying the message that he could break up the dollar amount by signing numerous contracts each for a smaller sum of money. In addition to the delays caused by the contracts, the roads also presented an additional problem. In order for the APCs to be used effectively they needed to be transported from Uganda to Rwanda. However, the MI-113s could not be driven all the way from Entebbe to Rwanda because, unlike the Mambas, they were tracked and would have destroyed every road in Uganda and Rwanda. Instead, the MI-113s had to be loaded onto trucks. This problem took several weeks to resolve and even weeks after the genocide, the MI-113s still remained at Entebbe airport.[85]

Vince Kern recalls that when he accompanied Secretary of Defense William Perry to Rwanda and Eastern Congo shortly after the genocide ended, their plane arrived in Entebbe where the APCs still remained. When the Secretary and his entourage arrived in Entebbe they flew by C-130 to Goma and then returned. However, when they returned, Ugandan President Yoweri Museveni requested a meeting with Secretary Perry. In order to get to Kampala, the Secretary and his convoy had to drive twenty to thirty minutes from Entebbe to Kampala. Kern remembers that on their way to Kampala, he and Under Secretary of Defense Slocombe were in the second car behind the Secretary and as they drove out of the airport, Kern said to Slocombe "Walt, don't look to the left because if you do, you will still see all those APCs that still haven't been delivered." Kern recalls Slocombe saying "no I don't want to look," as if he was in disbelief that they still had not been delivered after all their hard work in Washington to speed up the delivery.[86]

Following the eventual delivery of the APCs in early August, the first UNAMIR II troops arrived in Rwanda on August 10, almost one month after the genocide had ended. By the time the APCs arrived in Rwanda, disorganization and a lack of planning led to them being misused. Sewall recalls rumors circulating throughout the Pentagon and the State Department that because the UN troops never learned how to operate the APCs, they were actually being used by the Ghanaian UN troops as chicken coops instead of transportation units.[87]

THE REGIONAL SPREAD OF THE CONFLICT AND CHOLERA IN THE CONGO

By July 14, ten days after the genocide ended, the United States revisited the proposal for an airlift that they had denied in mid-May. At this time, one million refugees fled from Gisenyi, Rwanda into Goma, Zaire over the span of just two days. The unprecedented flood of refugees into Zaire, along with a cholera epidemic that claimed [5,000] lives a day, led the United States to consider a small-scale intervention that it had so strategically avoided during the genocide.[88] It took three months of genocide, unprecedented refugee migration, and cholera epidemic for the U.S. government to launch an intervention on the ground in the Great Lakes Region. Secretary of State Warren Christopher in his memoirs, *In the Stream of History: Shaping Foreign Policy for a New Era,* recalls:

> Because [the refugee camps in Zaire] lacked adequate food and clean water, starvation and cholera were rampant, and the death toll reached over 5,000 refugees per day. Although earlier in the year the Administration had judged that our European partners with long involvement in the region should take the lead in the Rwandan peacekeeping effort, we now felt compelled to act.[89]

In response to the cholera outbreak, Secretary of Defense William Perry approached President Clinton and explained, "We had the facilities, the engineers, the equipment, and the transport to get over to the refugee camps in just a few days to be up and operating and stop the cholera."[90] Perry explained that the million refugees were all drinking water from the contaminated lake and a water sanitation crew equipped with purification equipment could save hundreds of thousands of lives. In an effort to rebuff concerns the President may have about sending Americans into eastern Zaire, Secretary Perry informed him that, "The scale of a million people presented a serious logistical problem and the US was the only country in the world that had the equipment and the transfer ability to end the epidemic."[91] Perry also explained to the President that he would need "a few hundred army people to reopen Kigali airport, secure the area, and truck the sanitation team over to Zaire where the camps were." Anthony Lake, who was privy to these discussions was fully behind the effort and even played a significant role in orchestrating the Goma operation.

According to Perry, President Clinton expressed concern over the protection of those 200 sanitation specialists, whom Perry assured him would be protected by small arms. With the promise of protection from General Paul Kagame and assurance that the security situation in Rwanda had calmed, President Clinton gave Secretary of Defense Perry the authorization to send four planes to Kigali. Secretary of Defense Perry recalls "[getting] a firestorm from Congress about sending those 200 soldiers over there," but he testified before the Congressional floor that this was "not a long-term commitment, the job could be done in a matter of weeks, and the safety of the team could be guaranteed."[92] Secretary of Defense Perry remembers that he was enough concerned about the cholera epidemic that he decided to accompany the mission to Central Africa.

At this time, Chairman of the Joint Chiefs of Staff General John Shalikashvili called General Joulwan at U.S. European Command and informed him that the "President was going to give the Executive Order to go to Rwanda and stop the dying." General Joulwan recalls asking General Shalikashivili "How much time do I have? I need to put a joint task force headquarters together and that may take a week." The Chairman responded by relaying a direct order from the Oval Office: "The President wants you to deploy tomorrow." Ignoring the difficulty of an apparent unrealistic time frame of the order, General Joulwan acted immediately. He sent a reserve Colonel from EUCOM and a small plane with an assessment team of six men. Joulwan recalls getting a phone call shortly after the Colonel arrived in Goma in which he pleaded with the General, "Sir, you have to do something; the roads are stacked with bodies and there are so many of them that it is actually blocking the road from the airport to the city."[93]

The assessment team immediately determined that there was a cholera outbreak caused by the polluted water in Lake Kivu. At this time, General Joulwan requested that Secretary Perry make a stop in Brussels on his way back from the Middle East to be briefed on a plan of action in Goma. Joulwan recalls asking the Secretary, "what is my mission? Do you want me to take on rebels? Is it humanitarian?" According to Joulwan, the Secretary responded with "5–6,000 people are dying a day, let's get the water purified." Joulwan heard the order loud and clear and remembers writing on a board "stop the dying" and sharing that with the staff at the European Command headquarters.

It was at this time that the decision was made for Secretary Perry to personally accompany the inauguration of the mission. Security was a major issue and arranging the necessary precautions was a logistical undertaking, but in the end the Secretary made the trip. When Perry's C-130 arrived into Kigali International Airport, RPF General Paul Kagame approached the American Secretary of Defense and said, "I am General Kagame and I will see to your safety while you are here."[94]

The mission, which eventually consisted of 2,000 troops to aid the refugees in Goma and end the cholera epidemic, found great success and the cholera stopped "basically over night."[95] The sanitation team left after two or three weeks and equipped the NGOs to take over the operation upon their departure. From this small scale intervention, Secretary of Defense Perry realized the "effect that a relatively small American contingent could have, how much respect they got, and how much influence they had." True, the resistance Perry faced from Congress over this "minor operation" reassured him that "the earlier judgment that [the U.S. government] would not get support for a military operation from Congress was absolutely right." However, as Secretary of Defense Perry recalls, the small-scale operation in Goma revealed that, "Had we been willing, had we had the political support, we probably could have sent a force in. It is true that we did not have the logistics in that location to get a Bosnia size force, but it could well be that a brigade or even a lightly armed battalion, [simply by being American] may have been the psychological difference stopping the conflict."[96]

According to General Joulwan, the true hero in the swift combatting of the cholera epidemic was a fireman in blue overalls from San Francisco. General Joulwan remembers:

> When we finally got the water purification teams into Goma it was a truly remarkable sight. This "Red" Adair-type civilian fireman, who was an expert with water, had come in from San Francisco with some fire engines. I was standing there with this civilian, dressed in his blue overalls. He was in his late sixties or early seventies, and we were talking about what they had done. I remember I put my arm around him as I watched hoses going in all directions from these red fire trucks and I asked 'how did you do all this?' He said to me, "General, me and the Major worked that out, we are Americans and we know how to get things done." They had a mission and they did it. It was a magnificent thing to see. Here we were in Goma and hoses from the British, French, and other nationalities had all been hooked into the U.S. Army and fire truck system. It was just something you don't forget.[97]

IT'S TOO LITTLE, TOO LATE

By the time the United States sat down to discuss possible interventions in mid-May, the Rwanda Patriotic Front (RPF) had become frustrated with the international community's policy toward Rwanda. The French assisted the Rwanda government, the Belgians led a withdrawal of UNAMIR troops, and the United States refused to call the conflict in Rwanda a genocide. On May 13, 1994 RPF spokesman Denis Polisi announced to BBC that, "Should the UN force come in between the two warring sides then it will be treated as an enemy force and will be engaged."[98] Reflecting on this statement, Polisi explains, "We understood that we had to act on our own and try to stop the genocide, but around 12 and 13 May the better part of the genocide was already done. We believed that they would be coming between the two forces and it was clear that they were protecting the Genocidaires."[99] The RPF was very suspicious of the U.S. and the international community's interests in intervening during the month of May. They did not trust an intervention led by nations that "removed their forces in April and then wanted to intervene in the middle of the genocide." RPF officials believed that this was an indication that the international community still did not understand the nature of the violence in Rwanda. By mid-May, the RPF and the Rwandan Armed Forces (FAR) fought in the cities while the genocide continued "in the back, in the villages, the hills, and the areas of marginal symbolic importance."[100] The RPF understood that the FAR intended to stop the RPF from halting the genocide, and they feared that the engagement of the international community could jeopardize the RPF victory as they claim it had during the Arusha Peace Process.

NOTES

1. Personal Interview, Former Under Secretary of Defense for Policy Walt Slocombe, Via phone to Washington, DC, February 7, 2004.

2. Ibid

3. Ibid.

4. Ibid.

5. Personal Interview, Former National Security Advisor Anthony Lake, Washington, DC, November 20, 2002.

6. Personal Interview, Former White House Official [A], Washington, DC, November 21, 2002.

7. Personal Interview, Former National Security Advisor Anthony Lake, Washington, DC, November 20, 2002.

8. Press Release, Office of the Press Secretary, the White House, "Statement by the Press Secretary", April 22, 1994. Non-classified, in William Ferroggiaro, *A National Security Archive Briefing Book,* August 20, 2001, found in http://www.gwu.edu/~nsarchiv/NSAEBB/NSAEBB53/press.html.

9. See Michael Barnett, *Eyewitness to a Genocide,* pp. 145–7.

10. Linda Melvern, *A People Betrayed: The Role of the West in Rwanda's Genocide,* p. 199.

11. White House briefing, Federal News Service, July 15, 1994, in Samantha Power, *"A Problem From Hell:" America and the Age of Genocide,* p. 381.

12. Discussion Paper, Office of the Deputy Assistant Secretary of Defense for Middle East/Africa Region, Department of Defense, May 1, 1994. Secret, in William Ferroggiaro, *A National Security Archive Briefing Book,* August 20, 2001, found in http://www.gwu.edu/~nsarchiv/NSAEBB/NSAEBB53/press.html.

13. Personal Interview, Former White House Official [A], Washington, DC, November 21, 2002.

14. John Shattuck, Chapter 1 in unpublished book, expected date of publication September 1, 2003; cited with permission of the author.

15. Personal Interview, Former Deputy Assistant Secretary of Defense for Peacekeeping and Humanitarian Affairs Sarah Sewall, Via phone to Boston, MA, February 13, 2003.

16. Personal Interview, Former White House Official [A], Washington, DC, November 21, 2002, confirmed in Personal Interview, Former National Security Advisor Anthony Lake, Washington, DC, November 20, 2002.

17. Ibid.

18. This reluctance was based on skepticism about a unilateral French intervention in Rwanda.

19. A Chapter VII mandate permits the use of force to implement a mandate. Under the auspices of a Chapter VII mandate, UN troops can use firepower to maintain order or keep the peace. The parenthetic use of Chapter VII in this context implies that a Chapter VII mandate would be needed to "stop the killing." The parentheses in this quote were written into the document and are not the addition of the author.

20. Confidential International Security Affairs Briefing, "Rwanda Interagency Telecon," drafted by LtCol Harvin, May 9, 1994. Declassified by Director, Africa Region, Office of the Secretary of Defense. Secret. This document was declassified by Will Ferrogiaro, but was personally retrieved by the author from the Pentagon Freedom of Information Act Office. This memo was written in response to an options paper circulated by the State Department over the previous weekend, within which State presented the option of a robust force on the ground.

21. Secret International Security Affairs Briefing, "Rwanda Interagency Telecon," drafted by LtCol Harvin, May 11, 1994. Declassified by Director, Africa Region, Office of the Secretary of Defense. Secret. This document was declassified by Will Ferrogiaro, but was personally retrieved by the author from the Pentagon Freedom of Information Act Office.

22. Unlike a Chapter VII mandate, a Chapter VI mandate does not permit the use of force to maintain order or enforce peace.

23. Secret International Security Affairs Briefing, "Rwanda Interagency Telecon," drafted by LtCol Harvin, May 11, 1994. Declassified by Director, Africa Region, Office of the Secretary of Defense. Secret. This document was declassified by Will Ferrogiaro, but was personally retrieved by the author from the Pentagon Freedom of Information Act Office.

24. Secret International Security Affairs Briefing, "Rwanda Interagency Telecon," drafted by LtCol Harvin, May 12, 1994. Declassified by Director, Africa Region, Office of the Secretary of Defense. This document was declassified by Will Ferrogiaro, but was personally retrieved by the author from the Pentagon Freedom of Information Act Office.

25. Bruce Jones, *Peacemaking in Rwanda,* p. 122.

26. Memorandum to Secretary of Defense and Deputy Secretary of Defense from Principal Under Secretary of Defense for Policy Walter Slocombe, Subject: "Rwanda Update," 16 May 1994. Secret. Declassified by authority of: OSD, 18 November 1998, Case #: 95-F-0894. This document was declassified by Will Ferrogiaro, but was personally retrieved by the author from the Pentagon Freedom of Information Act Office.

27. Personal Interview, Alison Des Forges, Via e-mail to Buffalo, NY, May 18, 2002.

28. Samantha Power, *"A Problem From Hell:" America and the Age of Genocide,* p. 371.

29. Personal Interview, Former Director for African Affairs and Head of the Rwanda Task Force at the Pentagon, Vince Kern, Alexandria, VA, August 15, 2003.

30. Proposals to jam the hate radio began in late April and became more frequent by early May.

31. Personal Interview, Former Director for African Affairs and Head of the Rwanda Task Force at the Pentagon, Vince Kern, Alexandria, VA, August 15, 2003.

32. Personal Interview, RPF Director of Intelligence Major General Kayumba Nyamwasa, Kigali, Rwanda, December 18, 2002; see also, Alan Kuperman, *The Limits of Humanitarian Intervention,* Washington DC: The Brookings Institution, 2001.

33. Discussion Paper, Office of the Deputy Assistant Secretary of Defense for Middle East/Africa Region, Department of Defense, May 1, 1994. Secret, in William Ferroggiaro, *A National Security Archive Briefing Book,* August 20, 2001, found in http://www.gwu.edu/~nsarchiv/NSAEBB/NSAEBB53/press.html.

34. Ibid.

35. Personal Interview, Former Secretary of Defense Dr. William Perry, Stanford, CA, February 10, 2003.

36. Ibid.

37. Memorandum from Under Secretary of Defense for Policy to Deputy Assistant to the President for National Security, National Security Council, "Rwanda: Jamming Civilian Radio Broadcasts," May 5, 1994. Confidential, in William Ferroggiaro, *A National Security Archive Briefing Book,* August 20, 2001, found in http://www.gwu.edu/~nsarchiv/NSAEBB/NSAEBB53/press.html.

38. Memorandum from Under Secretary of Defense for Policy to Deputy Assistant to the President for National Security, National Security Council, "Rwanda: Jamming Civilian Radio Broadcasts," May 5, 1994. Confidential, in William Ferroggiaro, *A National Security Archive Briefing Book,* August 20, 2001, found in http://www.gwu.edu/~nsarchiv/NSAEBB/NSAEBB53/press.html.

39. Ibid.

40. Personal Interview, Former Director for African Affairs and Head of the Rwanda Task Force at the Pentagon, Vince Kern, Alexandria, VA, August 15, 2003.

41. Personal Interview, Former Director for African Affairs and Head of the Rwanda Task Force at the Pentagon, Vince Kern, Alexandria, VA, August 15, 2003.

42. Personal Interview, Deputy Assistant Secretary of State for African Affairs Prudence Bushnell, Washington, DC, December 9, 2002.

43. Personal Interview, Former Director for African Affairs and Head of the Rwanda Task Force at the Pentagon, Vince Kern, Alexandria, VA, August 15, 2003.

44. Congressional Record: April 26, 1994, in the Congressional Record Online via GPO Access [wais.access.gpo.gov]

45. Congressional Record: April 26, 1994, in the Congressional Record Online via GPO Access [wais.access.gpo.gov]

46. S. Res. 207, 103rd Congress, 2nd Session.

47. Personal Interview, United States Senator Paul Simon, Via telephone to Illinois, December 9, 2002.

48. Personal Interview, Human Rights Consultant Alison Des Forges, Via telephone to Buffalo, NY, October 22, 2003.

49. Ibid.

50. Congressional Record: June 10, 1994, in the Congressional Record Online via GPO Access [wais.access.gpo.gov]

51. Linda Melvern, *A People Betrayed: The Role of the West in Rwanda's Genocide*, p. 346. Confirmed in personal interview, Senator Paul Simon, Via telephone to Illinois, December 9, 2002.

52. Personal Interview, Former Senator Paul Simon, Via telephone to Illinois, December 9, 2002.

53. Ibid.

54. Personal Interview, Former Deputy Assistant Secretary of State for African Affairs Prudence Bushnell, Washington, DC, December 9, 2002.

55. Congressional Record: June 8, 1994, in the Congressional Record Online via GPO Access [wais.access.gpo.gov]

56. Congressional Record: June 8, 1994, in the Congressional Record Online via GPO Access [wais.access.gpo.gov]

57. Ibid.

58. H. Res. 453, 103rd Congress, 2nd Session.

59. Congressional Record: June 16, 1994, "The Genocide in Rwanda," in the Congressional Record Online via GPO Access [wais.access.gpo.gov]

60. Congressional Record: July 22, 1994, "The Massive Human Rights Tragedy in Rwanda, in the Congressional Record Online via GPO Access [wais.access .gpo.gov]

61. Congressional Record: July 27, 1994, "The Crisis in Rwanda," in the Congressional Record Online via GPO Access [wais.access.gpo.gov]

62. Congressional Record: August 11, 1994, "Flipping the U.N. Peacekeeping Coin: U.S. Participation in Multilateral Operations," in the Congressional Record Online via GPO Access [wais.access.gpo.gov]

63. Samantha Power, *"A Problem From Hell:" America and the Age of Genocide*, p. 342.

64. Michael Barnett, *Eyewitness to a Genocide*, p. 117.

65. A non-paper is a detailed memorandum.

66. U.S. Department of State, cable number 127262, to U.S. Mission to the United Nations, New York, "Rwanda: Security Council Discussions", May 13, 1994. Confidential, in William Ferroggiaro, *A National Security Archive Briefing Book,* August 20, 2001, found in http://www.gwu.edu/~nsarchiv/NSAEBB/NSAEBB53/press.html.

67. Despite the fact that the State Department received reports that hundreds of thousands of deaths had taken place by late April, many in Washington still continued to view the conflict in Rwanda as a civil war. This was in part a way for them to justify a continued pursuit of restoring the Arusha Peace Process.

68. U.S. Department of State, cable number 127262, to U.S. Mission to the United Nations, New York, "Rwanda: Security Council Discussions", May 13, 1994. Confidential, in William Ferroggiaro, *A National Security Archive Briefing Book,* August 20, 2001, found in http://www.gwu.edu/~nsarchiv/NSAEBB/NSAEBB53/press.html.

69. Personal Interview, Consultant for Human Rights Watch Alison Des Forges, Via telephone to Buffalo, NY, October 6, 2003.

70. U.S. Department of State, cable number 127262, to U.S. Mission to the United Nations, New York, "Rwanda: Security Council Discussions", May 13, 1994. Confidential, in William Ferroggiaro, *A National Security Archive Briefing Book,* August 20, 2001, found in http://www.gwu.edu/~nsarchiv/NSAEBB/NSAEBB53/press.html.

71. Ibid.

72. Michael Barnett, *Eyewitness to a Genocide,* p. 142.

73. Discussion Paper, Office of the Deputy Assistant Secretary of Defense for Middle East/Africa Region, Department of Defense, May 1, 1994. Secret, in William Ferroggiaro, *A National Security Archive Briefing Book,* August 20, 2001, found in http://www.gwu.edu/~nsarchiv/NSAEBB/NSAEBB53/press.html.

74. U.S. Department of State, confidential Bruce Jones interviews, June 1995; also, notes, U.S. Department of State, Astri Suhrke interviews, Washington, DC, June and July 1995, in Bruce Jones, *Peacemaking in Rwanda,* p. 123.

75. Personal Interview, Former Director for African Affairs and Head of the Rwanda Task Force at the Pentagon, Vince Kern, Alexandria, VA, August 15, 2003; see also, Joint Staff Action Processing Form to the Chairman of the Joint Staff through VCJS, DJS, and VDJS from Joint Staff J-5 CDR Casey Donlon, 13 June 1994. Secret. Declassified by authority of JCS.

76. Personal Interview, Former Director for African Affairs and Head of the Rwanda Task Force at the Pentagon, Vince Kern, Alexandria, VA, August 15, 2003.

77. In the 27 June 1994 SecDef Weekly Update on Rwanda, Secretary Perry was informed that "Support for the adopt a battalion concept is not moving. Of the likely equipment donors, the French are unwilling to lease equipment to the UN and there is only soft support in South Africa for aiding the Zimbabweans."

78. Personal Interview, Former Assistant Secretary of Defense for Peacekeeping and Humanitarian Affairs Sarah Sewall, Via telephone to Boston, MA, February 13, 2003.

79. Linda Melvern, *A People Betrayed: The Role of the West in Rwanda's Genocide,* p. 196.

80. Personal Interview, Former Director for African Affairs and Head of the Rwanda Task Force at the Pentagon, Vince Kern, Alexandria, VA, August 15, 2003. The embargo placed on South Africa during apartheid led the South African government to develop a very strong arms industry. It was one of those unintended consequences of the UN arms embargo against South Africa. When the embargo happened, South Africa said if we can't import arms, we will make our own. So they started to make their own equipment designed for Africa, particularly in Namibia and Angola.

81. Personal Interview, Former Director for African Affairs and Head of the Rwanda Task Force at the Pentagon, Vince Kern, Alexandria, VA, August 15, 2003.

82. Personal Interview, Former Director for African Affairs and Head of the Rwanda Task Force at the Pentagon, Vince Kern, Alexandria, VA, August 15, 2003; see also, SecDef Weekly Update on Rwanda, prepared by ISA/AF, 5 June 1994. Secret. Declassified by authority of: OSD, 18 November 1998, Case #: 95-F-0894.

83. Ibid.

84. Personal Interview, Former Director for African Affairs and Head of the Rwanda Task Force at the Pentagon, Vince Kern, Alexandria, VA, August 15, 2003.

85. Ibid.

86. Personal Interview, Former Director for African Affairs and Head of the Rwanda Task Force at the Pentagon, Vince Kern, Alexandria, VA, August 15, 2003.

87. Ibid.

88. Warren Christopher, in *In the Stream of History: Shaping Foreign Policy for a New Era,* argues that there were 5,000 deaths a day from cholera.

89. Warren Christopher, *In the Stream of History: Shaping Foreign Policy for a New Era,* Stanford, CA: Stanford University Press, 1998.

90. Personal Interview, Former Secretary of Defense Dr. William Perry, Stanford, CA, February 10, 2003.

91. Ibid.

92. Personal Interview, Former Secretary of Defense Dr. William Perry, Stanford, CA, February 10, 2003.

93. Personal Interview, Commander in Chief of U.S. European Command General George Joulwan, Washington, DC, September 7, 2004.

94. Ibid.

95. Ibid.

96. Personal Interview, Former Secretary of Defense Dr. William Perry, Stanford, CA, February 10, 2003.

97. Personal Interview, Commander in Chief of U.S. European Command General George Joulwan, Washington, DC, September 7, 2004.

98. Personal Interview, Former RPF Deputy Chairman and Spokesman Denis Polisi, Kigali, Rwanda, December 20, 2002.

99. Ibid.

100. Personal Interview, RPF Director of Intelligence Major General Kayumba Nyamwasa, Kigali, Rwanda, December 18, 2002.

8

Wrong Actions: What the United States Should Have Done

The intervention that eventually materialized in the form of the UN Assistance Mission for Rwanda II (UNAMIR II) was delayed by bureaucratic logistics and arrived in Rwanda too late to impact the genocide. Instead, the Rwanda Patriotic Front (RPF) was force to take matters into their own hands and expel the genocidaires from Rwanda on July 4, 1994. It took 37 days after the genocide concluded for the first UNAMIR II troops and the armored personnel carriers (APCs) to arrive in Rwanda. It would take another four months for the UN to make a decision to establish an International Criminal Tribunal for Rwanda (ICTR) in order to prosecute those responsible for the genocide.[1]

The U.S. refusal to intervene in the Rwanda genocide was blatant and obvious. While at the time many policymakers were influenced by the Somalia legacy, the marginal importance of Rwanda when compared with other pressing issues around the globe, and the varying opinions about what exactly was occurring in Rwanda, no policymaker could deny that their were hundreds of thousands of deaths taking place at a rapid pace. If one looks at the outcome of the Rwanda genocide, it is obvious that neither the United States, nor the international community wanted to intervene. However, what is even more shocking is the unwillingness to discuss Rwanda at senior levels.

FEELINGS OF REMORSE AND GUILT

Given the eventual realization that the crisis in Rwanda was genocide, the magnitude of 800,000 deaths, the horrific stories that became public, and the unprecedented refugee crisis that followed the genocide, it is not surprising that years later most policymakers are extremely apologetic and remorseful about what happened in Rwanda and the bystander role played by the United States. Assistant Secretary of State John Shattuck, who was one of the only senior officials who advocated an intervention in Rwanda, recalled that "by the time the genocide had run its course, and people had realized what a total disaster and failure it was not to do something about it, there was some degree of guilt."[2]

Despite the admissions of guilt across the U.S. government, many of these apologies are tainted with excuses and attempts to share the burden of responsibility. In an interview with PBS *Frontline* for its 1999 documentary "Triumph of Evil," State Department Political Advisor Tony Marley reflected back on the genocide by explaining,

> I think it was an enormous tragedy, preventable to some degree. I think the primary responsibility, of course, lies within the Rwandans themselves. The international community was not killing Rwandans, it was Rwandan killing Rwandan. It was a lack of political will to make the peace accord work driven by communal hatred to such a degree that neighbor turned on neighbor and would use hand tools to kill longtime neighbors and acquaintances. So I view it with a sense of tragedy, a great sense of regret.[3]

This reflection on the genocide indicates a lack of understanding that an entire ethnic group was left helpless, and Marley described the killings as if they were an inter-tribal conflict, when in actuality it was extremist Hutus intent to exterminate the Tutsis.

While most policymakers feel remorse over the failure of the United States to intervene in the Rwanda genocide, there are some who do not demonstrate this compassion. Despite formal acknowledgement that the 100 days of violence in Rwanda was a genocide, Secretary of State Warren Christopher appeared on television on July 24, 1994 and "continued to distort the reality of Rwanda" by stating "that there had been a tremendous civil war in Rwanda and that the USA had done all it could to try to support the UN, but that it was not a time for the USA to try and intervene."[4] While this does not mean that Secretary Christopher believed the genocide was actually a civil war, the carelessness of his statement reflects his attitude about Rwanda after the genocide was over. It appears that the Secretary of State was not alone in his carelessly insensitive statements after the genocide. According to Rwandan Foreign Minister Charles Murigande, Ambassador Rawson denied that a genocide occurred in Rwanda and during his return in August, he angered RPF officials with his "insensitivity and lack of compassion."[5] The persistent label of the genocide as a civil war was a particular sore spot for the RPF.

The inability to distinguish between the civil war and the genocide by Secretary Christopher and Ambassador Rawson was not the only way in which policymakers exonerated themselves of guilt. Other officials, most notably Dick Clarke, argued that they had a responsibility to adhere to their task. However, his definition of national interest did not include moral imperative. According to then National Security Advisor Anthony Lake, Dick Clarke reflected back on his role in Rwanda within a context that exempted him from any guilt. Lake explained that Clarke felt he was given a very specific purpose of restricting peacekeeping and he set out to achieve those objectives.[6]

In addition to offering justification for their actions, many policymakers have argued years after the fact that they did not know that genocide was taking place or did not appreciate the gravity of the killing. James Woods, who by the time the genocide began had retired as Deputy Assistant Secretary of Defense for Africa, offers a perspective that negates the use of ignorance as justification for inaction:

> [F]ailure to appreciate is an artful excuse for not wanting to appreciate the facts which, indeed, were presented to the White House and everybody else at the time. They knew. They chose not to know and they chose not to act . . . [W]e had a lot to apologize for, but it's not just the United States that owes the apology, it's the whole international community. We all failed to act and the facts were known in the capitals of Europe and in New York and in Washington.[7]

James Woods was correct in his assessment. The evidence was present and the entire international community shared the burden of the failure to intervene. Through an oppressive colonial rule in Rwanda where individuals were forced to carry ethnic identity cards, the Belgians set the precedent of labeling ethnicity and thus played a role in precipitating ethnic differences, yet when the Hutu capitalized on their ethnic majority and began the genocide of the Tutsis, the Belgians were the first nation to propose a withdrawal of the United Nations troops from Rwanda. Perhaps no other foreign nation was more accountable than the French, who supported the Rwanda government logistically and financially as it carried out the genocide. According to Foreign Minister Charles Murigande, French troops reportedly ran some of the road blocks and even built volleyball courts over some of the mass graves. Their eventual execution of Operation Turquoise toward the end of the genocide, while designed to save the lives of remaining Tutsis, actually helped many of the genocidaires escape into Zaire.

WHERE MISTAKES WERE MADE

The chronic feelings of remorse and guilt by senior officials at the State Department, the Pentagon, and the White House for their inaction during the genocide, reflects a general acceptance that mistakes were made. Those in the Clinton administration who had the influence and ability to stop the genocide, regardless of their reasoning at the time, have recognized the consequences of turning a blind eye to genocide. However, the mistakes that were made extend beyond inaction.

First, the United States encouraged, supported, and was instrumental in the pursuit of the Arusha Peace Process. While the notion of a peace process was a good idea, the approach was severely flawed. The failure of the international community to address the CDR as a spoiler to the Arusha Peace Process, resulted in repeated disruption of the implementation of transitional institutions.[8] But U.S. Ambassador David Rawson sought to focus on the politics instead of the reality that the Arusha Accords were progressing unsuccessfully in a changing context that was becoming less fit for the original peace process. While the international community repeatedly argued that the CDR should be part of the Arusha Peace Process, provided they sign a code of conduct, the RPF was wary from the beginning about their inclusion. The CDR had initially refused to sign the code of conduct, making it difficult for any party to argue for its inclusion. However, when the CDR decided to sign on to the code in 1994, the RPF blocked the implementation of the Accords. RPF officials argue that when the CDR initially refused to sign the code of conduct, this should have been alarming to diplomats that whether the CDR eventually signed on or not, they were going to play a spoiler role. There were numerous warning signs of the CDR becoming more extremist over time: inflammatory radio broadcasts, distribution of arms, and sporadic massacres of Tutsis and moderate Hutus. Because their focus had been on the effect the neighboring crisis in Burundi could have on Rwanda, maintaining the ceasefire, and inaugurating the transitional institutions, American diplomats were not prepared for the rapid change in context on April 6, 1994, from a civil war to genocide.

The U.S. decision to pressure the UN Security Council to withdraw UNAMIR from Rwanda during the most horrific phase of the genocide, marked the one instance in which the United States not only took the position of inaction, but actually made things worse. True, the ambush of ten Belgian soldiers during the second day of the genocide and the Belgian and Bangladeshi decisions to withdraw their troops from the mission made it difficult to have confidence that UNAMIR could be effective. However, the United States had the leverage to convince other member-states to contribute troops and ensure the sustainability of UNAMIR. Instead it did the opposite.

The withdrawal of all but 270 UN troops from Rwanda marked the point at which the United States had removed the final hope for the Tutsis and the RPF that the international community would stop the genocide. However, the consequences extended beyond a loss of hope. Tens of thousands of Rwandans who had sought the protection of UNAMIR were abandoned by the withdrawing troops from April 19 to 25 and left to fend against the machetes and clubs of the *Interahamwe*. The withdrawal of UNAMIR led the genocidaires to act more confidently. After all, if the international community had abruptly withdrawn the only international armed presence in Rwanda, it seemed unlikely that they would undertake any initiative to use force to stop the genocide. Essentially, the withdrawal of UNAMIR served as the green light for the genocidaires to further proceed with their campaign of extermination.

While the withdrawal of UNAMIR marks one of the most significant failures in U.S. policy toward Rwanda during the genocide, the general lack of interest in discussing Rwanda had even greater effect on the bureaucratic mechanisms that were needed to advocate a response to Rwanda. During the 100 days of genocide, senior officials, in large part because Rwanda was of marginal strategic importance to the United States, remained silent on the Rwanda issue. Neither President Clinton, nor National Security Advisor Anthony Lake called a single senior-level meeting during the period of the genocide to discuss the violence and a possible response by the United States. Secretary of State Warren Christopher explained that he "had other responsibilities," and Secretary of Defense William Perry would not get involved in Rwanda unless the President wanted to use the U.S. military. U.S. Ambassador David Rawson downplayed the crisis as a civil war and senior officials in the State Department and the Pentagon chose to adhere to the administration's position on Rwanda. For them, Rwanda was not worth the risk of the scrutiny they may have received for advocating an intervention in Central Africa just six months after eighteen Army Rangers had been killed in Mogadishu. This senior-level attention was a necessary prerequisite to move any proposal for a response through the bureaucracy. Without the interest of the President, the National Security Advisor, the Secretary of State, or senior officials, the proposals for intervention were developed from the lower ranks of the bureaucracy. These were the only officials who seemed able to think about interventions beyond the military commitments that the United States opposed. However, as junior officials, their proposals never gained traction and usually died in the interagency discussions. While some of these, in particular radio jamming, may have been effective, no proposal could realistically make it past the firewall created by senior officials' circumvention of the Rwanda issue.

The White House in particular stood firm on its opposition to intervention and seemed to find every excuse possible to reject the ideas being generated by the State Department. In a conversation with then Deputy Assistant Secretary of Defense for Africa Prudence Bushnell, she explained that the few policymakers that took part in discussions about Rwanda, regardless of whether or not they favored intervention, found themselves caught between doing what was bureaucratically normal, meaning determining what was of high-interest to the United States, and doing the right thing by permitting moral imperative to consider an otherwise marginal crisis a national interest. Unfortunately, more often than not, officials took the position of doing what was bureaucratically normal.

As the genocide worsened and the body count rose dramatically to half a million, senior officials refused to use the term "genocide" to describe the killings in Rwanda in fear that it would compel action. In the midst of the genocide, there were countless discussions about whether or not the violence was "genocide" or "acts of genocide." This debate provided those who opposed intervention with a convenient loop hole through which they felt they could legally argue against responding to the genocide, or as they liked to call it the "acts of genocide." The debate over calling the crisis genocide did not occur because policymakers felt unsure about what was occurring in Rwanda. While it would seem that this should be the only motivation for engaging in such a debate, it is far more likely that the principals, in particular Secretary Christopher, could ensure that Rwanda did not become a major issue consuming his bureaucracy and thus creating a tangent from North Korea, Bosnia, and Haiti.

WHAT COULD HAVE BEEN DONE DIFFERENTLY?

Rwanda is generally viewed as one of the greatest human failures in the twentieth century and with this in mind, one has to ask the question of what the United States should have done differently. Policymakers in Washington DC worked in a difficult political climate that presented a variety of obstacles against intervention in Rwanda, but even so, the ease at which extremists were able to begin the genocide could have been significantly mitigated with more strategic diplomacy. If Ambassador Rawson singled out the Coalition for the Defense of the Republic (CDR) as a potential spoiler to the peace process, pressured them to abandon an extremist platform, and placed greater pressure on the Habyarimana government to inaugurate the transitional institutions, then it is possible that the new government could have been in place before the onset of violence. However, without this pressure, the CDR became increasingly restless and as a result, Rwanda was vulnerable to a trigger effect in which any event could have set off a new wave of violence. Ambassador Rawson could have also pressured President Habyarimana to halt the inflammatory radio broadcasts over Radio Rwanda and RTLM, but Ambassador Rawson failed to see the danger in the propaganda and never spoke to Habyarimana about the issue. This may have prevented the CDR and MRND ideologies from popularizing among the peasantry and commoners.

Back in Washington, policymakers could have responded to the sporadic ethnically motivated massacres from 1990 to 1994, by publicly denouncing the violence and directly condemning those responsible. However, without this diplomatic response, there was hardly any deterrence against the violence until the deployment of UNAMIR in November 1993. A senior level diplomatic trip to Rwanda may also have had a tremendous effect on the events in the months before the genocide. Prudence Bushnell was the most senior official to visit Rwanda since 1992 and despite her position as a Deputy Assistant Secretary of State, she remembers that "they rolled out the red carpet" for her, indicating that a visit by the Assistant Secretary of State for African Affairs, or even an Undersecretary of State may have had an even greater reception in Rwanda and thus had more clout than a Deputy Assistant Secretary.

Congress would most likely not have supported an intervention in Rwanda and the American public would most likely have opposed military intervention like that of Somalia. However, neither the President, nor the National Security Advisor ever met, called a meeting, or requested information about other forms of intervention the United States could have either undertaken or assisted with logistically, financially, and politically. The later interest in Rwanda by Senators Simon, Jeffords, Kennedy, and Leahy, along with Congressman Payne, proves that when provided with sufficient information, members of Congress showed support for some kind of action in Rwanda. However, still neither President Clinton, nor Anthony Lake ever sat down to talk about Rwanda.

General Dallaire explained to the United Nations that he could stop the genocide with 5,000 well-equipped troops. Had the U.S. government entertained this possibility, it is likely that the necessary troop contributions might have been obtained from member-states, in particular a number of African nations which had already expressed a willingness to provide troops. If these troop contributions were obtained, the United States could have provided a symbolic colonel or lieutenant colonel to play a key role in the mission. After all, this was done in Liberia nearly ten years later.

If the United States did not want to commit forces, there are a number of other actions that might have had a tremendous effect on stopping the genocide. First, the United States maintained diplomatic relations with a government responsible for genocide until July 15, 1994. This was 11 days after the genocide had ended. Had the United States severed diplomatic ties, there would have been less legal hurdles with regard to small-scale military actions, most notably the jamming of the hate radio. Had this happened, the United States could have also bombed the Rwandan Army's headquarters, which Alan

Kuperman argues would have served two purposes: "If the threat alone initially failed to coerce them, subsequent US bombing would have served the dual purpose of further coercing Hutu leaders and providing a form of air support to the RPA, which was stemming the genocide as it advanced."[9] Even if the United States did not want to commit itself militarily, President Clinton could have placed a personal phone call to Augustin Bizimungu and Theoneste Bagosora, the two masterminds of the genocide. Prudence Bushnell was the only official to place personal phone calls to these leaders, and because she was a familiar face to them and not a senior official, the Rwandan leadership did not initially take her seriously. President Clinton's one-minute statement over the radio lacked forcefulness and served more as an appeal to the genocidaire leadership.

Secretary of Defense William Perry's efforts to find a solution to the cholera outbreak in Zaire indicated the influence that senior officials had over Congress when they were willing to take the lead on an issue. Despite fierce Congressional opposition, Perry testified before Congress and obtained support and funds to send a sanitation team to eastern Zaire to put an end to the epidemic. Had Anthony Lake, Warren Christopher, or even William Perry testified before Congress immediately after the evacuation to try and obtain Congressional support for a commitment of funds to either reinforce UNAMIR or support other forms of intervention, it is not inconceivable that Congress would have authorized the use of funds. This could have saved UNAMIR as the United States would have had the financial authorization to provide resources and equipment to member-states willing to be part of a coalition of the willing.

Where was the discussion? Where were the meetings? It is easy for policymakers to say in retrospect that intervention was not on the table and the political climate was difficult. However, this is a difficult explanation to accept given the fact that they did not even try. They did not test the boundaries of their political constraints, they did not attempt to think creatively about different types of actions that might have fallen within those constraints, and they did not embrace the prospect of other nations taking a lead on international action.

Has the U.S. government learned the lessons of Rwanda? If genocide occurred tomorrow, would the President be able to examine a broad spectrum of possible actions and interventions, or would the prospect of intervention once again be ruled out? The fact remains that the United States is unlikely to intervene in nations that are not of vital interest, and so long as there is an abundance of pressing foreign policy issues, this approach to foreign policy is unlikely to be changed. No matter how serious the crisis, whether it is in Rwanda or Sudan, the United States is always going to have "more pressing" domestic and international issues outside of Africa and the media is still going to prioritize European and Middle Eastern foreign policy issues.

The fundamental flaws are with the American system of reporting, the system of analysis, and the continued emphasis that the bureaucracy places on post-conflict rather than pre-conflict objectives. It is because of this reality that the U.S. government was able to stop the cholera outbreak almost overnight in the aftermath of 100 days of genocide, but it was not prepared to stop the genocide itself.

The U.S. government cannot send its troops into every ethnic conflict or humanitarian crisis. However, the United States, by demonstrating an interest and discussing various alternative actions beyond commitment of American troops, can raise the profile of a crisis. If the United States is to ensure that the claim of "never again" has credence, it must be proactive and ensure that these genocides do not develop in the first place. Genocide is difficult to predict, but the prospect for widespread, brutal, and ethnically motivated violence is usually more apparent. The distinction is only in words.

NOTES

1. The International Criminal Tribunal for Rwanda was established by the UN on November 8, 1994.

2. Personal Interview, Former Assistant Secretary of State for Democracy, Human Rights and Labor John Shattuck, Via telephone to Boston, MA, February 24, 2003.

3. Tony Marley, interview, "The Triumph of Evil," *Frontline,* PBS, January 26, 1999; available at PBS Online: http://www.pbs.org/wgbh/pages/frontline/shows/evil/interviews/marley.html.

4. Linda Melvern, *A People Betrayed: The Role of the West in Rwanda's Genocide,* p. 230.

5. Personal Interview, Foreign Minister of Rwanda Dr. Charles Murigande, Kigali, Rwanda, December 20, 2002.

6. Personal Interview, Former National Security Advisor Anthony Lake, Washington, DC, November 20, 2002.

7. James Woods, interview, "Triumph of Evil," *Frontline,* PBS, January 26, 1999; available at PBS Online: http://www.pbs.org/wgbh/pages/frontline/shows/evil/interviews/woods.html.

8. Stephen John Stedman, *Ending Civil Wars: The Implementation of Peace Agreements,* Boulder, CO: Lynne Rienner Publishers, Inc., 2002.

9. Alan Kuperman, *The Limits of Humanitarian Intervention,* p. 34.

Appendix A

Chronology of U.S. Policy Toward Rwanda

October 1, 1990:	The Rwanda Patriotic Front (RPF) invades Rwanda from Uganda, driving Rwanda into further chaos and civil war.
March 1992:	Extremist Coalition for the Defense of the Republic (CDR) party is established.
May 1992:	Assistant Secretary of State for African Affairs Herman "Hank" J. Cohen travels to Rwanda to stress "the importance of negotiations and highlight the readiness of the RPF to start talks, based on his discussion [with the RPF leadership] in Kampala."
August 1992:	U.S. mission in Kigali learns that civilian militias called *Interahamwe* are being trained in camps outside of Kigali.
January 20, 1993:	Bill Clinton is sworn in as the 42nd President of the United States. He calls for a foreign policy of assertive multilateralism.
November 23, 1993:	Ambassador Robert Flaten finishes his post in Rwanda.
October 3, 1993:	Eighteen American Army Rangers are killed by General Aideed's forces in an ambush in Mogadishu, Somalia.

January 6, 1994:   Ambassador David Rawson arrives in Kigali to replace
                     Robert Flaten.

January 11, 1994:   UN General Romeo Dallaire sends a cable to the UN
                     indicating that there is an informant who claims to
                     know the locations of arms caches. According to
                     Dallaire, the informant also described the speed at
                     which the *Interahamwe* militias could carry out
                     massacres. At the end of the cable, Dallaire stated that
                     the credibility of the informant could not be guaranteed.
                     (Dallaire later verified the report by sending UNAMIR
                     soldiers on a fact finding mission)

February 1994:   Assistant Secretary of State for International
                     Organizations Douglas Bennet, arrived in Rwanda "to
                     discuss issues coming before the Security Council. [He]
                     used this opportunity to stress to the Rwandans the
                     importance of their success in implementing the peace
                     process and thus the urgency of putting into place the
                     transitional institutions."

March 1994:   Deputy Assistant Secretary of Defense for
                     Humanitarian Affairs Patricia Irvin traveled to Rwanda
                     to discuss with the Foreign Minister and the Minister of
                     Defense the pressing issue of "de-mining the
                     countryside" and to identify "worthy humanitarian
                     projects" that would become eligible for "DoD excess
                     property, such as school desks for refugees."

                     Deputy Assistant Secretary of State Prudence Bushnell
                     comes to Rwanda to put pressure on the government to
                     implement the transitional government and pressure the
                     RPF to permit the joining of the CDR.

                     The CIA prepares a report indicating that if the
                     situation in Rwanda worsened, as many as
                     300,000–500,000 people could be killed.

April 6, 1994:   An unknown assassin shoots down a plane carrying
                     Rwandan President Juvenal Habyarimana and
                     Burundian President Cyprien Ntaryamira as it

comes into Kigali International Airport. The killings begin that night.

April 7, 1994: Extremists ambush ten Belgian UN Assistance Mission for Rwanda (UNAMIR) peacekeepers who had been tasked to protect the Prime Minister. The attack was undertaken in order to provoke an international withdrawal from Rwanda.

Evacuation of American expatriates takes place in one long convoy by way of road to Bujumbura, Burundi.

April 8, 1994: President Clinton issues a statement to the press: "I mention [Rwanda] only because there are a sizable number of Americans there and it is a very tense situation. And I just want to assure the families of those who are there that we are doing everything we possibly can to be on top of the situation to take all the appropriate steps to try to assure the safety of our citizens there."

April 10, 1994: The Deputy Chief of Mission, Joyce Leader, and Ambassador David Rawson close the door to the U.S. Embassy and are the final Americans evacuated to Burundi.

April 11, 1994: The International Red Cross estimates that tens of thousands of Rwandans have been murdered.

April 12, 1994: Interim government in Rwanda flees to Gitarama. The *Interahamwe* fills the vacuum and begins the most brutal phase of the genocide.

April 13, 1994: Last intervention proposal is removed from the UN Security Council under intense pressure from the U.S. Government.

The Rwanda Patriotic Front (RPF) declares that "genocide" was taking place in Rwanda.

April 18, 1994: First articles appear in popular U.S. magazines: *Time* article on Rwanda, "Rwanda Descends into Chaos"

and *Newsweek* article on Rwanda, "Corpses
Everywhere"

April 19, 1994: Human Rights Watch Executive Director Kenneth Roth
sends a letter to the UN Security Council in which he
describes the conflict in Rwanda as genocide.

April 20, 1994: The Belgians withdraw their contingent from the UN
Assistance Mission for Rwanda (UNAMIR)

April 21, 1994: The body count in Rwanda reaches 250,000.
International Committee for the Red Cross estimates
that hundreds of thousands have been killed.

April 24, 1994: Oxfam uses the word "genocide" to describe the
killings in Rwanda.

April 26, 1994: The Bureau of Intelligence and Research (INR) at the
State Department produces an intelligence report
entitled "Genocide in Partition," describing the conflict
in Rwanda as genocide and explaining the systematic
nature of the killings.

United States Senate Passes Resolution 207
condemning the violence in Rwanda.

April 27, 1994: The Pope issues a statement calling the violence in
Rwanda genocide.

April 28, 1994: Oxfam issues the following statement: "Oxfam fears
genocide is happening in Rwanda."

State Department spokeswoman Christine Shelley
responds to questions by reporters about whether the
violence in Rwanda constituted genocide: "Well, as I
think you know, the use of the term 'genocide' has a
very precise legal meaning . . . I'm not able to look at
all of those criteria at this moment and say yes, no. It's
something that requires very careful study before we
can make a final determination."

April 29, 1994: Deputy Assistant Secretary of State Prudence Bushnell
"telephoned Rwandan Ministry of Defense Cabinet

Director Colonel Bagosora . . . to urge him to stop the killings." She told Colonel Bagosora that "the world does not buy the [Government of Rwanda's] story on the killings and that credible eyewitness and respected organizations reported Rwandan military complicity in the killings . . . [and] criminal acts, aiding and abetting civilian massacres."

UNHCR reports that more than 250,000 refugees had fled from Rwanda into western Tanzania. This mass exodus results in a revitalization of discussions concerning a reinforced UN deployment in Rwanda.

May 1, 1994:   The Pentagon produces a discussion paper that discourages "[engaging] in additional propaganda activities to get a message into Rwanda to counter the radio stations that [were] urging the killings" because such actions presented the danger of a "significant increase in [the U.S.'] role."

May 3, 1994:   The White House releases Presidential Directive Decision 25 (PDD-25) in which the U.S. government outlines its new approach to peacekeeping. PDD-25 called for the United States to be more selective and effective in which peacekeeping operations it undertook.

May 5, 1994:   National Security Advisor Anthony Lake states at a press conference "When I wake up every morning and look at the headlines and the stories and the images on television of these conflicts, I want to work to end every conflict . . . But neither we, nor the international community have the resources, nor the mandate to do so. So we have to make distinctions. We have to ask the hard questions about where and when we can intervene. And the reality is that we cannot often solve other people's problems; we can never build their nations for them."

May 9, 1994:   The Defense Intelligence Agency (DIA) describes the violence in Rwanda as genocide.

May 13, 1994:   General Romeo Dallaire speaks with Senators Paul Simon and James Jeffords, who write to the White House urging action in Rwanda.

May 16, 1994:   Rwanda receives its first cover story in a popular U.S.
                  magazine: *Time* article on Rwanda, "Rwanda's Killing
                  Fields"

May 17, 1994:   The Pentagon, at the order of the Secretary of Defense
                  and the Under Secretary of Defense establishes the
                  Rwanda Task Force. Director for African Affairs Vince
                  Kern is appointed as its director.

                  After a heated debate in the Security Council and despite
                  initial opposition from the United States, the UN passes
                  Resolution 918, calling for an arms embargo on
                  Rwanda, the deployment of 5,500 UNAMIR II troops,
                  and a Secretary General's report on human rights abuses
                  in Rwanda.

May 20, 1994:   The International Committee for the Red Cross estimates
                  that more than 500,000 Rwandans have been killed.

May 25, 1994:   State Department Spokesperson Michael McCurry is
                  asked whether or not the violence in Rwanda constitutes
                  genocide. He responds: "I'll have to confess, I don't
                  know the answer to that. I know that the issue was under
                  very active consideration. I think there was a strong
                  disposition within the department here to view what has
                  happened there; certainly, constituting acts of genocide
                  that have occurred."

June 10, 1994:   At a State Department briefing, spokesperson Christine
                  Shelley is asked, "How many acts of genocide does it
                  take to make genocide?" She responds, "That's just not a
                  question that I'm in a position to answer."

June 22, 1994:   As the UN continues to delay deployment of UNAMIR
                  II, the French launch Operation Turquoise. The purpose
                  of the mission is to create safe zones for the government
                  controlled areas. The mission fails as killings persist in
                  the safe zones.

July 4, 1994:   RPF captures Kigali, the genocide officially ends.

July 13, 1994:   U.S. House of Representatives passes House Resolution 453 in which it describes the violence in Rwanda as genocide.

July 15, 1994:   The Clinton administration publicly declares that it no longer recognizes the interim government of Rwanda.

July 18, 1994:   The genocide and the Civil War comes to an end with the RPF defeat of the remnants of Rwandan government troops still in Rwanda.

July 19, 1994:   A new government of national unity is created and announces the end of compulsory identity cards.

Appendix B

List of Key Interviews

Date	Name	Position Held in 1994	Location of Interview
5/18/02 & 10/06/03 & 10/22/03	Alison Des Forges	Consultant of Human Rights Watch	Via e-mail
7/22/02	"Joseph"	Commander in the RPF	Pretoria, South Africa
11/18/02	Joyce Leader	Deputy Chief of Mission in Kigali	Washington, DC
11/20/02	Dr. Anthony Lake	National Security Advisor	Georgetown
11/21/02	White House Official [A]	Confidential	Washington, DC
12/9/02	Ambassador Prudence Bushnell	Deputy Assistant Secretary of State for African Affairs	Washington, DC
12/9/02	Senator Paul Simon	U.S. Senator	Via phone to Illinois
12/18/02	Major General Kayumba Nyamwasa	RPF Director of Intelligence	Kigali, Rwanda
12/18/02	Colonel Alexis Kanyarengwe	RPF Chairman	Kigali, Rwanda
12/19/02	FSN [A]	U.S. Embassy	Kigali, Rwanda
12/19/02	FSN [B]	UNICEF	Kigali, Rwanda
12/19/02	FSN [C]	FSN—USAID	Kigali, Rwanda
12/19/02	FSN [D]	FSN—USAID	Kigali, Rwanda

Date	*Name*	*Position Held in 1994*	*Location of Interview*
12/19/02	FSN [E]	FSN—USAID	Kigali, Rwanda
12/19/02	FSN [F]	FSN—USAID	Kigali, Rwanda
12/20/02	Dr. Charles Murigande	RPF liaison to the United States	Kigali, Rwanda
12/20/02	Tito Rutaremara	RPF Executive Committee	Kigali, Rwanda
12/20/02	Denis Polisi	RPF Deputy Chairman/RPF Spokesman	Kigali, Rwanda
12/23/02	FSN [G]	FSN—USAID	Kigali, Rwanda
12/24/02	Major General Marcel Gatsinzi	Army Chief of Staff for the Rwandan Army	Kigali, Rwanda
2/10/03	Dr. William Perry	Secretary of Defense	Stanford, CA
2/24/03	John Shattuck	Assistant Secretary of State for Democracy, Human Rights, and Labor	Via phone
2/13/03	Sarah Sewall	Deputy Assistant Secretary of Defense for Peacekeeping	Via phone
2/28/03	State Department Official [A]	State Department Official	Via phone
3/1/03	Department of Defense Official [A]	Department of Defense Official	Via e-mail
8/15/03	Vince Kern	Department of Defense Official	Alexandria, VA
9/10/03	Confidential Source	Confidential	Washington, DC
9/26/03	David Rawson	Professor	Via phone
11/02/03	Keneth Kaunda	Activist	Via phone
2/09/04	Walt Slocombe	Lawyer	Via phone
4/14/04	Douglas Bennet	President of Wesleyan University	Via phone
9/7/04	General George Joulwan	Commander in Chief of U.S. European Command	Arlington, VA

Appendix C

Flow Chart of Rwanda Decision-making Process

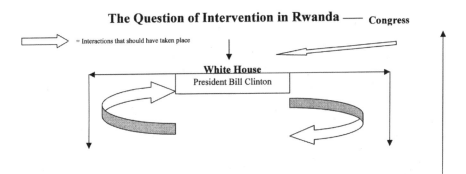

The Question of Intervention in Rwanda —— Congress

= Interactions that should have taken place

White House

President Bill Clinton

Appendix C

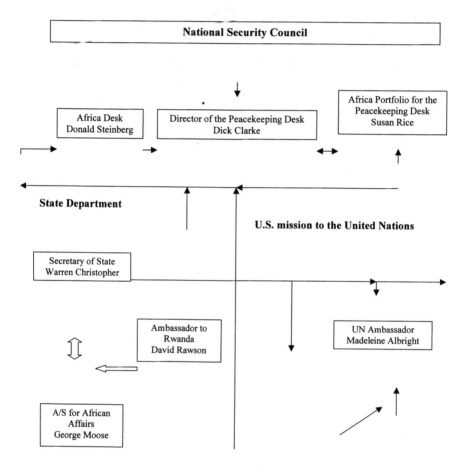

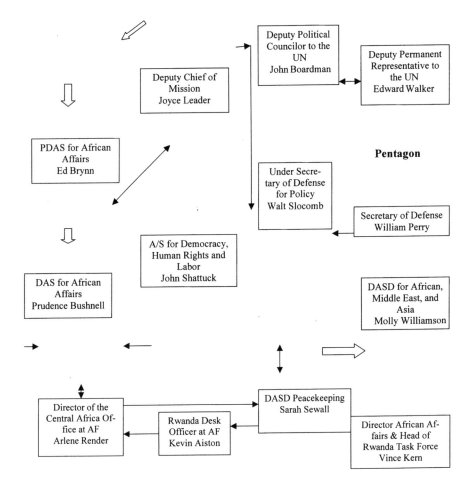

Appendix D

1948 Genocide Convention

UN CONVENTION ON THE PREVENTION AND PUNISHMENT FOR THE CRIME OF GENOCIDE

The Contracting Parties,

Having considered the declaration made by the General Assembly of the United Nations in its resolution 96(I) dated 11 December 1946 that genocide is a crime under international law, contrary to the spirit and aims of the United Nations and condemned by the civilized world; Recognizing that at all periods of history genocide has inflicted great losses on humanity; and Being convinced that, in order to liberate mankind from such an odious scourge, international co-operation is required,

Hereby agree as hereinafter provided:

ARTICLE 1

The Contracting Parties confirm that genocide, whether committed in time of peace, or in time of war, is a crime under international law which they undertake to prevent and to punish.

ARTICLE 2

In the present Convention, genocide means any of the following acts committed with intent to destroy, in whole or in part, a national, ethnic, racial or religious group as such:

(a) Killing members of the group;
(b) Causing serious bodily or mental harm to members of the group;
(c) Deliberately inflicting on the group conditions of life calculated to bring about its physical destruction in whole or in part;

(d) Imposing measures intended to prevent births within the group;

(e) Forcibly transferring children of the group to another group.

ARTICLE 3

The following acts shall be punishable:

(a) Genocide;

(b) Conspiracy to commit genocide;

(c) Direct and public incitement to commit genocide;

(d) Attempt to commit genocide;

(e) Complicity in genocide

ARTICLE 4

Persons committing genocide or any of the other acts enumerated in Article 3 shall be punished, whether they are constitutionally responsible rulers, public officials or private individuals.

ARTICLE 5

The Contracting Parties undertake to enact, in accordance with their respective Constitutions, the necessary legislation to give effect to the provisions of the present Convention and, in particular, to provide effective penalties for persons guilty of genocide or of any of the other acts enumerated in Article 3.

ARTICLE 6

Persons charged with genocide or any of the other acts enumerated in Article 3 shall be tried by a competent tribunal of the State in the territory of which the act was committed, or by such international panel tribunal as may have jurisdiction with respect to those Contracting Parties which shall have accepted its jurisdiction.

ARTICLE 7

Genocide and the other acts enumerated in Article 3 shall not be considered as political crimes for the purpose of extradition. The Contracting Parties pledge themselves in such cases to grant extradition in accordance with their laws and treaties in force.

ARTICLE 8

Any Contracting Party may call upon the competent organs of the United Nations to take such action under the Charter of the United Nations as they consider appropriate for the prevention and suppression of acts of genocide or any of the other acts enumerated in Article 3.

ARTICLE 9

Disputes between the Contracting Parties relating to the interpretation, application or fulfillment of the present Convention, including those relating to the responsibility of a State for genocide or any of the other acts enumerated in Article 3 shall be submitted to the International Court of Justice at the request of any of the parties to the dispute.

ARTICLE 10

The present Convention, of which the Chinese, English, French, Russian and Spanish texts are equally authentic, shall bear the date of 9 December 1948.

ARTICLE 11

The present Convention shall be open 31 December 1949 for signature on behalf of any Member of the United Nations and any non-member State to which an invitation to sign has been addressed by the General Assembly. The present Convention shall be ratified, and the instruments of ratification shall be deposited with the Secretary-General of the United Nations. After 1 January 1950 the present Convention may be acceded to on behalf of any Member of the United Nations and of any non-member State which has received an invitation as aforesaid. Instruments of accession shall be deposited with the Secretary of the United Nations.

ARTICLE 12

Any Contracting Party may at any time, by notification addressed to the Secretary-General of the United Nations, extend the application of the present Convention to all or any of the territories for the conduct of whose foreign relations that Contracting Party is responsible.

ARTICLE 13

On the day when the first twenty instruments of ratification or accession have been deposited, the Secretary-General shall draw up a proses-verbal and transmit a copy thereof to each Member of the United Nations and to each of the non-member States contemplated in Article 12. The present Convention shall come into force on the ninetieth day following the date of deposit of the twentieth instrument of ratification or succession.

ARTICLE 14

The present Convention shall remain in effect for a period of ten years as from the date of its coming into force. It shall thereafter remain in force for successive periods of five years for such Contracting Parties as have not denounced it at least six months before the expiration of the coming period. Denunciation shall be effected by a written notification addressed to the Secretary-General of the United Nations.

ARTICLE 15

If as a result of denunciations, the number of Parties to the present Convention shall become less than sixteen, the Convention shall cease to be in force as from the date on which the last of the denunciations shall become effective.

ARTICLE 16

A request for the revision of the present Convention may be made at any time by any Contracting Party by means of a written notification in writing addressed to the Secretary-General. The General Assembly shall decide upon the steps, if any, to be taken in respect of such a request.

ARTICLE 17

The Secretary-General of the United Nations shall notify all Members of the United Nations and the non-member States contemplated in Article 11 of the following:

(a) Signatures, ratifications and accessions received in accordance with Article 11;
(b) Notifications received in accordance with Article 12;
(c) The date upon which the present Convention comes into force in accordance with Article 13;
(d) Denunciations received in accordance with Article 14;
(e) The abrogation of the Convention in accordance with Article 15;
(f) Notifications received in accordance with Article 16.

ARTICLE 18

The original of the present Convention shall be deposited in the archives of the United Nations. A certified copy of the Convention shall be transmitted to each Member of the United Nations and to each of the non-member States contemplated in Article 11.

ARTICLE 19

The present Convention shall be registered by the Secretary-General of the United Nations on the date of its coming into force.

Appendix E

UN Charter, Chapter VI

CHARTER OF THE UNITED NATIONS
CHAPTER VI
PACIFIC SETTLEMENT OF DISPUTES

ARTICLE 33

1. The parties to any dispute, the continuance of which is likely to endanger the maintenance of international peace and security, shall, first of all, seek a solution by negotiation, enquiry, mediation, conciliation, arbitration, judicial settlement, resort to regional agencies or arrangements, or other peaceful means of their own choice.

2. The Security Council shall, when it deems necessary, call upon the parties to settle their dispute by such means.

ARTICLE 34

The Security Council may investigate any dispute, or any situation which might lead to international friction or give rise to a dispute, in order to determine whether the continuance of the dispute or situation is likely to endanger the maintenance of international peace and security.

ARTICLE 35

1. Any Member of the United Nations may bring any dispute, or any situation of the nature referred to in Article 34, to the attention of the Security Council or of the General Assembly.

2. A state which is not a Member of the United Nations may bring to the attention of the Security Council or of the General Assembly any dispute to which it is a party if it accepts in advance, for the purposes of the dispute, the obligations of pacific settlement provided in the present Charter.

3. The proceedings of the General Assembly in respect of matters brought to its attention under this Article will be subject to the provisions of Articles 11 and 12.

ARTICLE 36

1. The Security Council may, at any stage of a dispute of the nature referred to in Article 33 or of a situation of like nature, recommend appropriate procedures or methods of adjustment.

2. The Security Council should take into consideration any procedures for the settlement of the dispute which have already been adopted by the parties.

3. In making recommendations under this Article the Security Council should also take into consideration that legal disputes should as a general rule be referred by the parties to the International Court of Justice in accordance with the provisions of the Statute of the Court.

ARTICLE 37

1. Should the parties to a dispute of the nature referred to in Article 33 fail to settle it by the means indicated in that Article, they shall refer it to the Security Council.

2. If the Security Council deems that the continuance of the dispute is in fact likely to endanger the maintenance of international peace and security, it shall decide whether to take action under Article 36 or to recommend such terms of settlement as it may consider appropriate.

ARTICLE 38

Without prejudice to the provisions of Articles 33 to 37, the Security Council may, if all the parties to any dispute so request, make recommendations to the parties with a view to a pacific settlement of the dispute.

Appendix F

Clinton's 1998 Apology in Rwanda

PRESIDENT CLINTON APOLOGIZES
AS REPORTED BY THE ASSOCIATED PRESS, MARCH 25, 1998

Text of President Clinton's address to genocide survivors at the airport in Kigali, Rwanda, on March 25, 1998, as provided by the White House.

Thank you, Mr. President. First, let me thank you, Mr. President, and Vice President Kagame, and your wives for making Hillary and me and our delegation feel so welcome. I'd also like to thank the young students who met us and the musicians, the dancers who were outside. I thank especially the survivors of the genocide and those who are working to rebuild your country for spending a little time with us before we came in here.

I have a great delegation of Americans with me, leaders of our government, leaders of our Congress, distinguished American citizens. We're all very grateful to be here. We thank the diplomatic corps for being here, and the members of the Rwandan government, and especially the citizens.

I have come today to pay the respects of my nation to all who suffered and all who perished in the Rwandan genocide. It is my hope that through this trip, in every corner of the world today and tomorrow, their story will be told; that four years ago in this beautiful, green, lovely land, a clear and conscious decision was made by those then in power that the peoples of this country would not live side by side in peace.

During the 90 days that began on April 6 in 1994, Rwanda experienced the most intensive slaughter in this blood-filled century we are about to leave. Families murdered in their home, people hunted down as they fled by soldiers and militia, through farmland and woods as if they were animals.

From Kibuye in the west to Kibungo in the east, people gathered seeking refuge in churches by the thousands, in hospitals, in schools. And when they were found, the old and the sick, women and children alike, they were killed—killed because their identity card said they were Tutsi or because they had a Tutsi parent, or because someone thought they looked like a Tutsi, or slain like thousands of Hutus because they protected Tutsis or would not countenance a policy that sought to wipe out people who just the day before, and for years before, had been their friends and neighbors.

The government-led effort to exterminate Rwanda's Tutsi and moderate Hutus, as you know better than me, took at least a million lives. Scholars of these sorts of events say that the killers, armed mostly with machetes and clubs, nonetheless did their work five times as fast as the mechanized gas chambers used by the Nazis.

It is important that the world know that these killings were not spontaneous or accidental. It is important that the world hear what your president just said—they were most certainly not the result of ancient tribal struggles. Indeed, these people had lived together for centuries before the events the president described began to unfold.

These events grew from a policy aimed at the systematic destruction of a people. The ground for violence was carefully prepared, the airwaves poisoned with hate, casting the Tutsis as scapegoats for the problems of Rwanda, denying their humanity. All of this was done, clearly, to make it easy for otherwise reluctant people to participate in wholesale slaughter.

Lists of victims, name by name, were actually drawn up in advance. Today the images of all that haunt us all: the dead choking the Kigara River, floating to Lake Victoria. In their fate we are reminded of the capacity in people everywhere—not just in Rwanda, and certainly not just in Africa—but the capacity for people everywhere to slip into pure evil. We cannot abolish that capacity, but we must never accept it. And we know it can be overcome.

The international community, together with nations in Africa, must bear its share of responsibility for this tragedy, as well. We did not act quickly enough after the killing began. We should not have allowed the refugee camps to become safe haven for the killers. We did not immediately call these crimes by their rightful name: genocide. We cannot change the past. But we can and must do everything in our power to help you build a future without fear, and full of hope.

We owe to those who died and to those who survived who loved them, our every effort to increase our vigilance and strengthen our stand against those who would commit such atrocities in the future—here or elsewhere.

Indeed, we owe to all the peoples of the world who are at risk—because each bloodletting hastens the next as the value of human life is degraded and violence becomes tolerated, the unimaginable becomes more conceivable—we owe to all the people in the world our best efforts to organize ourselves so that we can maximize the chances of preventing these events. And where they cannot be prevented, we can move more quickly to minimize the horror.

So let us challenge ourselves to build a world in which no branch of humanity, because of national, racial, ethnic or religious origin, is again threatened with destruction because of those characteristics, of which people should rightly be proud. Let us work together as a community of civilized nations to strengthen our ability to prevent and, if necessary, to stop genocide.

To that end, I am directing my administration to improve, with the international community, our system for identifying and spotlighting nations in danger of genocidal violence, so that we can assure worldwide awareness of impending threats. It may seem strange to you here, especially the many of you who lost members of your family, but all over the world there were people like me sitting in offices, day after day after day, who did not fully appreciate the depth and the speed with which you were being engulfed by this unimaginable terror.

We have seen, too—and I want to say again—that genocide can occur anywhere. It is not an African phenomenon and must never be viewed as such. We have seen it in industrialized Europe; we have seen it in Asia. We must have global vigilance. And never again must we be shy in the face of the evidence.

Secondly, we must as an international community have the ability to act when genocide threatens. We are working to create that capacity here in the Great Lakes region, where the memory is still fresh.

This afternoon in Entebbe, leaders from central and eastern Africa will meet with me to launch an effort to build a coalition to prevent genocide in this region. I thank the leaders who have stepped forward to make this commitment. We hope the effort can be a model for all the world, because our sacred task is to work to banish this greatest crime against humanity.

Events here show how urgent the work is. In the northwest part of your country, attacks by those responsible for the slaughter in 1994 continue today. We must work as partners with Rwanda to end this violence and allow your people to go on rebuilding your lives and your nation.

Third, we must work now to remedy the consequences of genocide. The United States has provided assistance to Rwanda to settle the uprooted and restart its economy, but we must do more. I am pleased that America will become the first nation to contribute to the new Genocide Survivors Fund. We will contribute this year $2 million, continue our support in the years to come, and urge other nations to do the same, so that survivors and their communities can find the care they need and the help they must have.

Mr. President, to you, and to you, Mr. Vice President, you have shown great vision in your efforts to create a single nation in which all citizens can live freely and securely. As you pointed out, Rwanda was a single nation before the European powers met in Berlin to carve up Africa. America stands with you, and we will continue helping the people of Rwanda to rebuild their lives and society.

You spoke passionately this morning in our private meeting about the need for grassroots effort in this direction. We will deepen our support for those grassroots efforts, for the development projects which are bridging divisions and clearing a path to a better future. We will join with you to strengthen democratic institutions, to broaden participation, to give all Rwandans a greater voice in their own governance. The challenges you face are great, but your commitment to lasting reconciliation and inclusion is firm.

Fourth, to help ensure that those who survived in the generations to come never again suffer genocidal violence, nothing is more vital than establishing the rule of law. There can be no peace in Rwanda that lasts without a justice system that is recognized as such.

We applaud the efforts of the Rwandan government to strengthen civilian and military justice systems.

I am pleased that our Great Lakes Justice Initiative will invest $30 million to help create throughout the region judicial systems that are impartial, credible and effective. In Rwanda these funds will help to support courts, prosecutors, and police, military justice and cooperation at the local level.

We will also continue to pursue justice through our strong backing for the International Criminal Tribunal for Rwanda. The United States is the largest contributor to this tribunal. We are frustrated, as you are, by the delays in the tribunal's work. As we know, we must do better. Now that administrative improvements have begun, however, the tribunal should expedite cases through group trials, and fulfill its historic mission.

We are prepared to help, among other things, with witness relocation, so that those who still fear can speak the truth in safety. And we will support the War Crimes Tribunal for as long as it is needed to do its work, until the truth is clear and justice is rendered.

Fifth, we must make it clear to all those who would commit such acts in the future that they too must answer for their acts, and they will. In Rwanda, we must hold accountable all those who may abuse human rights, whether insurgents or soldiers. Internationally, as we meet here, talks are underway at the United Nations to establish a permanent international criminal court. Rwanda and the difficulties we have had with this special tribunal underscores the need for such a court. And the United States will work to see that it is created.

I know that in the face of all you have endured, optimism cannot come easily to any of you. Yet I have just spoken, as I said, with several Rwandans who survived the atrocities, and just listening to them gave me reason for hope. You see countless stories of courage around you every day as you go about your business here—men and women who survived and go on, children who recover the light in their eyes remind us that at the dawn of a new millennium there is only one crucial division among the peoples of the Earth. And believe me, after over five years of dealing with these problems I know it is not the division between Hutu and Tutsi, or Serb and Croatian and Muslim in Bosnia, or Arab and Jew, or Catholic and Protestant in Ireland, or black and white. It is really the line between those who embrace the common humanity we all share and those who reject it.

It is the line between those who find meaning in life through respect and cooperation and who, therefore, embrace peace, and those who can only find meaning in life if they have someone to look down on, someone to trample, someone to punish and, therefore, embrace war. It is the line between those who look to the future and those who cling to the past. It is the line between those who give up their resentment and those who believe they will absolutely die if they have to release one bit of grievance. It is the line between those who confront every day with a clenched fist and those who confront every day with an open hand. That is the only line that really counts when all is said and done.

To those who believe that God made each of us in His own image, how could we choose the darker road? When you look at those children who greeted us as we got off that plane today, how could anyone say they did not want those children to have a chance to have their own children? To experience the joy of another morning sunrise? To learn the normal lessons of life? To give something back to their people?

When you strip it all away, whether we're talking about Rwanda or some other distant troubled spot, the world is divided according to how people believe they draw meaning from life.

And so I say to you, though the road is hard and uncertain, and there are many difficulties ahead, and like every other person who wishes to help, I doubtless will not be able to do everything I would like to do, there are things we can do. And if we set about the business of doing them together, you can overcome the awful burden that you have endured. You can put a smile on the face of every child in this country, and you can make people once again believe that they should live as people were living who were singing to us and dancing for us today. That's what we have to believe. That is what I came here to say. That is what I wish for you. Thank you and God bless you.

Source: www.rudyfoto.com/ClintonApology.html.

Bibliography

BOOKS

Adelman, Howard & Suhrke, Astri. *The Path of a Genocide: The Rwanda Crisis from Uganda to Zaire*. (New Brunswick, NJ: Transaction Publishers, 1999).

Albright, Madeleine. *Madam Secretary: A Memoir*. (New York: Easton Press, 2003).

Barnett, Michael. *Eyewitness to Genocide*. (Ithaca, New York: Cornell University Press, 2002).

Berkeley, Bill. *The Graves Are Not Yet Full: Race, Tribe, and Power in the Heart of Africa*. (New York: Basic Books, 2001).

Boutros-Ghali, Boutros. *The United Nations and Rwanda 1993–1996*. (New York: Department of Public Information at the United Nations, 1996).

Campbell, Kenneth J. *Genocide and the Global Village*. (New York: Palgrave, 2001).

Christopher, Warren. *In the Stream of History: Shaping Foreign Policy for a New Era*. (Stanford, CA: Stanford University Press, 1998).

Clarke, Walter. *Learning from Somalia: The Lessons of Armed Humanitarian Intervention*. (Boulder, CO: Westview Press, 1997).

Dallaire, Romeo. *Shake Hands with the Devil: The Failure of Humanity in Rwanda*. (New York: Carroll & Graf Publishers, 2003).

Des Forges, Alison. *Leave None to Tell the Story*. (New York: Human Rights Watch, 1995).

Destexhe, Alain. *Rwanda and Genocide in the Twentieth Century*. (New York: New York University Press, 1995).

Findlay, Trevor. *The Use of Force in UN Peace Operations*. (Oxford: Oxford University Press, 2002).

Gellately, Robert and Ben Kiernan. *Spector of Genocide: Mass Murder in Historical Perspective*. (New York: Cambridge University Press, 2003).

Gourevitch, Philip. *We Wish to Inform You That Tomorrow We Will Be Killed With Our Families*. (New York: Farrar, Straus and Giroux, 1998).

213

Hatzfeld, Jean. *Machete Season: The Killers of Rwanda Speak.* (New York: Farrar, Straus and Giroux, 2003).

Jett, Dinnis. *Why Peacekeeping Fails.* (New York: St. Martin's Press, 1999).

Jones, Bruce D. *Peacemaking in Rwanda.* (London: Lynne Rienner Publishers, 2001).

Keane, Fergal. *Season Of Blood: A Rwandan Journey.* (London: Penguin Books, 1995).

Klinghoffer, Arthur Jay. *The International Dimension of Genocide in Rwanda.* (New York: New York University Press, 1998).

Kuperman, Alan J. *The Limits of Humanitarian Intervention: Genocide in Rwanda.* (Washington, DC: Brookings Institution Press, 2001).

Leader, Joyce. *Rwanda's Struggle for Democracy and Peace.* (Washington, DC: The Fund for Peace, 2001).

MacKinnon, Michael. *The Evolution of US Peacekeeping Policy Under Clinton: A Fairweather Friend?* (London: Frank Cass, 2000).

Melvern, Linda. *A People Betrayed: The Role of the West in Rwanda's Genocide.* (London: Zed Books, 2000).

Melvern, Linda. *Conspiracy to Murder: The Rwanda Genocide and the International Community.* (New York: Verso, 2004).

Mamdani, Mahmood. *When Victims Become Killers: Colonialism, Nativism and the Genocide in Rwanda* (Princeton: Princeton University Press, 2001).

Neuffer, Elizabeth. *The Key to My Neighbor's House: Seeking Justice in Bosnia and Rwanda.* (New York: St. Martin's Press, 2001).

Omaar, Rakiya. *Rwanda: Death, Despair, Defiance.* (London: African Rights, 1995).

Prunier, Gerard. *The Rwanda Crisis.* (New York: Columbia University Press, 1995).

Powers, Samantha. *A Problem from Hell: America and the Age of Genocide.* (New York: Basic Books, 2002).

Schabas, William. *Genocide and International Law: The Crimes of Crimes.* (New York: Cambridge University Press, 2000).

Stedman, Stephen John; Donald Rothchild, and Elizabeth M. Cousens. *Ending Civil Wars: The Implementation of Peace Agreements.* (Boulder, CO: Lynne Rienner Publishers, Inc., 2002).

Taylor, Christopher. *Sacrifice as Terror: The Rwandan Genocide of 1994.* (New York: Berg Publishing, 1999).

Uvin, Peter. *Aiding Violence: The Development Enterprise in Rwanda.* (West Hartford, CT: Kumarian Press, Inc., 1998).

Valentino, Benjamin A. *Final Solutions: Mass Killing and Genocide in the Twentieth Century.* (Ithaca, New York: Cornell University Press, 2004).

Vassall-Adams, Guy. *Rwanda: An Agenda for International Action.* (Ireland: Oxfam Publications, 1994).

CONGRESSIONAL DOCUMENTS

Congressional Letter from U.S. Senator Paul Simon and U.S. Senator James Jeffords to President Clinton, May 13, 1994.

Congressional Record: April 26, 1994, Crisis in Rwanda

Congressional Record: April 26, 1994, Regarding the Catastrophe in Rwanda

Congressional Record: April 26, 1994, Senate Resolution 207—Relative to Rwanda

Congressional Record: June 8, 1994, The International Community's Failure in Rwanda

Congressional Record: June 10, 1994, Getting Rwanda Wrong

Congressional Record: June 10, 1994, Stop the Genocide in Rwanda

Congressional Record: June 15, 1994, Rwanda

Congressional Record: June 16, 1994, The Genocide in Rwanda

Congressional Record: June 16, 1994, What the United States can do to Improve the Present Situation in Rwanda

Congressional Record: July 22, 1994, The Massive Human Tragedy in Rwanda

Congressional Record: July 27, 1994, The Crisis in Rwanda

Congressional Record: August 1, 1994, Rwanda

Congressional Record: August 1, 1994, The Rwanda Tragedy

Congressional Record: August 1, 1994, The Situation in Rwanda

Congressional Record: August 8, 1994, Tragic United States Policy in Rwanda

Congressional Record: August 11, 1994, Flipping the UN Peacekeeping Coin: US Participation in Multilateral Operations

H. RES. 497, July 28, 1994

H. RES. 453, June 13, 1994

S. RES. 160, November 2, 1993

S. RES. 207, April 26, 1994

S. 2208

S. 2370

S. 2475

H.R. 4541, June 8, 1994

H.R. 4541

H.R. 4541, September 20, 1994

H.R. 4541, September 19, 1994

ARTICLES AND REPORTS

AACC Update on Rwanda Crisis for Members and Partners, June 22, 1994.

Amnesty International, *Raise the Roof! Rwanda: The Killings Must Stop*, July 1, 1994.

Amnesty International, "Rwanda: Amnesty International Calls for an End of the Recent Outbreak of Violence," Mass e-mail sent out by Amnesty International, 25 February 1994.

Amnesty International, "Rwanda's Military and Government Authorities Complicit in Atrocities," 26 April 1994.

Charlene Jendry, "A Petition for Peace in Rwanda—Your Help is Needed!" May 9, 1994.

International Affairs Desk (Refugee and Emergency Services), "Update 4: Update on Rwanda Crisis for AACC Partners," April 14, 1994.

International Affairs Desk (Refugee and Emergency Services), "Update 5: Update for AACC Partners on Rwanda Crisis," April 14, 1994.

Information Desk, AACC, "AACC Fears World Community Has Abandoned Rwanda," urgent press release, April 22, 1994.

International Affairs Desk, "Update 3: Update on Rwanda Crisis to AACC Partners," April 12, 1994.

Information Desk, International Affairs Desk, Refugee and Emergency Services Desk, "Urgent Rwanda Update for AACC Members and Partners," May 24, 1994.

Information Desk, International Affairs Desk, Refugee and Emergency Services Desk, "Urgent Rwanda Update for AACC Members and Partners," May 30, 1994.

Information Desk, International Affairs Desk, Refugee and Emergency Services Desk, "Urgent Rwanda Update for AACC Members and Partners," June 6, 1994.

Information Desk, "Update 2: Memorandum to AACC Partners Re Rwanda," April 8, 1994.

Information Office, International Affairs, Refugee and Emergency Desk, "Update No. 6: For AACC Partners on Rwanda Crisis, April 21, 1994.

Information, Refugee and Emergency, International Affairs, "Update 7: Rwanda Emergency Team," April 29, 1994.

Janes Defense Weekly Interview, Vol. 24, No. 14, 7 October 1995.

Janes Defense Weekly Interview, Vol. 25, No. 10, 6 March 1996.

Kenneth Roth (Executive Director of Human Rights Watch), "Rwanda Urgent Action," letter from Human Rights Watch to President of the Security Council His Excellency Colin Keating, April 19, 1994.

Letter from Rwandese citizens of Byumba, North-Eastern Rwanda, to Secretary General of the UN.

Letter to President Clinton from U.S. Senate Foreign Relations Committee, June 16, 1994.

Michael Chossudovsky, IMF-World Bank Policies and the Rwanda Holocaust, January 24, 1995.

Press Release, Steering Committee for Joint Evaluation of Emergency Assistance to Rwanda, Geneva, Nairobi, New York, 12 March 1996.

Proposed Talking Points on Rwanda, prepared by InterAction, June 22, 1994

Rev. Jose Belo Chipenda, "Letter to Dr. Boutros Boutros Ghali," May 4, 1994.

Rev. Jose Belo Chipenda, "Message to AACC Partners Re. Rwanda and Burundi," April 7, 1994.

Rev. Jose Belo Chipenda, Press Release, May 19, 1994.

Rev. Jose Belo Chipenda, "Update 1: Message to the People of Rwanda," April 7, 1994.

Testimony of Holly Burkhalter, Physician for Human Rights Subcommittee on Human Rights and International Operations, May 5, 1998.

The Most Rev. Desmond M. Tutu, "To the Churches and People of Rwanda," April 12, 1994.

Washington Notes on Africa Update, *Conflict Resolution a High Priority in Rwanda and the Region,* July 23, 1994.

MAGAZINE ARTICLES

Alison Des Forges, "The Method in Rwanda's Madness; Politics, Not Tribalism, Is the Root of the Bloodletting," *Washington Post,* April 17, 1994.

All Things Considered, NPR, July 22, 1994.

"At Last, Rwanda's Pain Registers," *New York Times*, July 23, 1994, p. A18.

Bob Dole, "Peacekeeping and Politics," *New York Times*, January 24, 1994, p. A15.

"Cold Choices in Rwanda," *New York Times*, April 23, 1994, p. A24.

David Rieff, "The Big Risk," *New York Review of Books*, October 31, 1996.

Helen Fein, "Rwanda 1994: What the US knew and Why it Stood By," Institute for the Study of Genocide: International Association of Genocide Scholars, 2001.

Helen Fein, "The Prevention of Genocide: Rwanda and Yugoslavia Reconsidered," New York: Institute for the Study of Genocide, 1994.

Helen M. Hintjens, "Explaining the 1994 Genocide in Rwanda," *Journal of Modern African Studies*, 37:2 (1999), pp. 241–286.

Holly Burkhalter, "The Question of Genocide: The Clinton Administration," *World Policy Journal*, Winter 1994, p. 50.

J. William Snyder, Jr., "Command Versus Operational Control: A Critical Review of PDD-25" 1995.

James Bennet, "Clinton Declares U.S., with World, Failed Rwandans," *New York Times,* March 26, 1998, pp. A6, A12.

Ken Ringle, "The Haunting: He Couldn't Stop the Slaughter in Rwanda. Now He Can't Stop the Memory," *Washington Post*, June 15, 2002.

Mark Fritz, "Death By Design: Planning for the Apocalypse," Associated Press, May 21, 1994.

"One, Two, Many Rwandas?" *Washington Post,* April 17, 1994, p. C6.

Paul Richter, "Rwanda Violence Stumps World Leaders; Africa: Though Clinton and Boutros Boutros-Ghali Have Made Guarded Threats, Calls for Action Have Been Eerily Absent," *Los Angeles Times*, April 30, 1994, p. A13.

Peter Landesman, "A Woman's Work," *New York Times Magazine*, September 15, 2002.

Philip Gourevitch, "Annals of Diplomacy: The Genocide Fax," *New Yorker*, May 11, 1998, pp. 42–46.

Robert C. DiPrizio, "US Humanitarian Interventions in the Post-Cold War Era", August-September 2001.

Samantha Power, "Bystanders to Genocide", *The Atlantic Monthly*, September 2001.

OFFICIAL DOCUMENTS

Action memorandum from Assistant Secretary of State for African Affairs George E. Moose, Assistant Secretary of State for Democracy, Human Rights and Labor John Shattuck, Assistant Secretary of State for International Organization Affairs

Douglas J. Bennett, and Department of State Legal Adviser Conrad K. Harper, through Under Secretary of State for Political Affairs Peter Tarnoff and Under Secretary of State for Global Affairs Tim Wirth, to Secretary of State Warren Christopher, "Has Genocide Occurred in Rwanda?", May 21, 1994. Secret.

Defense Intelligence Report, Defense Intelligence Agency, "Rwanda: The Rwandan Patriotic Front's Offensive", May 9, 1994. Secret/NOFORN (not releasable to foreign nationals).

Discussion Paper, Office of the Deputy Assistant Secretary of Defense for Middle East/Africa Region, Department of Defense, May 1, 1994. Secret.

Draft Legal Analysis, Office of the Legal Adviser, Department of State, drafted by Assistant Legal Adviser for African Affairs Joan Donoghue, May 16, 1994. Secret.

Facsimile from Maj. General Romeo Dallarie, Force Commander, United Nations Assistance Mission for Rwanda, to Maj. Gen. Maurice Baril, United Nations Department of Peacekeeping Operations, "Request for Protection for Informant", January 11, 1994.

Memorandum from Assistant Secretary for Intelligence and Research Toby T. Gati to Assistant Secretary of State for African Affairs George Moose and Department of State Legal Adviser Conrad Harper, "Rwanda—Geneva Convention Violations", circa May 18, 1994. Secret/ORCON (originator controlled).

Memorandum from Deputy Assistant Secretary of Defense for Middle East/Africa, through Assistant Secretary of Defense for International Security Affairs, to Under Secretary of Defense for Policy, "Talking Points on Rwanda/Burundi"; April 11, 1994. Confidential.

Memorandum from Prudence Bushnell, Principal Deputy Assistant Secretary, Bureau of African Affairs, through Peter Tarnoff, Under Secretary for Political Affairs, to Secretary of State Warren Christopher, "Death of Rwandan and Burundian Presidents in Plane Crash Outside Kigali", April 6, 1994. Limited Official Use.

Memorandum for the Vice President, et. al., "PDD 25: U.S. Policy on Reforming Multilateral Peace Operations", May 3, 1994. Confidential with Secret attachment.

Memorandum from Under Secretary of Defense for Policy to Deputy Assistant to the President for National Security, National Security Council, "Rwanda: Jamming Civilian Radio Broadcasts", May 5, 1994. Confidential.

Memorandum of Conversation, Office of the Deputy Assistant Secretary of Defense for Middle East/Africa Region, Department of Defense, "Rwanda Interagency Telecon", drafted by Lt. Col. Michael Harvin, circa May 11, 1994. Secret.

Press Release, Office of the Press Secretary, The White House, "Statement by the Press Secretary", April 22, 1994. Non-classified.

U.S. Department of State, cable number 099440, to U.S. Mission to the United Nations, New York, "Talking Points for UNAMIR Withdrawal", April 15, 1994. Confidential.

U.S. Department of State, cable number 113672, to U.S. Embassy Bujumbura and US Embassy Dar es Salaam, "DAS Bushnell Tells Col. Bagosora to Stop the Killings", April 29, 1994. Limited Official Use.

U.S. Department of State, cable number 127262, to U.S. Mission to the United Nations, New York, "Rwanda: Security Council Discussions", May 13, 1994. Confidential.

White paper, Department of State, "The Clinton Administration's Policy on Reforming Multilateral Peace Operations", May 1994. Non-classified.

ONLINE SOURCES

people.brandeis.edu/~teuber/rwanda.html
pro.harvard.edu/papers/020/020011DiPrizioRo.pdf
www.access.gpo.gov/su_docs/aces/aces150.html
www.iss.co.za/Pubs/ASR/7No5/PeaceInforcement.html
www.pennyhill.com/foreignpolicy.html
www.usatoday.com/news/index/nns053.htm
"The Triumph of Evil" *Frontline*, PBS, January 26, 1999
www.pbs.org/wgbh/pages/frontline/shows/evil
J. William Snyder, Jr., *"Command" versus "Operational Control": A Critical Review of PDD-25,* 1995, www.mikenew.com/review-pdd25.html
Human Rights Watch, *Ignoring Genocide*, www.hrw.org/reports/1999/rwanda/Geno15-8-01.htm

OFFICIAL REPORTS

Human Rights Watch, "Arming Rwanda: The Arms Trade and Human Rights Abuses in the Rwanda War," Vol. 6, Issue 1, January 1994.
Human Rights Watch. "Genocide in Rwanda: April–May 1994." Vol. 6, No. 4, May 1994.
Organization of African Unity. "International Panel of Eminent Personalities to Investigate the 1994 Genocide in Rwanda and the Surrounding Events," 1999.
"Report of the Independent Inquiry Into the Actions of the United Nations During the 1994 Genocide in Rwanda," December 15, 1999.
Report of the Secretary-General, "An Agenda for Peace, Preventive Diplomacy, Peacemaking and Peace-keeping, June 17, 1992," A/47/277–S/24111.
United Nations, "Comprehensive Report on Lessons Learned From United Nations Assistance Mission for Rwanda (UNAMIR)," 1996.

Index

About the Author

Jared Cohen received his BA from Stanford University in 2004 and his M.Phil in International Relations from Oxford University in 2006, where he studied as a Rhodes Scholar. Jared's interest in Africa began at an early age when in high school and college he began traveling to various parts of the continent to learn about its cultures, history, and languages. This interest led him to travel to twenty-one different African countries where his activities ranged from conducting research on Maasai socialization of youth to the politics of rebel groups in the Congo. He has worked for the Institute for Democracy in South Africa, the Forum on Early Warning and Emergency Response, PBS *Frontline*, the Department of Defense, and the State Department. He is fluent in Kiswahili, conversant in Maa and its dialects, and has studied Arabic, Farsi, Korean, Amharic, and Spanish.

At present, Jared focuses on the Middle East and the Islamic world at large. He has conducted research in Iran, Iraq, Syria, Lebanon, and Afghanistan, where he focuses on promotion of democracy, counter-terrorism, and outreach to Middle-Eastern youth. He has consulted in various capacities both in the public and private sectors on issues related to the Middle East and public diplomacy. He is author of "Iran's Young Opposition: Youth in Post-Revolutionary Iran" (*SAIS Review*, September 2006) and co-author of "The Passive Revolution: Is Political Resistance Dead or Alive in Iran" (*Hoover Digest*, Fall 2005)

Jared has appeared on the BBC, Discovery Channel, and ABC Radio to discuss issues related to the Middle East. Following this same theme, he is author of the forthcoming book *Children of Jihad: Journeys Into the Hearts and Minds of Middle Eastern Youth*.

In addition to his interests in Africa and the Middle East, Jared enjoys playing soccer, surfing, painting, and traveling. Jared Cohen currently works at the U.S. State Department* and lives in Washington, DC.

*This book was written before the author joined the U.S. Government. The views presented in this book do not necessarily reflect those of either the U.S. State Department or the U.S. Government.